Ach

Mountain Bike Training
for Beginners and Professionals

For Beate

Achim Schmidt

Mountain Bike Training

for Beginners and Professionals

Meyer & Meyer Sport

Original title: Mountainbiketraining: für Anfänger und Profis
-Aachen : Meyer und Meyer, 1998
Translated by Paul D. Chilvers-Grierson

British Library Cataloguing in Publication Data
A catalogue record for this book is available from the British Library

Schmidt, Achim/
Mountain Bike Training: for Beginners and Professionals
- Oxford : Meyer & Meyer Sport (UK) Ltd.,1999
ISBN 1-84126-007-X

Oxford, Aachen, Olten (CH), Vienna,
Québec, Lansing/ Michigan, Adelaide, Auckland, Johannesburg
e-mail: verlag@meyer-meyer-sports.com
Cover Photo: Stephan Bögli (SSG Europe) und iko
Photos: See credits under the illustrations
Diagrams: See credits under the illustrations
Graphics: René Marks, Köln
All others: Achim Schmidt
Editorial: John Coghlan, Dr. Irmgard Jaeger
Cover design: Walter J. Neumann, N&N Design-Studio, Aachen
Cover and Type exposure: frw, Reiner Wahlen, Aachen
Typesetting: Quay
Printing: Burg Verlag Gastinger GmbH, Stolberg
Printed and bound in Germany
ISBN 1-84126-007-X

Contents

1 Introduction

1.1 Using this Book

This book, with its great variety of topics, is designed for active mountain bikers, whether they participate in races or practise the sport for fitness reasons, as well as for racing sport trainers, instructors and coaches.

In contrast to numerous books on mountain biking already available, this book is not dedicated to technology or the repairing of bikes but is focused solely on training the various factors of performance in mountain biking. Cycling technique is also covered in numerous other books and in the chapter "Technique Training" it is only dealt with exceptionally; here too the focus is rather on the training possibilities of the correct techniques.

In order to understand the special chapters better, chapter 2 "Physiology and Anatomy of Mountain Bikers" is especially recommended for readers who have no basic knowledge of physiology and anatomy. This basic knowledge is absolutely necessary to understand the chapters that follow. Just as important as the physiological and anatomical basics are training methodology principles which are explained in chapter 3 at the beginning of each relevant section.

The aim of this book is to enable readers to create their own individual training schedules after reading it intensively.

The comprehensive contents page allows the reader to quickly find specific subjects so that the book can also be used as a reference book.

A note on the use of language: to make the book more readable, only the male form has been used, which of course stands for the female form as well.

Training Schedules

The training schedules found in various chapters are only training schedule suggestions which are designed for an average athlete in the particular class. Individually different objectives and varying time budgets, as well as differing levels of fitness mean, however, that individual adaptation or correction is indispensable. The schedules are in no way designed for members of national teams but are aimed at the larger group of "normal" mountain bikers in the fields of racing, hobby and fitness riding.

As described in chapter 3, the degree of difficulty in planning and carrying out training increases with increasing performance capacity. The path to be covered in the field of performance is very narrow, and details can decide top form or loss of form and thus victory or defeat.

It should be pointed out to newcomers to the sport that while training progress in an endurance sport is very rapid at the beginning, after six to nine months the jumps in performance get increasingly smaller. To reach a regional level of performance, however, requires several years of wellthought out, regular and consistent training if an athlete has not previously been involved in another endurance sport. This is not a phenomenon peculiar to mountain biking, it can be observed in all other endurance sports as well.

It is even more difficult in road cycling, which is mentioned here because of common training means. Here the races with closed fields of cyclists do not have the single timed ride characteristics of a mountain bike race, or e.g. a triathlon. If newcomers fall behind the cyclist field they have to abandon the race as a rule, but in mountain biking every cyclist rides more or less for himself.

1.2 Developments in Mountain Biking

The Beginning

When in 1974 the first freaks around Gary Fisher and Tom Ritchey began to ride down the mountains around Mount Tamalpais near San Francisco (California) on old classical American cruisers, nobody could foresee what a boom the invention of the mountain bike would lead to. Shortly afterwards the same freaks fixed gears to their bikes and thus created the first bikes that were really suitable for off-road cycling. Now they could not only ride downhill, but back up again as well.

In the late seventies the first mountain bikes were produced in great numbers in California. It was not long before first industrial production centres were set up in Asia, and thanks to high production numbers and low prices the triumphal march of the mountain bike reached Europe too. Numerous technical innovations in the field of mountain bikes also led to the growth of the components giant Shimano.

The first mountain bike races at Mount Tamalpais were downhill races with mass starts, but soon cross-country and uphill races took place. The first World Cup was held in 1991, and in 1990 mountain biking was officially recognised by the international organisation UCI (Union Cycliste International).

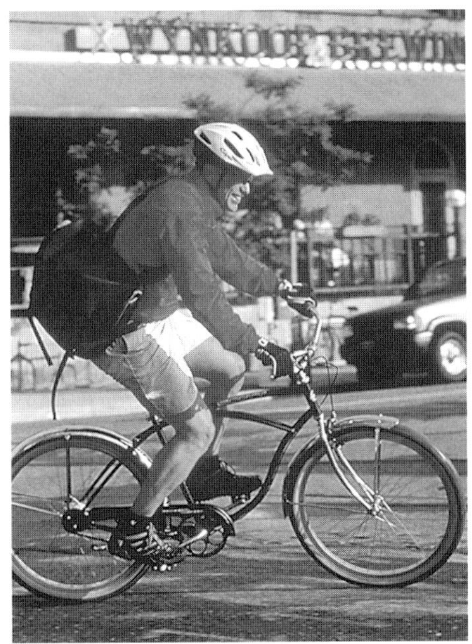

Cruisers were the predecessors of mountain bikes. Photo: John Kelly, Trisport

In the three years before, from 1987 onwards, there had been two competing world championships run by two separate organisations.

Today, in addition to the above-mentioned race types, there are the dual slalom and various trial, fun and stunt competitions as well as speed biking, where speed records are set.

But not only in the field of racing have there been changes as a result of the "invention" of the mountain bike. In the fitness, leisure and hobby fields cycling has experienced a real boom in central Europe which seems to have no end. The bicycle will certainly become even more popular as a means of transport as a result of environmental and traffic problems.

What Is so Special about Mountain Biking?

What is special about the mountain bike is its cross-country suitability, thanks to which it is possible to leave sealed roads and go one's own way along rough tracks. The spirit of discovery which everyone seems to have also plays a role. An area that was previously only marginally known from the car can be experienced and explored on a mountain bike: hidden natural beauties create new impressions.

The slower speed of the mountain bike in contrast to cars makes possible an incomparable experience of nature away from major roads on narrow tracks and paths. Beautiful landscapes can be explored and actively experienced.

The greater range in comparison to walking makes it possible to reach even distant places within a day. At any time you can stop, look and enjoy the view.

On long trips, which can occasionally take you to your physical limits, you experience anew feelings such as hunger and thirst that are often forgotten in our perfect and rationalised daily surroundings. The feeling of sinking into bed tired and worn out after physical exertion is an aspect of a new feeling for life that is not without significance.

In addition to these more contemplative appeals of mountain biking there is of course the excitement of a fast descent, the feeling of gliding as in skiing which attracts the biker into the mountains again and again.

The difficulty of riding down a narrow trail on a mountain bike, despite all the perils of gravity and centrifugal force, or mastering a steep climb with all one's strength and skill, inspires the biker anew every time and the feeling of having done it increases the desire for more.

Stunts and Trial

Playing with gravity particularly fascinates young people, who unfortunately take less and less interest in cross-country racing with its tough training demands and instead prefer endless training of stunts and tricks. Jumps across the edges of fields and self-made ramps, fast descents into old shingle pits and bomb holes, as well as trial manoeuvres over old cars and on steps, have a magic attraction for young bikers.

They invest all their money in the newest equipment and matching outfits and spend all day on their bikes without giving a single thought to racing.

Popular and Health Sport

When you consider the sales figures of mountain bikes it becomes obvious that mountain biking is not just a competition sport for a small racing elite. Only a small proportion of the bikes sold are used for racing, while by far the most bikes are used for cycling tours on and off the road.

Mountain biking away from the road is excellent for families with children; experiencing nature without being endangered by cars. Not so good, however, is that on weekends mountain bikes often spend more time on the car roof than on their own wheels.

Even close to the cities there are usually places worth going to which can be reached directly by bike via tracks and paths.

Often blind destruction of nature can be observed. Mountain bikers should stick to tracks and trails, because away from these they destroy the plant cover and disturb deer and other animals in their habitats.

In health sport and in rehabilitation the mountain bike is used to expose body and soul to positive stimuli. Using great gear flexibility on mountain bikes it is almost always possible to find the right level of strain in the preventive area. In the field of co-ordination too the mountain bike places significant demands on the cyclist. Longer trips at low intensity across relatively flat country are an experience for every health sports person. An upright position without any stretching, and if necessary a suspension fork or a full suspension bike, increase cycling comfort considerably.

Performance Sport

Initially the mountain bike racing scene was dominated by ex-racing cyclists and freaks, but since then the racing scene has developed further and many new mountain bikers have taken up the sport. Since the introduction of the World Cup the sport has become very professional and the degree of commercialisation increases constantly.

There can be few other sports that are as physically and psychologically exerting as a cross-country race on a difficult course. Already at the mass start the pulse races because of the effort of struggling for a good starting position. During the race you constantly reach your limits, are overtaken by cyclists, overtake other cyclists, people will not let you pass, you may fall off and you try to negotiate technically difficult stretches as safely and quickly as possible.

Anyone who wants even to be up with the leaders will have to accept very high levels of training, have a great deal of talent and above all be highly motivated to put up with the strain.

In the early to mid eighties, practically anyone could participate in international races in cross-country racing because apart from a few top riders the standard was very low. Today a broad, high performance elite has developed which views the sport professionally and therefore does everything to be right up the front. Every year at the World Cup new young riders appear, dominate the racing scene for a brief period and then disappear for a while again.

Most of these riders got their first racing experience on the road and belong, or belonged at least, to the national elite on the road as well.

As the competition sport mountain biking develops, the first "pure mountain bikers" meanwhile play a greater part. By "pure mountain bikers" is meant those cyclists who did not come to the sport via road racing. In order to be up with the world's leaders, however, these riders too must take part in road races and tours.

If one considers the professionalisation initiated and pushed by the world cycling organisation, which can be damaging to performance sport at the lower levels, it can be seen that in mountain biking too performance levels in general are increasing.

If some mountain bike races become so lucrative that they can compete with the classic road races, then it is certain that strong road professionals with thousands of racing kilometres behind them will participate in such cross-country races and, if they can cover the distances well technique-wise and also concentrate their training on shorter periods of exertion, there is no question that they will be superior to the mountain bikers to date.

The same thing occurred in recent years in track cycling, which was also opened up to professionals at the Olympic Games and world championships. Suddenly professionals raced away from the "state amateurs" of the past in the endurance disciplines, individual and team pursuit, and cycling for points, and in some cases set fabulous world records. This was, and is, possible because they are used to exertion such as that of the great tours which require a completely different level of performance than is possible in the amateur field. A similar development is definitely possible in mountain biking too in the near future.

In the technical disciplines such as downhill, dual slalom and the various trial competitions, however, this development will not take place because here abilities other than endurance and strength are called for. Cycling technique and co-ordinative abilities must be trained just as intensively, but are more closely linked to the individual mobility talent of an athlete than are endurance and strength. A co-ordinatively less gifted athlete will as a rule not make a very good trial rider, while a very average cross-country rider can achieve very high performance through years of well-planned training. In the technical disciplines performance development is increasingly determined by material development, which in downhill and dual slalom at least is often the limiting factor.

2 Physiology and Anatomy of Mountain Bikers

2.1 From Beginner to Professional from a Physiological Perspective

If you begin mountain biking as a person with little endurance training, within the body certain processes of change are initiated which are aimed at matching bodily functions to the increased demands on performance. In addition to visible signs such as better shape of the muscles or loss of weight, a whole range of further adaptive processes to increase the performance capability of the system "body" takes place unnoticed.

For a mountain biker seriously interested in his hobby it should be a basic need to find out as much as possible about his body, which allows him to carry out the sport. Understanding of and feeling for the body are becoming increasingly insignificant in an age of computer guided training, and so it is a logical consequence that many performance athletes strain their bodies more than they should, until they cannot take any more.

In the following sections the anatomical and physiological foundations for endurance sport mountain biking are described. Also considered here are the adaptive processes resulting from endurance training in order to help mountain bikers grasp processes in their bodies, injuries, but also improvements in performance. This knowledge also helps in getting a basic understanding of training and all factors connected with it.

This book is not long enough to go into the smallest details, but there are a number of good books on anatomy and physiology where they are described very extensively (e.g. DE MARÉES: Sportphysiologie; SILBERNAGEL: Physiologie; FALLER: Der Körper des Menschen).

2.1.1 Effects of Training on the Cardio-Vascular System and Moving Apparatus

The adaptive process of the body (adaptation) can be divided into two parts. In the first phase, involving small amounts and low intensity of training, e.g. in popular and health sport, there is only *functional* adaptation which is characterised by an improvement in metabolism resulting in economisation of the cardio-vascular system.

The second phase of adaptation is *dimensional* adaptation during which the dimensions (size) of the organs change.

The Performance Capacity of the Heart Increases

Regular endurance training over several years leads to an adaptive process in the heart, the result of which is the development of a sport heart. The *sport heart* is characterised by an increase in size and, linked with this, a lowering of the heart rate.

This adaptive process is a result of increased metabolism, especially in the muscles, whose increased need for oxygen and nutrients can only be met by increased blood circulation and thus requires a heart that performs better. While the heart of an untrained person weighs about 300 g, an endurance sport heart can weigh as much as 500 g. With the weight the heart volume also increases. It rises from about 800 ml in men and 500 ml in women to 900-1,200 ml, in rare cases even over 1,500 ml. The largest sport hearts are found in road cyclists and are a result of the often extreme endurance work they undergo.

As a result of the increased heart volume, a greater beat volume is possible. The *beat volume* is the amount of blood per heartbeat that the heart expels into the aorta (in untrained people 80 ml, in trained athletes up to 150 ml). Because, however, the body does not need more blood for the same level of performance, the heart can beat at a slower rate. The maximum possible *heart volume per minute*, by which is meant the amount of blood per minute transported by the left half of the heart (heart rate x beat volume; e.g. 70 x 80 ml = 5.6 l/min at rest), rises in contrast to the untrained person so that a greater amount of blood per unit of time is available to the muscles. The maximum heart rate only goes down a little as a result of years of endurance training.

This means that the greater maximum beat volume leads to a greatly increased maximum heart volume per minute. Under greatest exertion an untrained person reaches a heart volume per minute of about 20 l whereas an endurance trained athlete can reach values of over 30 l.

The maximum heart rate is generally calculated using the formula 220 less age in years, but this only gives approximate information and is therefore practically useless in performance sport. More about the measurement and significance of the maximum heart rate can be found in chapter 3.

A clear indication of development of a sport heart is the lowering of the *resting heart rate* from about 60-70 (women 70-80) beats per minute in untrained people to 40-50 in performance athletes. In the high performance field of the professionals, resting heart rates of under 40 are common and occasionally under 30.

When a "mountain bike career" ends, training should definitely not be stopped completely because this would result in symptoms of strain withdrawal in the heart which can even be dangerous.
The functioning of the heart is explained in figure 2.1.

Advantages of a Sport Heart

- Higher performance capacity.
- The same performance can be achieved at a lower heart rate.
- Lower rest and working heart rate, thus less wear on the heart (comparable to low revolutions per minute or rpm in a car engine).
- Economisation of the vascular system (circulation).
- During the development of a sport heart other positive adaptive processes take place in the organism.

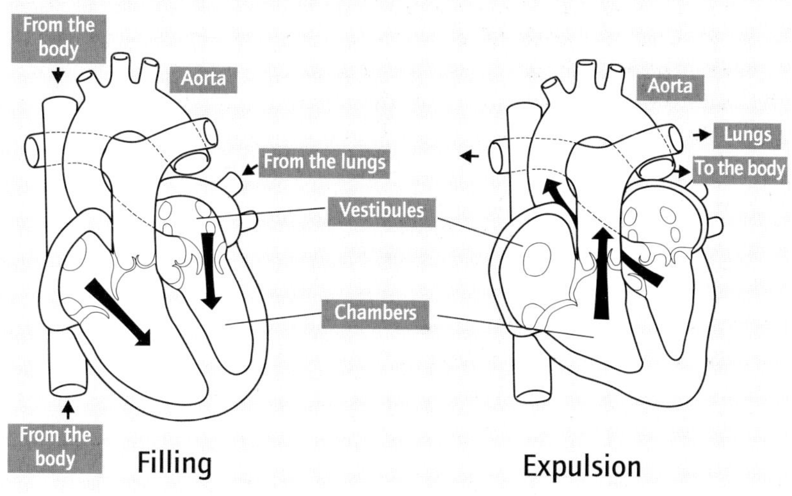

Fig. 2.1: Anatomy and working phases of the heart

Vascular System (Blood Vessels)

The distribution of oxygen-rich blood in the body takes place via the aorta (body artery), the arteries and the arterioles (small arteries). At rest the arterioles and capillaries of the muscles are actively narrowed and thus prevent unnecessary provision of blood to the muscles, for at rest the blood is mainly needed for other organs (digestive tract, kidneys, liver).

When you begin to move, the vessels in the working muscles dilate and more blood, and thus more oxygen and nutrients, can flow through the muscles. Accordingly the flow of blood in the digestive system is reduced during movement. The muscles' increased blood requirements during movement are met by increased pumping of the heart. Linked to the capillaries, the smallest vessels and at the same time the place where the exchange of substances is carried out (oxygen ⟷ carbon dioxide, nutrients ⟷ metabolic end products), are the venules and finally the veins, which lead into either the upper or lower main vein. The veins transport blood back to the heart.

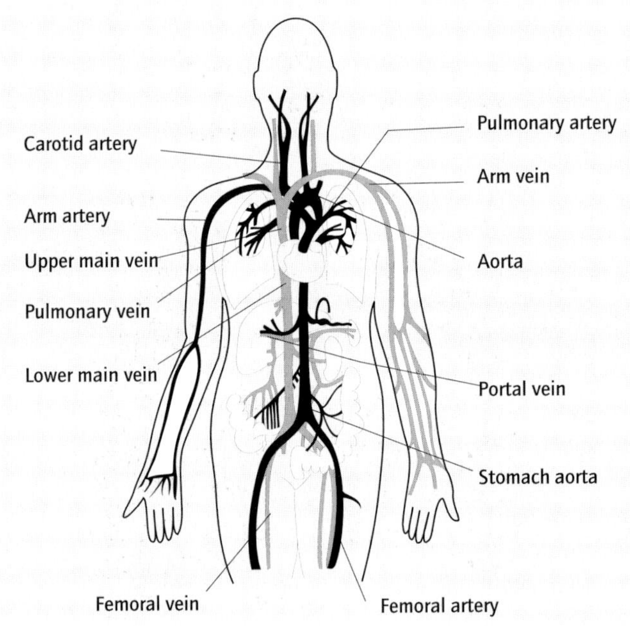

Fig. 2.2: Vascular System

Breathing

Oxygen-poor, carbon dioxide-rich blood flows around the pulmonary alveoli in extremely thin walled capilliaries within the lungs, expels its carbon dioxide there and in return takes in oxygen. This process is called external breathing, while the exchange between blood and body cells is called internal breathing.

With the aid of the breathing muscles, at rest this is mainly the diaphragm, the lungs are expanded during the course of breathing, air flows via the windpipe and bronchial tubes into the pulmonary aveoli, where the exchange of gases takes place, and finally the carbon dioxide-rich air leaves the lungs again (breathing out). Not until there is exertion (cycling) - with increased breathing - does chest breathing support the diaphragm breathing described. A whole range of breathing support muscles then strengthen both breathing in and breathing out and increase the energy requirements of the breathing muscles to 10% of total energy requirements. When exerted to the utmost, the oxygen needs of these muscles even rises to 15-20% of maximum oxygen intake.

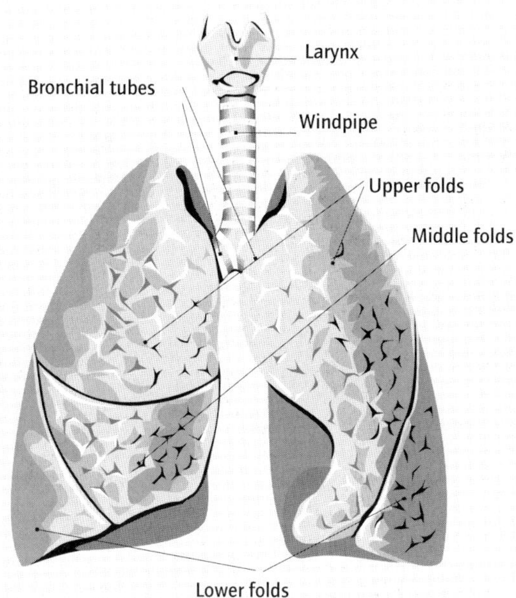

Fig. 2.3: Anatomy of the lungs

At rest only about 0.5 litres of air per breath are breathed in and out 15 times a minute (= 7.5 l); under maximum strain, for example after the sprint to the finish, a trained mountain biker can breathe in and out over 190 l of air per minute.

Vital capacity (the maximum volume to be breathed out after maximum breathing in) is dependent to a great degree on age, gender and body size. Vital capacity is generally between 3 and 7 litres, but it tells us very little about the absolute endurance capability of a mountain biker. Africa's top runners, for example, have smaller lungs than Europeans and yet they usually run faster.

Blood

The 5-6 l of blood is made up of about 55% blood plasma (fluid) and 45% consists of the various blood cells. The blood represents about 5-6% of body weight. As a result of endurance training such as mountain biking, blood volume increases by about 15%.

The following main functions are attributed to the blood:

- Transport (oxygen, carbon dioxide, nutrients, metabolic waste products, hormones)
- Transport and distribution of heat
- Blood coagulation
- Immune defence.

1mm^3 of blood, i.e. a tiny amount, contains 4.5-5 million red corpuscles, an unbelievable figure, and about 5,000-8,000 white corpuscles for immune defence. In 100 ml of blood there are also about 7 g of proteins. The red corpuscles (erythrocytes) are the oxygen and carbon dioxide transporters of the blood.

The *haematocrit value* indicates the proportion of solid components (blood cells) in the total volume of the blood. More recently the haematocrit has been used in road racing in particular to provide evidence of the frequently used doping substance "Erythropoetin" (EPO). Erythropoetin leads to increased red corpuscle production which increases an athlete's ability to take in oxygen.

The result is significantly increased endurance capability, but also a significantly greater risk of dying from thrombosis (blood clot). In road cycling, where this doping substance is more frequently abused than in mountain biking, there have been a number of sudden deaths attributed to intake of this hormone.

Maximum Oxygen Intake

Maximum oxygen intake **(VO_2 max.)** is a very interesting physiological value for mountain biking, for it is considered the decisive criterion for endurance capability. Maximum oxygen intake means the greatest amount of oxygen - not air - taken in by a mountain biker via his lungs to his blood when under maximum strain.

The exact ascertainment of maximum oxygen intake is carried out on a cycle ergometer as part of a performance diagnostic examination. The normal value for an untrained person is about 3 l of oxygen per minute and with appropriate training can be increased to values of 5-6 l. The VO_2 max. is dependent on the athlete's training state, age, gender and weight. Thus a bigger person needs a greater oxygen intake for the same external performance than a smaller person because he has to move a greater weight. For this reason the weight related VO_2 max. is used to get an exact indication of performance capacity and to be able to compare several athletes. The weight related or relative VO_2 max. indicates the oxygen intake per kilogramme body weight and minute. Here professionals reach values of over 80 ml of oxygen per minute and kg of body weight, untrained 20- to 30-year olds, on the other hand, only reach about 40 to 45 ml of oxygen per minute and kg of body weight. The maximum oxygen intake of untrained men goes down by 1% per year, women lose only 0.8% per year. What most "non-athletes" do not know, however, is that this process can be stopped and even reversed by endurance sport. Thus a trained 70-year old can achieve the same values as an untrained 30-year old.

Factors influencing VO_2 max. (in addition to age, weight, gender):
- Transport capacity of the circulation (heart volume per minute)
- Oxygen transport capacity of the blood
- Breathing and exchange of gases in the lungs
- Blood supply to the muscle (capillarisation)
- Muscle metabolism (enzyme stock).

Moving Apparatus

Muscles

The roughly 430 muscles in the human body usually make up between 40 and 45% of its weight and at rest they need about 20% of energy. During maximum work (top sporting performances) this value rises up to 90%. Muscles have the ability to convert chemical energy (nutrients) to mechanical energy (tension), similar to a combustion engine.

A muscle or muscle group never works alone during a movement, but is dependent on one or more antagonists. Example: in the leg the extensors (agonists) are opposite the flexors (antagonists).

In figures 2.4 to 2.7 all the important human muscles are shown.

These illustrations are important in connection with chapters 4 "Strength Training" and 5 "Stretching", in which individual muscles are also dealt with in detail. In the explanations of the illustrations the muscles are described in English and using their Latin names and their functions are briefly described as related to mountain biking.

Torso

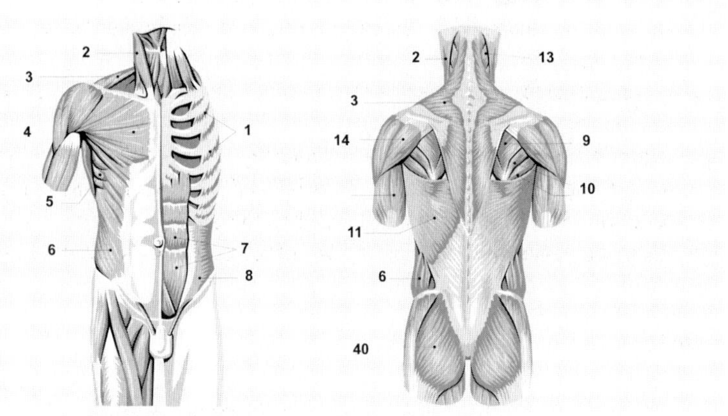

Fig. 2.4: Illustration of the torso muscles with descriptions of the most important muscles (left: torso seen from the front, right: rear of torso)

1 **External muscles between the ribs** (mm. intercostales externi): breathing support muscles for chest breathing.

2 **Head turner** or sternocleidomastoid muscle (m. sternocleidomastoideus): turns the head to the side, e.g. when looking around on the bike.

3 **Hood or trapezius muscle** (m. trapezius): muscle with three parts; raises and fixes the shoulders and stabilises the shoulder blades; when pedalling standing up it raises the shoulders.

4 **Large chest muscle** (m. pectoralis major): draws the arm to the body; when biking it is strained excentrically during intense downhills and concentrically when cycling standing up.

5 **Saw muscle** (m. serratus anterior): draws the shoulder blades forwards and allows raising of the arm above the horizontal; slight significance in cushioning shocks.

6 **Oblique stomach muscles** (mm. obliquus externus/internus abdominis): turn and bend the torso sideways; when biking they stabilise the pelvis and support thrust when pedalling standing up.

7 **Straight stomach muscle** (m. rectus abdominis): bends the torso forwards, stabilises the pelvis when pedalling; part of the muscle loop when pedalling energetically.

8 **Transverse stomach muscle (**m. transversus abdominis): tenses the stomach wall.

9 **Infraspinatus muscle** (m. infraspinatus): with various parts for drawing up and extending the arm; used when absorbing major unevenness with the arms.

10 **Large and small scapula muscles** (m. teres major/minor): turn the arm outwards and draw it close to the torso; used when pedalling standing up going uphill.

11 B**roadest back muscle** (m. latissimus dorsi): draws the arm downwards to the body from being held high.

12 **Deep back extensors** (m. erector spinae): (no illustration) deeper muscles located close to the vertebrae, especially left and right of the spinal column; keep the back straight, hold it firm when pedalling.

13 **Deep neck muscles:** deeper muscles, (not marked) turn and twist the head.

Arms

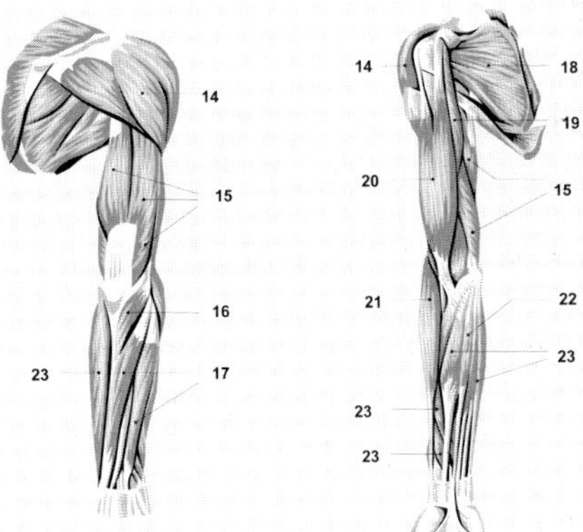

Fig. 2.5: Illustration of the arm muscles of the right arm with descriptions of the most important muscles (left: rear of arm with elbow, right: front of arm with crook of the arm)

14 **Deltoid or shoulder muscle** (m. deltoideus): moves the arms forwards, sideways and backwards; used when pedalling standing up going uphill and downhill.

15 **Triceps brachii muscle of the upper arm** (m. triceps brachii): stretches the arm at the elbow; important shock absorber on downhills, where it is strained excentrically.

16 **Knot muscle** (m. anconaeus): extensor in elbow joint; functions like the triceps.

17 **Hand and finger extensors** (mm. extensor carpi/digitorum): stretch the wrist and the fingers; used in holding the handle bars and absorbing shocks.

18 **Lower shoulder blade muscle** (m. subscapularis): stabilises in the shoulder joint and turns the arm inwards.

19 **Coracobrachial muscle in the upper arm** (m. coracobrachialis): raises the arm, stabilises in the shoulder joint under great effort.

20 **Biceps** (m. biceps brachii): bends the arm at the elbow; concentrically strained when pedalling standing up going uphill and on the flat, but also when sitting.

21 **Brachioradial** (spoke) **muscle of the upper arm** (m. brachioradialis): bends the arm at the elbow; used when pedalling standing up, but also when sitting.

22 **Long palm tensor** (m. palmaris longus): bends the fingers; used when holding the handle bars.

23 **Hand and finger flexors (**mm. flexor carpi/digitorum): bend the fingers and wrist; concentrically strained especially when holding the handle bars.

Front of Leg

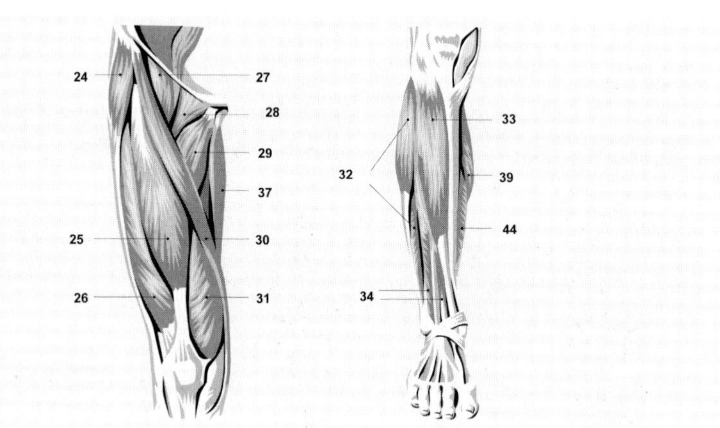

Fig. 2.6: Illustration of front leg muscles with descriptions of the most important muscles (right leg)

24 **Thigh tensor** (m. tensor fasciae latae): bends at the hip joint; used during upward movement of the pedal.

25 **Straight thigh muscle** (m. rectus femoris): stretches the knee joint, bends at the hip as well; concentrically strained when pushing down the pedal.

26 **Outer thigh muscle (**m. vastus lateralis): stretches and stabilises the knee joint, also bends at the hip; concentrically strained when pushing down the pedal.

27 **Ilium muscle** (m. iliopsoas): bends at hip joint, part of the muscle loop when pedalling hard.

28 **Crest muscle** (m. pectineus): bends at the hip joint; used during upward movement of pedal.

29 **Long adductor muscle** (m. adductor longus): draws the outspread leg towards the central axis and supports bending.

30 **Sartorius muscle** (m. satorius): bends at the hip, turns the lower leg inwards and the upper leg outwards, supports bending at the knee.

31 **Inner thigh muscle** (m. vastus medalis): stretches and stabilises the knee joint, also bends at the hip; concentrically strained when pushing down the pedal.

32 **Long/short calf muscles** (mm. peronaeus longus/brevis): raise the foot forwards and outwards, support the ankle extensors; strain during upward movement of pedal before upper standstill (pulling).

33 **Front shin muscle** (m. tibialis anterior): raises the foot; strain during upward movement of pedal before upper standstill (pulling).

34 **Toe extensors** (m. extensor digitorum): stretch the toes; strain during upward movement of pedal (pulling).

Back of Leg

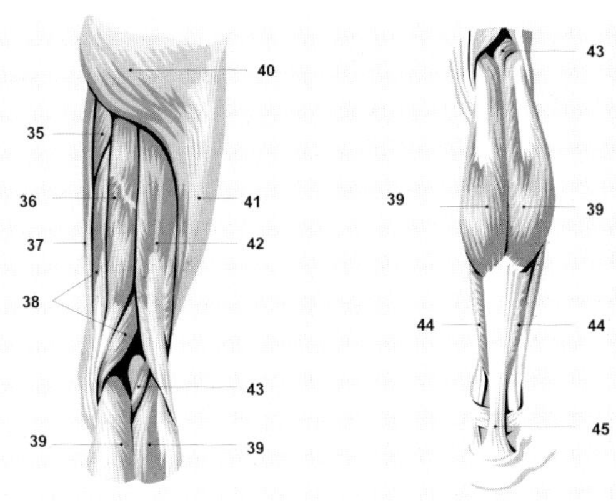

Fig. 2.7: Illustration of back leg muscles with descriptions of the most important muscles (right leg)

35 **Large adductor** (m. adductor magnus): draws the outspread leg towards the central axis and stretches at the hip; of medium significance in stretching the leg during the pedalling cycle.
36 **Semitendon muscle** (m. semitendinosus): bends at the knee joint and stretches at the hip; particularly significant for bending during the pedalling cycle.
37 **Gracilis muscle** (m. gracilis): bends at the hip joint and at the knee joint; used during upward movement of the pedal.
38 **Semimembrane muscle** (m. semimembranosus): bends at the knee joint and stretches at the hip; especially significant for bending in the rear part of the pedalling cycle, maximum at lower standstill point of pedalling cycle.
39 **Twin calf muscle** (m. gastrocnemius): stretches at the ankle and bends at the knee joint; especially strained when pushing the pedals down, but also when pulling up.
40 **Gluteal muscle** (m. glutaeus maximus): stretches at the hip joint; strong support of the quadriceps during leg stretching, forward part of pedalling cycle.
41 **Ilium-shin tendon** (tractus iliotibialis): not a muscle but a connective tissue reinforcement of the muscle fibre for tensing of the long thigh bone.
42 **Femoral biceps** (m. biceps femoris): bends at the knee joint and turns outwards, stretches at the hip; especially significant for bending in the rear of the pedalling cycle, but also for stretching of the hip in the front cycle.
43 **Foot sole muscle** (m. plantaris): insignificant in the pedalling cycle.
44 **Sole muscle** (m. soleus): stretches at the ankle; used when treading on the pedal, supports the twin calf muscle.
45 **Achilles' tendon** (tendo calcaneus): connects calf muscles and ankle.

There are two underlying ways the muscles work: *a) static functioning, b) dynamic functioning*. Static means without movement; for the mountain biker these are the muscles that do the holding work. Arm, neck and back muscles keep the upper body and head firm when sitting calmly and thus function mainly statically. Pedalling on the other hand is a dynamic function, or to be more exact, this is dynamic-concentric muscle functioning which means that during contraction the muscle is actually shortened, it overcomes a force. The opposite, excentric strain (giving function) occurs for example when landing after jumping from a wall, when the legs have to give, the muscles resist, but are nevertheless stretched (lengthening).

The exclusively concentric pedalling movement in the main leg muscles is the main reason mountain bikers get sore muscles when they have to run a sector they are not used to, for example during a cross-country race. The leg's extensor muscles are greatly stretched during the phase of excentric exertion when running under strain (absorption of body weight), which these are not at all used to. Microscopically small muscle injuries occur (microtraumata) which are generally known as strained muscles.

That is one of the reasons mountain bikers should also do regular running training.

In the human muscle system there are slow and fast muscle fibres as well as an intermediate type. The slow, so-called "red muscle fibres" are the endurance fibres; they are most common among mountain bikers (70-90%). The fast or "white muscle fibres" are thicker, tire more quickly and are mainly found among resilience and strength athletes.

Untrained people have a varied distribution of fibres, depending on their constitution type, which, however, can only be shifted to a limited extent by training. How the transformation process from white to red fibres or vice versa actually takes place has not yet been fully explained; what is known, however, is that a change is probably triggered by the type of strain (endurance or strength). A shift to the endurance fibres happens more easily than towards resilience fibres. It is thus considerably easier to train a high level of endurance than a good sprinting ability.

Also, in the course of specialisation, young people with a high proportion of endurance fibres will probably be more likely to opt for an endurance sport because they are more successful in it.

This is even more so in the resilience area, where selection needs not be done according to the criterion of muscle fibre distribution, but rather the selection process takes place on its own on the basis of performance.

In the course of endurance training capillarisation (number of capillaries per muscle fibre) of the muscle tissue improves, which means that the surfaces for the exchange of gases and substances between muscle fibres and blood increase in size and metabolism can function more quickly and economically.

Bones

The bones of humans follow the principle of lightweight construction; a firm outer, compact layer surrounds the spongy looking internal layer. Bones, although they seem very stiff and inflexible, are relatively elastic. Pulling, pressure, bending and twisting are tolerated to an amazing degree. Mountain biking is a sport that "spares bones and joints" because there are no strain high points as a result of impact and compression as in running. The strains of biking in fact lead to a strengthening of the bone substance in the legs in particular.

Joints

With their cartilage-covered ends the bones form the joints which allow the mobility of the body. Usually two, rarely three, bones meet in a joint, linked by tendons, muscles, capsules and ligaments. The cartilage-covered bone ends form the joint surfaces within the joint. The cartilage is a substance that is very elastic under pressure, with a lifespan not yet achieved by technology. The joint gap, the space between the bone ends, is surrounded by a double layered capsule which on the one hand provides additional support to the joint and on the other hand produces so-called "joint grease".

Digestion

Using a muesli bar as an example, here is a description of the digestive process from ingestion of food to excretion. The time indications are general only and differ according to situation and circumstances.

3.30 p.m.: A test cyclist begins a three to four hour training ride. The last meal was three hours ago and was not very big.

5.00 p.m.: The cyclist eats a muesli bar. With the aid of the teeth the food is broken up mechanically and changed by the saliva into a flowable paste (chyme). ❶ The saliva enzymes immediately begin to split the complex carbohydrates in the mouth.

5.01 p.m.: The muesli paste slides through the gullet into the stomach. Contracting waves in the approximately 30 cm long gullet speed up transportation. ❷

5.02 p.m.: Now in the stomach, the "muesli bar" stimulates the production of hydrochloric acid and enzymes which as stomach juice chemically process the chyme. ❸ About 1.5 to 2 l of stomach juice are produced daily. Only fats and proteins are processed by the enzymes, while carbohydrates are not broken down further at this stage. The hydrochloric acid continues the process of breaking down the rough muesli paste.

5.03 p.m.: Water secretion leads to thinning of the chyme which is well mixed up by the movements of the stomach wall as if in a concrete mixer. At a high cycling speed the body would not sacrifice any energy for digestion and would postpone the digestive process until there is a calmer cycling section.

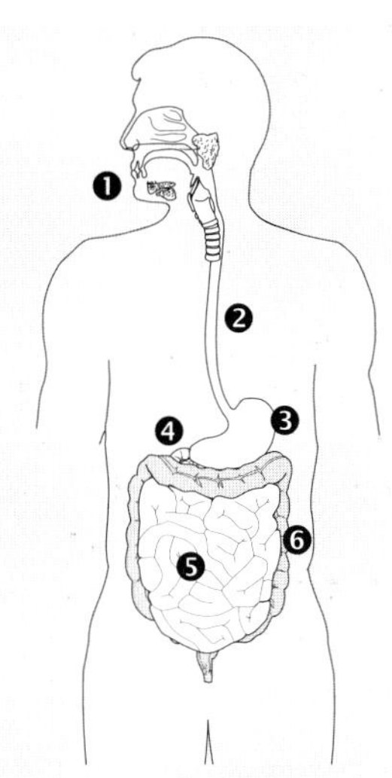

Fig. 2.8: digestive system

5.09 p.m.: The stomach continues to function like a mixer, but gradually the fats come to the surface of the chyme while the carbohydrates are deposited on the bottom of the stomach.

5.25 p.m.: The chyme is further liquefied and still needs a few minutes before it can leave the stomach. Carbohydrate-rich drinks would already be in the intestines.

5.40 p.m.: Finally, shortly before a blood sugar deficit begins, the stomach opens the pylorus muscle at its lower end and passes the chyme in small portions through to the duodenum. ❹ The pancreas releases enzymes to split carbohydrates, proteins and fats in the duodenum; bile secretion also begins for fat digestion.

5.43 p.m.: Rhythmic (peristaltic) movements transport the "muesli bar" onwards to the small intestine which immediately follows. The complex carbohydrates of the bar have meanwhile been split into glucose which is now taken into the blood via villi which project into the intestine, and begins its way to the liver via the portal vein system. Parts of the fats have already been split into free fatty acids and glycerine and the proteins too have meanwhile been largely broken down into individual amino acids. Their absorption gradually begins.

5.46 p.m.: The chyme carries on through the small intestine, whose first third mainly serves the purpose of glucose absorption. ❺ Via the portal vein system the glucose gets to the liver where glycogen is built up from the glucose molecules. The liver stores part of the glycogen itself (stored amount: 100-130 g of glycogen) while the rest goes to the muscles where it is either deposited in depots or burnt immediately. In the small intestine, amino acids, fatty acids, vitamins A, B, C, E and K as well as minerals are absorbed into the blood.

6.30 p.m.: The remains of the bar are still in the small intestine.

7.00 p.m.: End of the training ride. Meanwhile almost all the glucose has been absorbed and the proteins have been partially absorbed. Fat digestion and absorption continue for quite some time.

7.30 p.m.: When the evening meal is eaten the process begins again. The amino acids from the bar now also reach the liver where they are reassembled as proteins - so-called "plasma proteins" - and go into the blood. Excess protein (when calorie intake is too high or there is not enough food) would be burnt or transformed into fat and stored (see chapter 7).

10.30 p.m.: The remains of the muesli bar leave the small intestine in the direction of the colon. ❻ Up to this point about 80-90% of the nutrients have been absorbed from the chyme. In the colon the main function is to re-absorb the water used for digestion. Thus the consistency gets firmer and drier during passage through the colon. At the beginning of the colon some minerals and nutrients are also still absorbed.

The next morning

The muesli bar leaves the body in the form of stool. In the case of fatty foods digestion would take about ten hours longer.

Nervous System

All processes in our body and our actions are steered by our nervous system, partly consciously, partly unconsciously. Reception of stimuli, processing them and reacting to them are done by the nervous system with the aid of the organs of sense and effect which allow contact to the environment in the first place. The nervous system consists of many billions of cells which have lost their ability to divide.

In terms of space and anatomy a difference is made between the central nervous system (CNS: brain and spinal cord) and the peripheral nervous system (PNS) with the nerves that provide the links with the organs of sense and effect. Functionally one differentiates between the voluntary (animal) and involuntary (vegetative) nervous system. The *animal nervous system* passes on all deliberate commands of movement to the appropriate organs of effect, usually muscles.

Whereas the brain represents the control centre of the nervous system, the spinal cord is in a way the "cable bundle" which is responsible for the information transfer through the nerves that run down the spinal cord channel protected by the vertebrae to and from the organs of effect. Furthermore, in a similar way to the brain, the spinal cord functions as a control centre for secondary processes such as the reflexes for example.

The *vegetative nervous system*, which regulates all unconscious processes in the body, consists of two separate sub-systems with completely different functional areas. The parasympathetic nervous system is responsible for all bodily functions at rest (digestion, regeneration). The sympathetic nervous system on the other hand is responsible for the body in movement and increases the performance preparedness of the organ systems which serve to move the body forwards.

Kidneys

The kidneys are of great importance to the body as blood filters and excretive organs. During cycling in particular they have to work considerably harder because their filtering activity increases with calorie consumption, which is linked to physical activity. Salts, waste products of protein metabolism, water but also foreign matter are removed from the blood and thus the body with the help of the kidneys. From the 1,500 l of blood which flows through the kidneys daily, about 150 l of primary urine is filtered which is ultimately concentrated to 1.5 l of urine and excreted.

2.1.2 Metabolism

Contrary to the belief that the cardio-vascular system limits performance capacity, the actual bottle neck of performance development is muscle metabolism. Only the contractile elements of the body (muscles) are able to transform chemical to mechanical energy and thus make movement possible at all. Thus metabolism, the structure and the regulation (co-ordination) of the muscles limit the performance capacity of mountain bikers.

Three methods of energy metabolism are available to the muscles. Here they are shown separately for easier understanding but actually they fit together like cogwheels. The transitions from one metabolic form to the other are fluid. We are talking here about **aerobic energy release** and **anaerobic energy release**, which in its turn is divided into *anaerobic-alactacid* and *anaerobic-lactacid energy release.*

Aerobic Energy Release (Aerobic Glycolysis, Lipolysis)

What does *aerobic* mean? Aerobic means that energy is released with the assistance of oxygen. *Aer* comes from Greek and means air. For mountain bikers, aerobic energy release is the most important metabolic form because it can function over a longer period of time, it releases relatively large amounts of energy and even refills and regenerates the two anaerobic metabolic forms after their "use".

During aerobic metabolism fats and carbohydrates are burnt or oxidised. The most important fuel is glucose (aerobic glycolysis), a simple carbohydrate with the chemical formula $C_6H_{12}O_6$. Glucose is the product of the splitting of complex carbohydrates (see chapter 7 "Dietary Considerations"). Greatly oversimplified, glucose is combined with oxygen and is split into carbon dioxide (breathed out through the lungs) and water.

During this process a relatively large amount of energy is released in the form of ATP (adenosine triphosphate, a very energy-rich molecule).

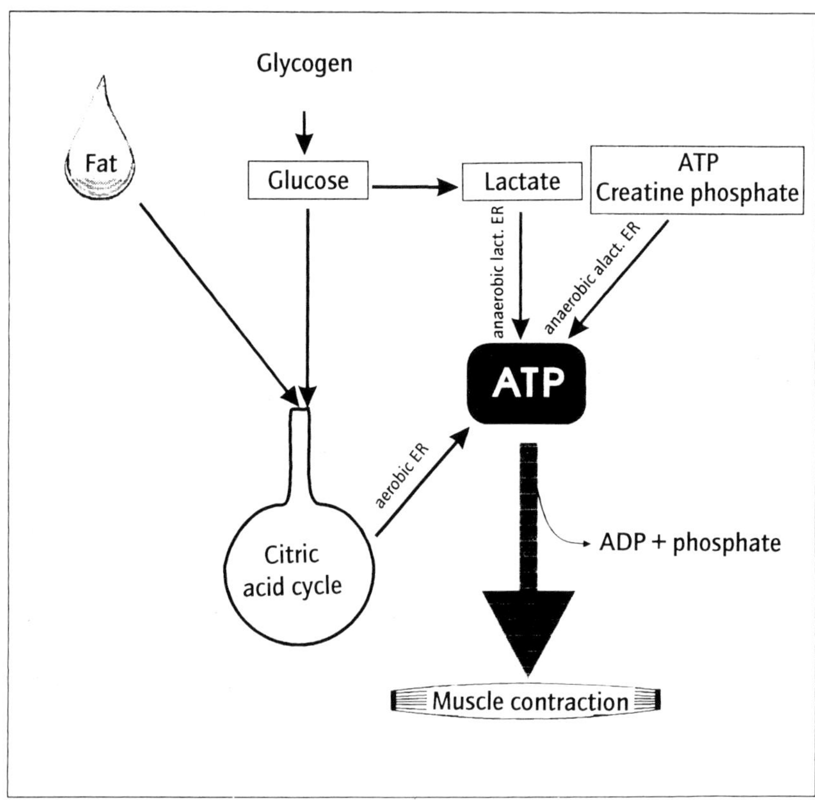

Fig. 2.9: Simplified diagram of energy metabolism

ATP Is the Fuel for Contraction

ATP is the direct energy store of the cell and is used as the "muscle fuel" which actually triggers muscle contraction. Only ATP is capable, through the separating of a remaining phosphate, of causing a muscle contraction on the molecular level by binding, folding off and dissolving certain structures (myosin heads).

ATP must, however, be at the appropriate link locations before the contraction so that the muscle is always ready for action. If the ATP supply in the muscle cell declines, especially when new synthesis is not sufficient, the links between the contractile structures are not dissolved and the muscle hardens. This is what happens when rigor mortis sets in for example. In mountain biking, cramps, especially in the leg muscles, are a sign of increasing exhaustion and thus also of an ATP shortage in the relevant muscle fibre; the links are no longer dissolved. The lay person usually immediately thinks there is a lack of magnesium because magnesium makes the splitting off into ADP possible. Very often, however, cramps are only a sign of overtaxing and depleted ATP stores, i.e. they are an energetic problem and disappear as training condition improves. In the muscle fibre all transformation processes involving energy-rich substances ultimately serve the securing of the ATP production.

Simplified Diagram of Energy Release

The release of energy can be compared to a steam engine. The fuels (fats and glucose) represent the water; the fire, sometimes larger, sometimes smaller, symbolises the metabolic form. The steam that comes from the water stands for the ATP. In order to move something or drive it on, the cell uses the ATP supply, the steam engine uses steam. As in the body the ATP supply, so too is the supply of steam in the engine (boiler), limited and must be constantly created anew.

The place where aerobic energy is won is in the muscle fibre, and within it the mitochondrium, the so-called power station of the cell. The glucose is either drawn from the blood and broken down or it comes from the glycogen stores of the cell (glycogen is the stored form of glucose), from where it is transported into the mitochondrium after the transformation and splitting processes.

Fat Metabolism (Lipolysis)

As well as carbohydrates, fats are also burnt aerobically. This process is called lipolysis. Fats are made up of glycerol and fatty acids. The fatty acids are channelled into a particular place in the carbohydrate metabolism and burnt together with the carbohydrates.

This is why the energy from fats can only be made use of when carbohydrates are burnt. When the fatty acid coenzyme A (comes from the fatty acid) is channelled into the mitochondrium, carnitin is needed as a carrier. Research has not, however, been able to demonstrate any increase in performance caused by additional carnitin being introduced.

The disadvantage of fat combustion is that it is only available at low intensities of effort because a great deal of oxygen is required. The amount of energy stored or the calorific value of fats is, however, twice as high as that of carbohydrates, namely 9.3 kcal to 4.1 kcal per gramme.

The fat metabolism (lipolysis) of a mountain biker has to be trained in order to spare the glycogen stores, which to a great extent limit performance because they are more or less empty after about two hours of intensive exertion. Whereas an untrained person can cover about 40% of energy requirements at medium intensity through fat metabolism, an endurance trained mountain biker can cover 60% or more from this source. With increasingly better endurance training condition, at the same intensity the proportion of energy won from fats increases. The valuable glycogen reserves are thus protected and saved for highly intensive phases that can decide the race. The endurance trained mountain biker can deposit two to three times more fat for the obtaining of energy in the muscle cell than an untrained person.

Glycogen Stores

If basic stamina or endurance is not at a high level the muscle cell immediately turns to the glycogen stores at relatively low levels of effort. Between 400 g and 500 g of glycogen are stored in the muscles and the liver, most of which is in the muscles.

An important factor for performance on the bike is the amount of muscle glycogen stored. If the glycogen stores are empty after a race they must be refilled. This can take between 24 and 48 hours on an optimum diet (see chapter 7 "Dietary Considerations").

Endurance training leads to an improvement in the metabolic situation in the muscle fibre itself. The enzyme stocks in the mitochondria are higher and the substrates (glucose, fatty acids) are available in higher concentration for breaking down than in untrained people. The number of mitochondria per fibre also increases, and through the improved capillarisation (number of capillaries per muscle fibre) oxygen can be used more simply and in greater amounts for obtaining energy. Aerobic metabolism takes place more quickly and economically as a result of the factors mentioned.

Anaerobic Energy Release

a) Anaerobic-lactacid Energy Release (Anaerobic Glycolysis)

Anaerobic means the release of energy without the involvement of oxygen. In this metabolic form lactate, the salt of lactic acid, is produced, as expressed by the adjective "lactacid". Lactate causes overacidity of the muscles and finally forces a drop in performance. The muscles use the metabolic form of lactate creation whenever aerobic combustion is insufficient as an energy source to achieve the performance level required.

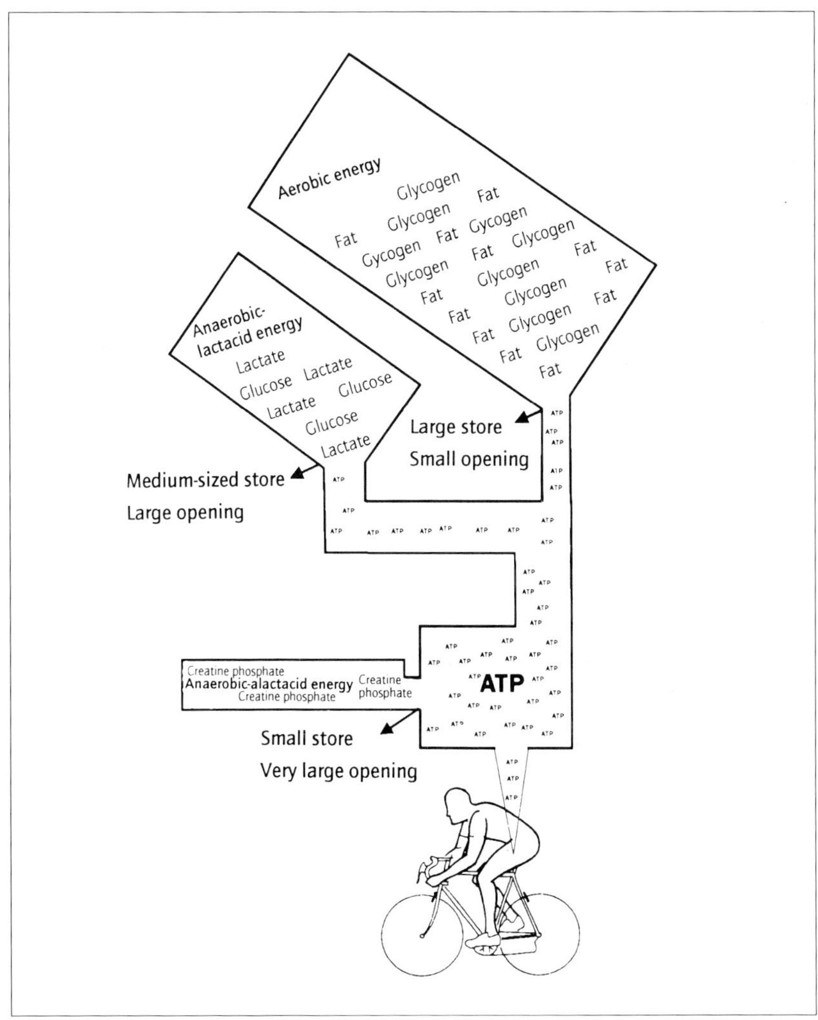

Fig. 2.10: The human energy stores (schematised). The means of providing energy overlap. The large supply of aerobic energy can only flow away slowly; when greater amounts of energy are needed the anaerobic-lactacid store is used which, however, empties quickly. Short (a few seconds) movements with very high energy consumption use up the anaerobic-alactacid store (creatine phosphate). In all three ways ATP is created which is split into ADP for muscle contraction. The various stores then refill the ATP pool.

In the cells, in the absence of oxygen, glucose is broken down into lactate. This continues until the "glycotic enzymes" (responsible for the breaking down) are restricted by the overacidity the lactate causes and have to cease their activity. In this breaking down of the glucose, energy is again released in the form of ATP. The resulting lactate goes into the blood a short time later. Here for example the concentration can be used for performance diagnostic purposes. The lactate created is partially synthesised back into glucose in the liver or metabolised by the heart muscle.

It is surprising at first that the anaerobic splitting of a glucose molecule only supplies about 5% of the combustion energy of the anaerobic metabolic form and that on top of that the lactacid energy release blocks itself, yet nevertheless a greater amount of energy per time unit is released. This is because theoretically any number of glucose molecules can be split at the same time, whose combined energy leads to a very high performance level for a relatively short period of 40 to 60 seconds.

Metabolism under Strain

At the beginning of a period of strain, especially in races, the aerobic release of energy does not yet function to best advantage, even more so when the cyclist has not warmed-up sufficiently. Here the energy deficit is covered by the anaerobic-lactacid form with acceptance of oxygen "debt".

The lactate that arises is called starting lactate; as aerobic metabolism gets going properly it is burnt up again. An intermediate sprint or a challenge are similar situations in which more lactate is created. If, however, the lactate concentration exceeds a certain level then the pressure has to be temporarily reduced or removed - from that point on, namely when the lactate concentration has risen so high that it blocks the rest of metabolism and the lactate can no longer be burnt off aerobically. The muscles become overacidic and the cyclist is forced to reduce exertion considerably.

A the beginning of a movement, as we see below, the first few seconds are covered from the ATP/CP pool, only then does the body work anaerobically depending on the intensity of exertion. As mentioned earlier, the three forms of metabolism do not take place in isolation from each other but intermesh to a great degree and determine and make each other possible. The work of the muscles is thus made possible in the following order of energy supplying processes: ATP - CP - anaerobic glycolysis - aerobic glycolysis, lipolysis. At the beginning of movement these processes overlap like cascades. Figure 2.11 illustrates the approximate time these processes take.

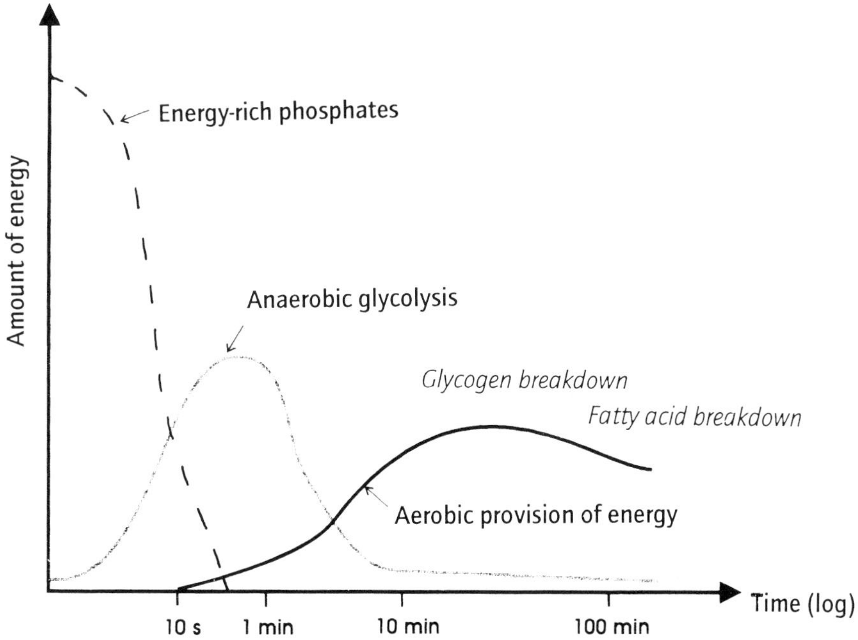

Fig. 2.11: The types of energy provision in relation to length of exertion

Protein Metabolism

If the energy stores are not enough for long and intensive training, racing sessions and phases, the body turns to its own structures and metabolises protein. In such a catabolic phase the breakdown of body substance can cause great damage which requires weeks of reduced exertion for regeneration. Such phenomena occur especially in cases of glycogen poverty caused by incorrect diet and hard training (see chapter 7 "Dietary Considerations"). In non-homogeneous training groups the weakest (young people) are affected. Frequently they reach a state of overtraining.

b) Anaerobic-alactacid Energy Release

Anaerobic-alactacid energy release only plays a subordinate role in mountain biking. For strength sports such as weight lifting and shotput, but also for all kinds of jumping, it is however of special significance. "Alactacid" means that here, in contrast to anaerobic-lactacid energy release as just described, no lactate is created.

The ATP and creatine phosphate stores (energy-rich phosphate compound) are used up during this type of energy release which lasts a maximum of five to eight seconds, and is only enough for a few muscle contractions which, however, are at a maximum.

It is important to know that ATP is absolutely necessary for every muscle contraction; without ATP the muscle cannot develop tension. For this reason the cell's ATP store must be regenerated again and again, mainly through aerobic metabolism. ATP is also needed for other processes in the cell which consume energy, such as regeneration processes or cell growth.

When a small amount of phosphate is split from the ATP, the stored energy is released and the muscle contracts. The remaining ADP (adenosine diphosphate) is later "recycled" into ATP by the creatine phosphate through the splitting of an amount of phosphate again.

The CP stores can be enlarged by doing a series of short, about eight second long, sprints at maximum exertion, which especially benefits the mountain biker on hills or in spurts (assault, after bends). More recently more significance has been attributed to these energy stores in endurance sport too.

Metabolic Phases

In endurance sport and mountain biking four different metabolic phases can thus be differentiated. In the following sections these phases are described as in a stage test on the ergometer.

1st Phase

At low strain there is an aerobic metabolic situation in which mainly fats are metabolised. The lactate values are in or even slightly below the rest area, and thus provide no information about the intensity of effort.

2nd Phase

With growing intensity the proportion of metabolised carbohydrates increases. In this area there are slightly increased lactate values which, however, do not increase if effort remains constant. With increasing effort a growing proportion of metabolism must come from anaerobic glycolysis. As long as lactate elimination and production are in balance there is a "steady state". The maximum lactate steady state is the highest level of effort at which this balance occurs.

This point is often equated with the anaerobic threshold and thus limits the second phase upwards.

3rd Phase

In the third phase during constant effort there is an accumulation of lactate in the blood which is coupled with rising lactate values because more lactate is produced than can be eliminated. The proportion of anaerobic glycolysis in energy provision is already very high here.

4th Phase

In a 4th phase the provision of energy would be covered purely anaerobically by anaerobic glycolysis. Shortly after ending strain the highest lactate values can be measured.

Beginners and Professionals Have Dissimilar Starting Conditions

The information in this chapter shows how great the physiological differences are between a mountain bike beginner, a cross-country cyclist who has been active for several years, and a professional.

Years of adaptive processes have made the professional superior in all physiological performance criteria. If professionals race against amateurs the results are generally very predictable - comparable to a touring car in a Formula One race.

2.2 Requirements of the Individual Disciplines

Training planning and co-ordination in performance and in popular sport first call for an analysis of the requirements of the particular sport. A requirement profile gives information about the exact performance structure of the sport or sporting movement under examination. The performance structure of a sport is determined by performance factors.

The emphasis is placed on the use made of the fitness performance factors i.e. strength, endurance or stamina, speed, mobility and co-ordination, in practising a sport. This includes determining certain physiological performance characteristics of the sport. Both racing and training are taken into consideration.

Additionally a profile of psychological, cognitive and social performance factors is often compiled. To this are added external performance factors such as the profile and length of the course, and material factors which include the mountain bike and all other equipment the biker uses.

Performance factors in mountain biking:

- Fitness performance factors
- Psychological performance factors
- Cognitive performance factors
- Social performance factors
- External performance factors
- Material factors.

In mountain biking only a start has been made with compiling a requirement profile. In the coming years there will certainly be detailed results available.

Within the framework of this book we will briefly sketch the requirement profiles of the individual disciplines involved in mountain biking, taking into special consideration the physiological performance factors. The profiles do not claim to be complete, but as discussed above, they are of great importance in creating a training schedule.

Some of the performance factors are valid for all the disciplines in mountain biking and are therefore only covered once under "cross-country".

2.2.1 Cross-country

External Factors

Without a doubt the field of cross-country is the most popular and therefore has the most active participants, whether in racing or in popular sport with cross-country tours. In racing sport a difference is made between races over round courses with varying numbers of laps and the rarer route races (from one place to another). These often include marathons which play a special role, not only because of their long duration of exertion.

The duration of exertion is rarely over three hours even in the World Cup (this applies only to cyclists at the rear; the leaders rarely take more than 2-2.5 h), which places the races in the field of long-term endurance III and long-term endurance II (up to 90 minutes). Most cross-country races, however, are in a field of between 30 and 120 minutes.

In addition to very different course lengths there is also a wide range of course profiles from practically flat to very uneven. There are often laps with altitude differences of several hundred metres which place more demands on a mountain biker than a flat race.

The great variation in these external performance factors only allows a partial characterisation of the other performance factors.

Cross-country field in the women's class shortly after the start (Paola Pezzo) Photo: Klaus Eweleit

Fitness Factors

The metabolic situation during a cross-country race is generally in the aerobic-anaerobic transitional area for most of the course. The shorter the riding time, the greater the proportion of anaerobic metabolism, which will, however, always remain under 20%, and in a normal cross-country race will make up about 5% of total cycling time. Cyclists are only in the aerobic area during longer downhill sections.

In long races such as marathons, aerobic metabolism takes place 70-95% of the time depending on the duration of exertion. Anaerobic mobilisation decreases in significance and is only relevant in the final dash, on very steep slopes or during challenges in the course of the race, and here it is much less than in shorter races.

Corresponding to the metabolic situation, depending on motivation and the race situation, heart rates under strain in cross-country races are just under the anaerobic threshold with a few brief rises into the anaerobic area, as well as occasional short phases in the aerobic area (downhills). A well-trained biker with a maximum heart rate of about 200 has a race heart rate of about 185 beats per minute. The metabolic situation is thus comparable with that of a timed race on a profiled road race course, although the heart rate oscillates much more strongly because of the only rarely constant demands on performance.

In training it is therefore necessary to concentrate on creating as good an aerobic capacity as possible without neglecting anaerobic mobilisation, which plays a decisive part in mountain biking.

Cross-country races place especially high demands on strength. The cross-country cyclist has relatively low pedalling rates (< 80) but with a high use of strength. The course of pedalling frequency in a cross-country race is characterised by an alternation between rates of 80 and phases of no pedalling.

In addition to excellent strength endurance to cope with the necessary gearing over the total course of the race, resilience and maximum strength must be at a high level to overcome very steep sections both on the bike and on foot. In considering the exertion profile (SRM system) on page 132ff the significance of strength endurance and resilience in the many performance peaks on short uphill slopes and spurts becomes clear. This exertion criterion calls for training methodology that considers the area of resilience to a great degree. The size of the creatine phosphate stores thus has a decisive influence on performing ability.

As can be seen in figure 3.29ff., pedalling frequency and performance undergo constant change. In training it is therefore necessary to increase the contractability of the pedalling muscles in order to realise the necessary movements as economically as possible. Also decisive is the ability to repeat these very brief acceleration phases very often during a race (sometimes several hundred times). In the high performance field this requires very high repeat numbers in interval training.

The arm muscles are subject to much higher strain in comparison to road cycling, which should be considered in planning training (strength training). The same applies to the torso muscles which also need to be kept in a good state of training.

The highest demands are placed on the co-ordinative abilities of cross-country cyclists because they have to negotiate both difficult uphill sections and tricky downhill rides. Many cyclists lose a huge amount of time on downhills and other difficult sections as a result of deficits in cycling technique which cannot be caught up even through excellent aerobic/anaerobic provision of energy. This highlights the importance of training technique.

Psychological Factors

The psychological performance factors are characterised by the ability to concentrate on often difficult sections, and the necessary high degree of motivation. Psychological training must be applied in order to ensure these performance prerequisites.

Social Factors

The social factors are comprised of an optimal environment regarding family, friends and the club or team. Here one should strive for well-ordered circumstances.

Cognitive Factors

Demands are placed cognitively on the mountain biker in particular in the tactical field and in planning and co-ordinating of training. Certain race situations have to be mastered tactically. This is not a problem cognitively, but as a rule it can only be realised in races when experience is available.

Equipment Factors

Equipment factors play a significant role in mountain biking. Especially in difficult country the equipment must be optimally adapted to conditions in order to lose as little time as possible. Matching equipment to conditions also increases cycling safety.

Stage Races

In stage races, which are becoming increasingly popular in mountain biking but are only for the absolute elite, physiological factors in particular take on special significance in addition to the performance factors already mentioned. Because of the required best possible regenerational ability in the course of a tour, the significance of aerobic capacity grows. With increasing length of the stage and the tour, anaerobic mobilisation decreases in significance, but is used at the finish and in challenges. If excellent regenerational ability has not been developed through special preparation and planning of the season, there will be great drops in performance in the fields of aerobic and aerobic/anaerobic energy provision, as well as in the field of strength, because the body can no longer regenerate the required amounts of energy from one stage to the next.

Motivation and the will to perform are stretched to a great degree during a stage race.

The variety of factors listed here, which are only a rough overview, show how complex performance structures are in a physiologically and technically very demanding sport like cross-country biking. Without a doubt cross-country must be very diverse, and combine the requirements of all the other disciplines to a high degree.

If you compare performance structure with other cycling disciplines, the majority of similarities can be found in short laps in road cycling, in point races, and two man team races in track cycling. In these disciplines there is usually also an irregular alternation between intensive and less intensive phases. Especially in lap races very high performance is required over short laps. Anaerobic mobilisational ability also needs to be very well developed in these disciplines.

Further interesting information on performance structure can be obtained from the graphs in chapter 3.9 created using the "Schober Measuring System".

2.2.2 Downhill

Downhill races usually place demands on fitness performance factors in a different way to cross-country races. In a relatively short race of several minutes to rarely more than 20 minutes aerobic capacity loses significance. Of great importance on the other hand is perfect co-ordination which must be constantly available even at highest heart rates under strain. Thus a great deal of training time is spent learning and perfecting technical cycling skills.

From the point of view of performance physiology high demands are placed on anaerobic capacity and strength. Because of the course, very often brief accelerations are necessary which require a high degree of resilience and maximum strength. There are parallels to the performance structures of 1,000 metre cyclists and track sprinters which should be reflected in the training of downhillers.

In addition to the pedalling muscles the rest of the muscles are placed under very high strain for brief periods. Strength training for the arms and upper body should therefore be carried out regularly. A strengthened muscle corset protects when falls occur, and also provides a certain performance reserve when extreme demands are placed on strength.

Concentration, mental anticipation and fearlessness are psychological characteristics of performance structure in downhill racing. Mental training for visualising the courses and reducing fear is absolutely necessary.

In the downhill in particular the performance factor "material" can be decisive to the race outcome because rapid developments in technology mean that a disadvantage through equipment that is dated, or not suited to course conditions, is especially noticeable. The equipment is taxed in borderline situations so that technical innovations which increase safety reserves directly lead to faster times.

Photo: Stephan Bögli© SSG Europe

Dual Slalom

The dual slalom requires a similar degree of control over the bike to the downhill. Physiological performance factors are not so prominent here because of the short race times. Fast accelerations are decisive and training should be targeted to developing excellent resilience and resilience endurance without, however, negatively influencing co-ordination through too much strength training. Equipment also plays a significant role here.

2.2.3 Uphill

Uphill races can be equated with timed hill races or hill races with mass starts. The duration of strain ranges from a few minutes (timed hill races) in low mountain ranges up to over an hour in high mountains. Uphill races are only carried out on rare occasions and usually only cross-country riders participate.

To overcome the downhill force both excellent aerobic capacity and especially good strength characteristics are needed. The low pedalling rates, and the usually lacking regeneration phases with pedalling breaks require extremely well-developed strength endurance.

Uphill races demand all a biker has to give.
Photo: Trek Deutschland

The shorter an uphill race is, the more significant is anaerobic mobilisation, especially towards the end of the race. Heart rate readings are near the anaerobic threshold during a race, and at the end of the course actually rise above it.

In timed hill climbs riders need to have marked psychological hardness and a will to perform in combination with definite lactate tolerance.

Lower cycling speeds mean that aerodynamic considerations are unimportant, but the weight of the mountain bike is of significance.

2.2.4 Technical Races

The term "technical races" refers to all kinds of trial competitions. As the name indicates, co-ordinative control of the mountain bike (trial bike) is most important here. All other fitness performance factors are only of subordinate significance. Mobility and strength (resilience and "explosive" strength) have the greatest influence on performance structure.
Here too the right choice of equipment plays an important role.

3 Training

3.1 Basic Training Principles

Training is a planned process with the aim of achieving an improvement in or maintaining the sporting performance capacity of an athlete through the use of suitable training means.

Sporting performance capacity not only means purely physical (fitness) performance capacity. Tactical, technical and psychological aspects must be considered and improved as well.

The term **fitness** is characterised by five different capabilities which are addressed to varying degrees depending on the sport. Principally though none of these capabilities should be neglected in training.

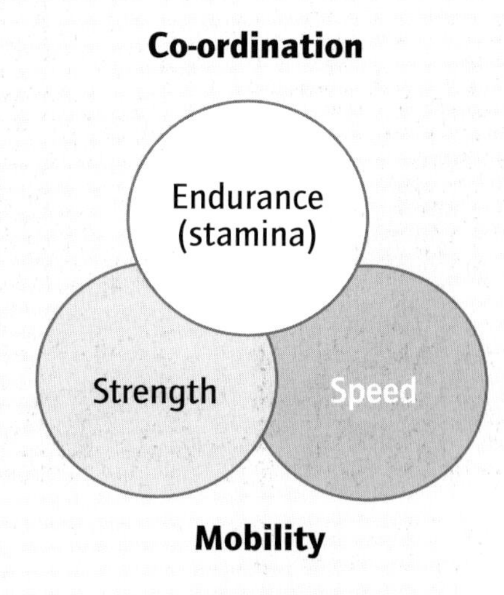

Fig. 3.1: The fitness capabilities

Biologically, training is the reaction of the body to effort. If demands are placed on the human body it develops its physical abilities, but if no more demands are placed on it, these abilities decline again. The sensible alternation of effort and relief (break for rest) is decisive for the training effect. Effort mixes up the biological balance of the body with the result that after recovery (regeneration) the body adapts to the effort and is able to perform better than before.

The following diagram explains the principle of **super compensation**, one of the most important training principles. Training stimulus, tiredness, recovery and super compensation must occur with the right periods of time between them. **Regeneration** is the process which compensates the exhaustion of the organism and lasts until restoration of the previous level of performance capacity is complete. Super compensation is the term for the performance increase after

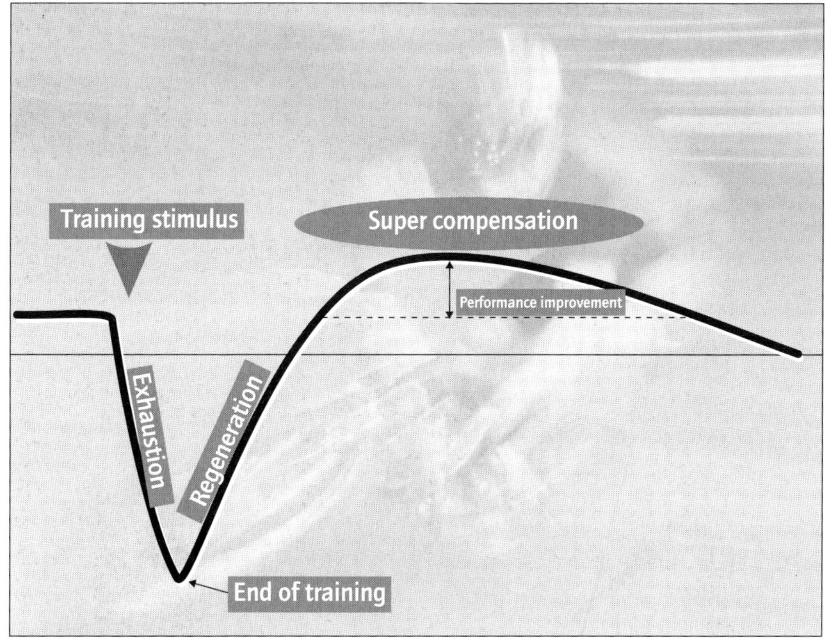

Fig. 3.2: Super compensation

regeneration, in a way it is a kind of "over-regeneration". The increased level of performance is achieved because regeneration does not stop at the previous level of performance but continues until a level is reached that makes it possible to deal with the same amount of effort again without difficulty. This process is called adaptation.

Once training has reached a high level, the jumps in performance ability get smaller until finally a plateau of constant performance capability has been developed.

This circumstance is the reason that trained mountain bikers need very large amounts of training and clever training schedules in order to maintain, or even increase, their performance level. Only the greatest exertion, well-dosed over many years, makes it possible to achieve top placings at international level. Because of the already very high standard there can be no surprise winners (completely

Time

Fig. 3.3: Development of performance through many years of endurance training with increasing exertion (simplified)

unknown) in the cross-country World Cup who have not already achieved top performances in a related sport (road, cross). More about the physiological adaptation processes can be found in chapter 2.1.

In **adaptation,** metabolic adaptation is distinguished from morphological adaptation (roughly: physical adaptation, e.g. muscles, heart). Mountain biking often leads to major adaptation processes both on the metabolic and the morphological sides which are more closely examined in chapter 2.1 "From Beginner to Professional from a Physiological Perspective".

3.1.1 Description of Training Strain

Training Intensity

refers to the force of the strain from a strain stimulus or a training session. In mountain biking, training intensity is most easily measured with the aid of the heart rate (high intensity = high heart rate). Other intensity values are lactate concentration and speed.

Amount of Training

The amount of training is the sum of all effort or training stimuli within a training session or within a certain training period (week, preparatory period). In mountain biking the amount of training can be equated to the kilometres cycled or even better with the duration of training (e.g. 22 h/week or 6 h basic training); if there are also training sessions without the bike (indoor training, gymnastics, running training, strength training etc.) these are included in the amount of training.

Density of Strain

indicates the relationship between effort and relief (recovery) and thus also the length of breaks between individual strain stimuli; a difference is made between complete and incomplete breaks. When there is a *complete break*, you wait before applying the next strain stimulus until you have completely recovered, which in turn is determined using the heart rate or by one's feeling. An *incomplete* or *worthwhile break* is finished when the heart rate has gone back down to a reading of 120-130 beats per minute; now the next stimulus is applied (e.g. 1,000 m at speed).

Duration of Strain

is the duration of an exertion stimulus, for example of an interval (three minutes) or a series of sprints (six times 20 seconds).

Training Frequency

indicates how often you train per week.

These five basic factors of sports training allow an exact description of the training process and will be used again and again on the following pages.

If the exertion stimuli are applied correctly, performance capacity can be increased to an *individual performance limit* which in an endurance sport like mountain biking can only be reached after many years of training. It is therefore impossible to achieve absolute top performance within one year, especially if you have not previously been involved in an endurance sport. This is often difficult for mountain bikers to understand and frequently leads to frustration.

The following diagram shows a sequence of strain that is too short; during regeneration the next strain stimulus is applied immediately so that performance capacity cannot improve and instead even deteriorates.

A stagnation of performance would be the result of not enough strain stimuli; the following strain stimulus is not applied until the super compensation has deteriorated again and finds the athlete in practically the same state as before training. Here little or no improvement in performance is achieved. The lower illustration (3.4) shows that the new strain must be in the middle area (high point) of the super compensation phase in order to assure an optimum improvement in performance.

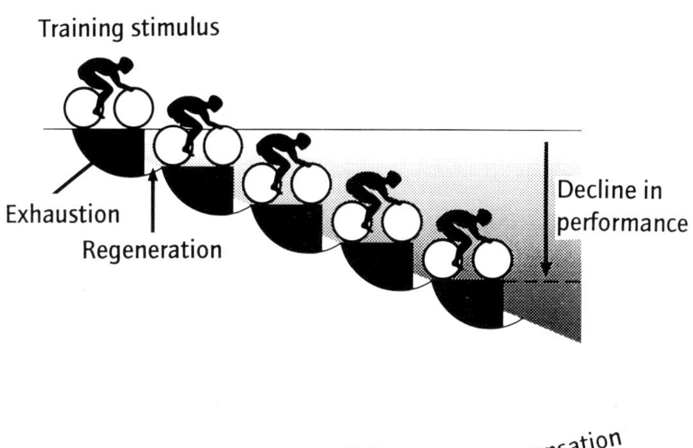

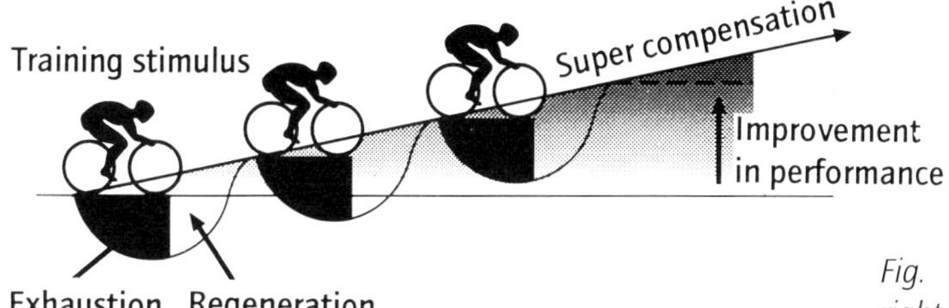

Fig. 3.4: The right and the wrong sequence of strain stimuli

Not only the length of the regenerational break between the training sessions must be chosen correctly, the training and competition strain itself must be right in order to increase performance; more about this in the next chapter. A stimulus that is not strong enough does not trigger an adaptive process - too great a stimulus can lead to a state of overtraining over time; only a correct stimulus will lead to the desired adaptation and super compensation. In connection with this "correct" stimulus, amount and intensity must be right, but the breaks in between must also be ideally co-ordinated.

In choosing the breaks from strain, and also in creating the training schedule, one's feeling for one's own body plays a decisive role. Training schedule suggestions such as those in this book must be adapted to individual circumstances. A training schedule must not be seen as a rigid structure.

3.1.2 Regeneration

If it were possible to be successful just through hard and exhausting training on a daily basis, then a large number of mountain bikers would probably have much greater performance capacity. But in addition to the necessary training exertion, recovery or regeneration is just as much a part of a structured training programme. The following lines deal with getting the relationship between exertion and recovery right.

Photo: Trek Deutschland

What Determines the Duration of the Regeneration Phase?

A simple basic principle of regeneration says that the harder or more exhausting the training or competition, the longer the regeneration phase needed by the body should be because the body needs more time to equalise the "muddle" in its tissues, the biological imbalance.

Illnesses such as infections or inflammations usually influence regeneration negatively. Even normal daily training can then not be dealt with and the recovery phase takes longer. After heavy colds, regeneration can be disturbed for up to two or three weeks, which has a major effect on performance capacity.

How Can Regeneration Be Influenced?

Regeneration can only be influenced by optimising the prerequisites for training and racing; there is, however, no "miracle drug" that causes immediate recovery when taken. Especially when training and race strain are high, such as at a training camp or on race weekends, regeneration should not be left to itself but rather actively supported.

Factors Favourable to Regeneration

- Sufficient rest (sleep)
- Regenerative diet
- Stretching
- Massage
- Hot bath, shower
- Sauna
- Active recovery (walks)
- Relaxation techniques
- Regenerative training

Sufficient rest means that after exertion you should not involve yourself in any unnecessary effort; but sufficient sleep is also meant by this. **Diet** must be very rich in carbohydrates, vitamins and minerals (see chapter 7 "Dietary Considerations") in order to replenish used energy reserves. **Stretching** lowers muscle tone, stimulates metabolism, maintains flexibility and should be carried out daily.

A **regenerational massage** also ensures lower muscle tone, accelerated removal of metabolic waste products and above all relaxation. A **hot bath** for about 15 minutes lowers muscle tone, stimulates metabolism, relaxes and calms. **Relaxation techniques** will be dealt with in chapter 9.

Above all, **regenerative training** on the bike (CO, see 3.2) contributes to faster removal of metabolic waste products from the muscles and is thus the most important means of supporting regeneration. Active recovery when going for a walk has a similar effect.

As a general rule regenerational ability can be increased through endurance training. After a hard race trained mountain bikers are usually fresh and recovered only a few minutes after crossing the finish line; training beginners for example hardly recover after a hill section, and may even have to pull out of the race or training session.

How Do You Feel the Regenerational State?

As described above, regeneration is an individual process which can differ in time from one mountain biker to another after the same course. In addition to the factors described the duration of regeneration is also related to age. Young bikers regenerate more quickly than older bikers (same training level). Bikers with much training experience (high training age) also regenerate faster, and women regenerate more quickly than men.

One's body feeling during training and races gives the most information about the state of regeneration. Further indications of completed regeneration are a positive attitude, the desire to train and achieve performance, good sleep, a good appetite, normal resting heart rates, heart rates under strain, and the feeling of being healthy.

Deficiencies in one or more of these factors should motivate the mountain biker to extend the regeneration phase. The aim of the "self-training mountain biker" should be to find out his own regeneration requirements for various kinds of exertion.

Hightech Regeneration

In modern sports medicine care of endurance athletes a number of blood parameters are also determined, in addition to the regeneration indicators mentioned, which allow a very detailed characterisation of the state of regeneration.

Concentrations of creatine phosphate, urea and other metabolic waste products are examined as well as the concentration of minerals.

Phase	Regeneration process	Comments
Early phase End of strain up to about 6 h	- Replenishment of the CP and ATP stores - Elimination of blood lactate - Beginning of replenishment of glycogen stores - Normalisation of heart and breathing rates	Important phase for glycogen resynthesis; sufficient carbohydrates and liquids must be consumed. Warning: increased danger of infection after getting cold and excess exertion.
Late phase About 6-36 h	- Replenishment of glycogen stores - Regeneration of protein structures (mitochondria) - Practically regenerated immune defence	Further consumption of sufficient carbohydrates. Also various regenerative measures, especially compensatory training (30 min) and stretching (see text).
Super compensation About 36 h to several weeks	- Electrolyte compensation, potentially super compensation - Restoration of hormonal balance - Super compensation of structural proteins - Super compensation of hormones and enzymes	Super compensation, especially of the protein structures, can be spread over several weeks e.g. after a training camp or a stage race. This must be taken into consideration in training.

Fig. 3.5: Duration of various regenerational processes

An immunological assessment of regeneration is also possible through the determination of cell numbers and the activity of various immune cells.

In this respect science is still in an early phase, and it is only in recent years that larger projects to research regeneration have begun; results will probably lead to first steps towards regeneration-dependent training co-ordination and regulation.

Meanwhile, however, with the aid of the methods discussed here and a little experience, it is not a problem to assess regeneration in performance mountain biking.

3.1.3 Training Principles for Mountain Biking

Training principles relate to the physiological effect of training and the adaptive processes in the body after strain stimulus, and make up the foundation of training planning.

Principle of Effective Strain Stimulus

This principle means that a strain stimulus must have a minimum intensity in order to have a training effect at all. The degree of this intensity in endurance training depends on performance capacity state and individual form on a particular day. For example, in a trained biker there would not be any adaptive processes from doing 30 minutes daily mountain bike endurance training at a heart rate of 110 beats per minute. This would only serve regeneration, whereas for a rehabilitation patient it could represent a training stimulus that is too high.

Principle of Progressive Increase of Strain

In order to achieve an improvement in performance capacity over a longer period of time, training and competition strain must correspond to current performance capacity. As performance capacity increases, effort must be increased in order to improve or maintain form. Over several years the strain is increased gradually. When the level of performance is very high this is not enough and effort must be increased rapidly to trigger adaptation.

Principle of Variation of Strain

Similar to the above-mentioned principle, over the years strain must not only be increased but also changed. This applies especially to mountain bikers with a very high performance level who need to use completely new training methods (e.g. cross-training) in order to break through so-called performance barriers caused by uniform training.

Principle of Optimal Structuring of Strain and Recovery

This principle has already been extensively discussed in sections 3.1 and 3.2. Super compensation and recovery are key factors in sports training.

Principle of Periodisation and Cyclisation

Because a mountain biker cannot be in top form all season long, the training year must be divided into periods of varying strain in order to reach a top performance level at a given time. This principle will be dealt with extensively in chapter 3.4.

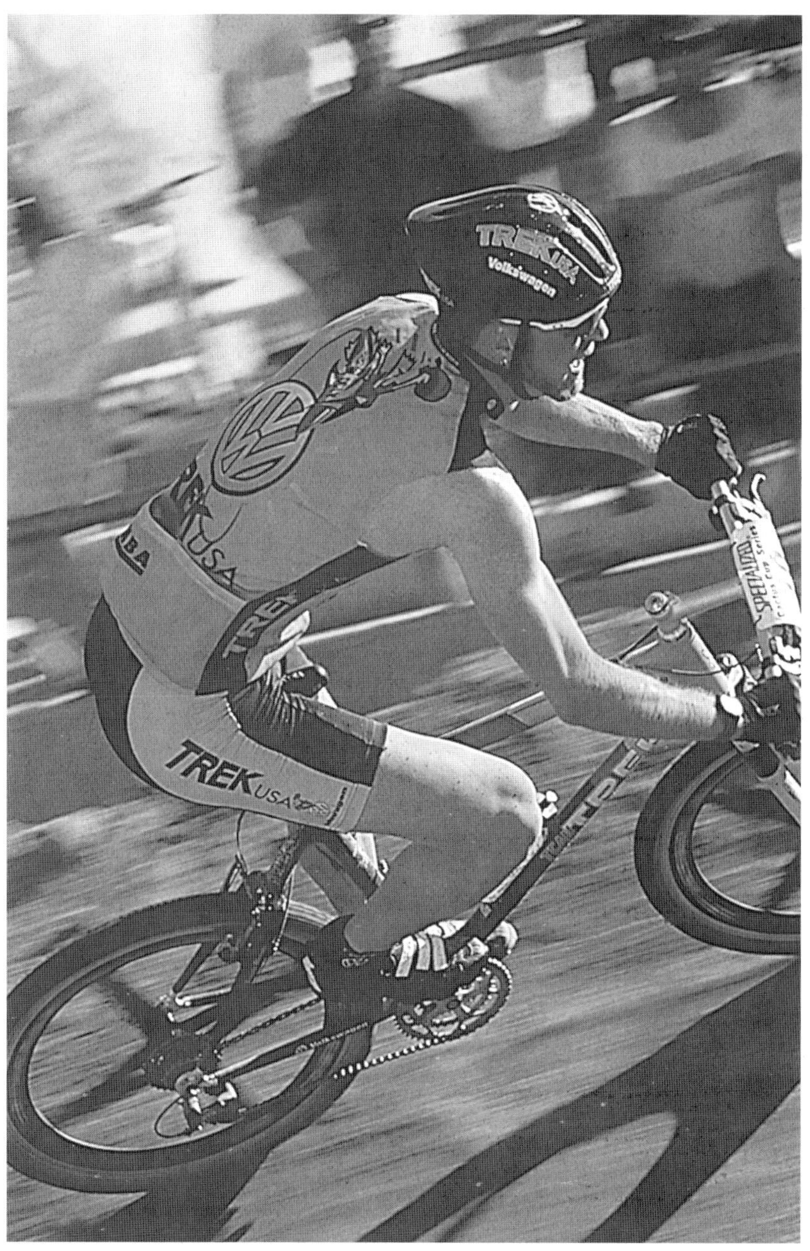

Photo: Trek Deutschland

Principle of Individuality and Appropriateness to Age

Because every mountain biker has different biological prerequisites, each has to train differently. The personal situation and abilities of the athlete must be considered in training planning. For young people age plays a major role in the choice of the type of work, for adults the training age is significant.

Principle of Increasing Specialisation

In the course of a training year, but also of a "mountain biking career", special training means take on increasing significance. If for example at the beginning of the year a lot of cross-training is still carried out, during the season you would concentrate on cycling training. Similarly, the proportion of cycling training increases constantly from young people in basic training to World Cup riders doing high performance work.

Principle of Conscious Training

The principle of conscious training, which calls for occupying oneself mentally with training content, is decisive. Before a training session one should be conscious of the objectives served by the session and of what should and should not be done in order to achieve this objective. Often people train without even knowing what specifically is supposed to be trained. This principle applies especially to trainers.

3.1.4 Training Methodology

Endurance

Endurance or **stamina** is generally used to describe the increased ability of the body to resist tiredness and to recover after it (ability to resist tiredness). This robustness is not only a physical feature, but the psychological aspects are also meant here.

There are several forms of endurance.
Local endurance is the opposite of *general endurance*; local endurance is limited to less than 1/6 of all muscles. When cycling, the use of large muscle groups (legs) means that *general endurance* is addressed. *Aerobic* and *anaerobic endurance* are differentiated according to the form of energy provision; in mountain biking both aerobic and anaerobic endurance are necessary.

	STE	MTE	LTE I	LTE II	LTE III	LTE IV
Duration	35 s - 2 min	2 min - 10 min	10 min - 35 min	35 min - 90 min	90 min - 6 h	> 6 h
Competition form in mountain biking	(Downhill) Uphill Sprints	Downhill Uphill	(Downhill) Uphill Cross-country	(Uphill) Cross-country	Marathon Cross-country	Marathon
HR/min	185 - 200	190 - 210	180 - 190	170 - 190	150 - 180	120 - 170
% VO_2 max.	100	95 - 100	90 - 95	80 - 95	60 - 90	50 - 60
Aerobic proportion	20 - 35	40 - 60	70 - 80	80 - 90	95	99
Anaerobic proportion	80 - 65	60 - 40	30 - 20	20 - 10	5	1
Energy supplying Main substrates	Glycogen Phosphates	Glycogen	Glycogen	Glycogen Fats	Fats, glycogen Amino acids	Fats, glycogen Amino acids
Limiting factors	High level of speed and strength Aerobic performance capacity Co-ordination (technique) High acidity tolerance	High aerobic and anaerobic capacity High level of speed and strength High acidity tolerance VO_2 max. co-ordination	Anaerobic threshold VO_2 max. Acidity tolerance Lactate elimination	Anaerobic threshold VO_2 max. Glycogen stores Thermo-regulation	Anaerobic threshold VO_2 max. Glycogen stores Water balance Lipolysis	Lipolysis Water balance Carbohydrate consumption

Fig. 3.6: Endurance types according to duration of strain (modified from NEUMANN, G./BERBALK, A., 1991)

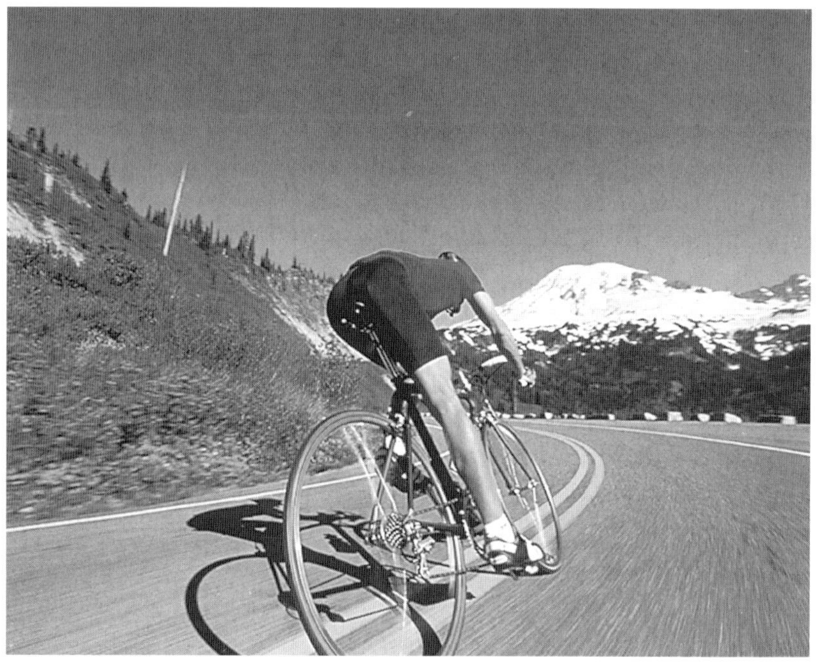

Training with the duration method on the road also has its attractions.
Photo: Trek Deutschland

Furthermore there is a difference between *static* (holding the body without moving) and *dynamic endurance* (movement).

The values shown in figure 3.6 are approximate values for the corresponding duration of endurance. The heart rates shown are based on a maximum heart rate of about 210 beats/minute. Only the most important factors limiting performance are mentioned.

The downhill only enters the endurance field when practically continuous maximum pedalling is required.

On technically difficult courses with only brief, intensive pedalling phases, categorisation is difficult and is oriented to the sum of the pedalling sections and their temporal sequence.

Methodology of Endurance Training

1) The **duration training method** mainly serves the development of basic endurance.

a) *Continuous method:* constant intensity; regulation of effort using the heart rate is most exact. The continuous duration training method is the main training method in mountain biking, especially in the preparatory period, because with the appropriate intensity it improves aerobic capacity and regenerational ability. The duration of exertion should be over two hours and can be up to 5-8 hours. Training intensity can either be constant or vary within a small framework.

b) *Alternating method:* on predetermined sectors speed is increased up to the mixed aerobic-anaerobic area.

c) *Fartlek:* speed is adjusted to the course and wind conditions. The biker plays with speed and thus with intensity. Fartlek is done particularly in rough country or in the forest.

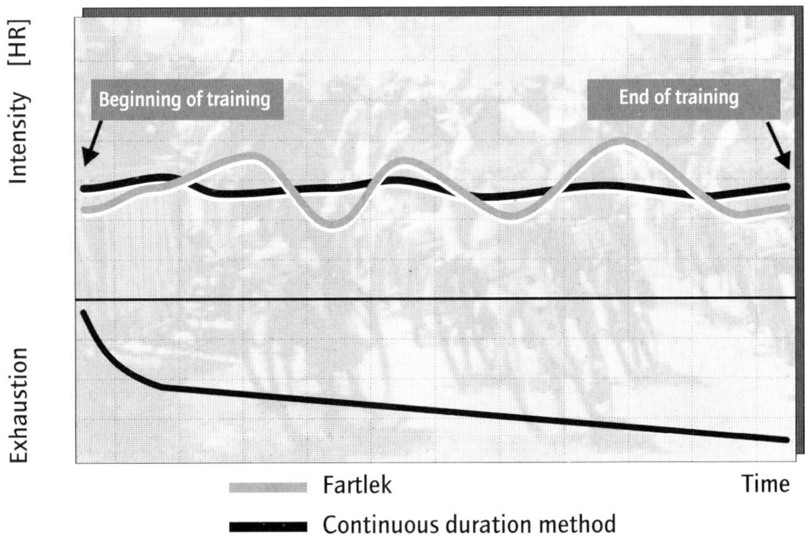

Fig. 3.7: Diagram of continuous method and fartlek

2) The **interval methods** feature planned alternation of effort and recovery; the recovery phase, however, does not last until complete recovery but is followed by another strain interval when the heart rate is about 120 to 140 (see fig. 3.8). This break is called a "worthwhile break". The interval method is used in sprint training for example (e.g.: 8 x 7 s or 6 x 30 s). If a number of series is carried out there should be longer recovery breaks between the individual series of 4-8 repeats. For short sprints (resilience training), the breaks should last 1-2 minutes and, depending on fitness, 5-10 minutes for long intervals of 4,000 metres. The breaks should be active, at greatly reduced intensity (slow pedalling in easy gears in the CO field).
   The interval methods are differentiated according to interval length:

a) Short interval (SI): 7-60 s (e.g. 10 x 7 s, 6 x 30 s)
b) Medium interval (MI): 1-3 min (e.g. 4 x 1:30 min)
c) Long interval (LI): 3-15 min (e.g. 4 x 10 min)

Short intervals are also referred to as the **intensive interval method,** long intervals as the **extensive interval method**; medium intervals are classed under both methods depending on intensity.

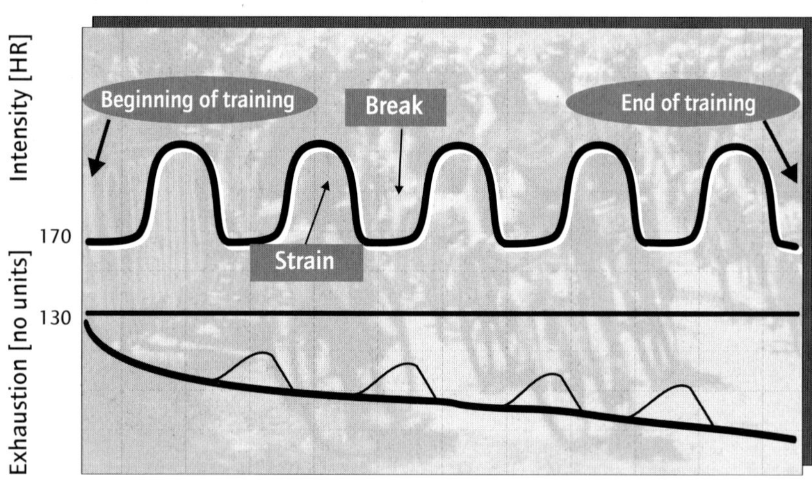

Fig. 3.8: Diagram of interval method (worthwhile break)

The extensive interval methods serve to raise the anaerobic threshold, improve aerobic capacity and improve anaerobic mobilisation.

The intensive interval methods improve lactate tolerance, raise anaerobic-lactacid and anaerobic-alactacid capacity (see chapter 2), improve regenerational ability on short, steep climbs and address speed and resilience.

3) **Repetition Method**

The repetition method is characterised by complete recovery breaks (heart rate under 100) between the strain phases ridden at or above competition intensity. In cross-country this method is used less often, in track sport on the other hand it is frequently chosen (e.g. 3 x 1,000 m).

In cross-country the repetition method can be used for strength training on hills, after about 2-3 minutes of maximum effort there is a first active then passive break until the heart rate has gone down to about 90.

The repetition method too is differentiated into short, medium and long units. This method is used particularly in the downhill, where pedalling sections at top speed are involved.

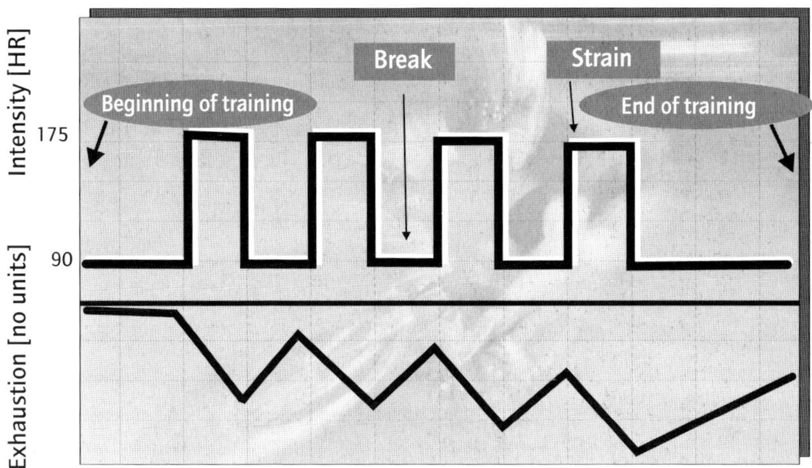

Fig. 3.9: Diagram of repetition method (complete breaks until recovery)

4) **Race and Monitor Method**

The race and monitor method involves a single effort of race intensity and duration.

The physiological training strain is very similar to race strain over the same distance and speed, in over-distance training (longer than race distance) the effort/intensity is slightly lower than race intensity, in under-distance training it is slightly higher. High motivation is a prerequisite for the race method in order to be able to simulate the toughness of the race.

Unorganised training races on a round course are good for this because then they can "properly" simulate races not only physically, but also technically, tactically and pyschologically.

The race method should, however, only be used at the end of the preparatory period or even at the beginning of the competition period. To monitor performance (monitor method) and for easy performance diagnosis, timed races and uphills are carried out.

The race method allows playful practising of tactical behaviour. At the same time it improves psychological "race toughness". For this, though, it is important to train in a homogeneous group.

Strength

Strength is the underlying physical characteristic for the realisation of movement. Without a certain degree of strength no movements can be carried out. The various types of muscular contraction have already been discussed in chapter 2.

Here we will just explain the various types of strength. Sport science traditionally differentiates three main forms of strength in addition to numerous subforms. Although recent research differentiates even more, for the sake of easier understanding we will use the traditional model here. In chapter 2 the functioning of muscles important to strength training was explained.

a) Maximum Strength

The strength an athlete can voluntarily exert using maximum muscle contraction is referred to as *maximum strength*.

Recent research has found that maximum strength as the "foundation" for the other types of strength is of far greater significance than was previously assumed – for mountain biking as well.

b) Resilience

Resilience is the athlete's ability to overcome great resistance with fast muscle contraction; it is greatly dependent on the level of *maximum strength. Resilience* is significant in cross-country for it is needed especially for steep ascents, sprints and challenges. Overcoming obstacles and jumps is also made easier by a high level of *resilience.*

c) Strength Endurance

Strength endurance describes the athlete's ability to resist tiring from repeated demands on strength. One speaks of strength endurance or stamina when about 30-50% of maximum strength is applied in a dynamic way. *Strength endurance* is of great importance for uphill sections and dashes away from the field which require high to top gearing using all one's strength. A simple comparison can be made which puts strength and pedalling rate in a relationship to each other: the higher the pedalling rate is at constant speed, the less strength is needed; the lower the pedalling rate at constant speed, the more strength is required. In mountain biking the pedalling rate is relatively low.

Methodology of Strength Training

In strength training, training strains are assigned in repeats and sets; a set can consist of one to 20 repeats or more which are carried out after each other without a break. Between the sets there are breaks.

Chapter 4 deals with the "Methodology of Strength Training" more extensively.

Speed

Speed is defined as the ability to contract a muscle as fast as possible. Speed is divided into two main forms: the speed of a single movement (speed of movement - pedalling rate) and the motion speed (riding speed) of an athlete. Depending on the type of movement, a difference is made between *cyclical* and *acyclical* speed.

Cycling involves a movement that happens again and again, i.e. it is *cyclical*, which means that *cyclical speed* has the most significance for mountain bikers. *Cyclical speed* (speed of movement) depends on gearing. If gearing is high, pedalling rate and thus speed of movement are low; motion speed, however, can be very high. If a high pedalling rate coupled with a very high strength level (high gear, strength endurance) can be maintained for a longer period of time, then high motion speed can be achieved. This shows how much speed is dependent on strength; high speed performance cannot be realised without a correspondingly high strength level anyway. In training importance should be attached both to developing strength and improving speed.

Speed training is of less importance in cross-country, while the speed ability of the muscles is needed for brief maximum accelerations in downhill and slalom and is a deciding performance factor here.

Methodology of Speed Training

In speed training the repetition method is used at high intensities and with movements that are as specific as possible (on the mountain bike or racing bike). The duration of effort should correspond to competition demands (short accelerations of 6-8 seconds and longer pedalling sections downhill of up to 40 seconds). For a better stimulus effect, speed training should be carried out in blocks several days in a row.

For more on this subject see "Speed Training" in chapter 3.2.

Mobility

Mobility is a person's ability to carry out a movement with as great an amount of movement as possible. Good mobility is an absolute prerequisite for movement of high quality.

Insufficient development of mobility makes people more prone to injury. If joints and ligaments only have little room to move when there is a fall, then ligaments and tendons can more easily be pulled or even torn and broken bones are also more frequent. Insufficient mobility hinders the development of an athlete's fitness and co-ordinative abilities.

Mobility economises the moving processes of cycling and helps develop regenerational ability. In the technical disciplines, and in downhill in particular, mobility is a fundamental prerequisite for good control of the bike.

Mobility depends to a great extent on the elasticity of the muscles. For this reason a whole chapter of this book is dedicated to stretching.

Methodology of Mobility Training

High mountain bike-specific and sufficient general mobility should be aimed for. When optimal mobility has been achieved, training should not be stopped because mobility can very quickly fall back to the starting situation. Exercises should be chosen that are suitable for the race- or training-specific form of strain. The exercises are done either in the warm-up part of the training session or after exertion. In performance sport it goes without saying that training should be daily.

Chapter 5 "Stretching for Mountain Bikers" contains more about mobility.

Co-ordination

Co-ordination is an athlete's ability to achieve a maximum effect with the aid of minimal and deliberate use of his muscles.

In mountain biking, and in downhill in particular, a high degree of cycling-specific co-ordination is required, while mountain bikers' general co-ordination is usually not well developed. Often co-ordination and mobility training are neglected at the beginning of a "career" and the saying "you cannot teach an old dog new tricks" is valid here too.

Nevertheless, cycling-specific co-ordination is often excellent; for example the rounded pedal thrust, jumping, taking-off, riding through bends and attempting to stand still show that there certainly are highly developed co-ordinative abilities around.

In order to combat the loss of general co-ordination through "mindless pedalling", general co-ordination should be developed straight away at a young training age; for example in winter indoor training. In chapter 8 "Technique Training", ways of improving co-ordination are discussed.

Methodology of Co-ordination Training

Co-ordination and cycling technique are closely linked and for this reason there are many hints on co-ordinative training in the technique section. Co-ordination training without the bike takes place in winter indoor training, but should also be continued during the season.

Co-ordination training should always be carried out when the body is well recovered, i.e. not at the end of a hard training session when it could do more harm than good.

For example a session to train a rounded pedal thrust can be excellently combined with a compensatory/regenerative training session. Exercises for training cycling technique such as overcoming hurdles, touching the rear wheel of the cyclist in front with your front wheel or other tricks and stunts can be done on days off (training camp).

Here too it must be emphasised that in addition to cycling-specific co-ordination, general co-ordination must not be neglected because it positively influences the learning of new skills on the bike.

3.2 Training Fields

In order to structure training better it is divided into training fields which are mainly classified according to intensity and the type of strain.

Derivation of the Training Fields from the Metabolic Processes

Using the metabolic processes described in chapter 2 as a basis, the training fields will now be formulated which address and train the various metabolic areas.

Basically there are three areas of metabolism:

- Aerobic area
- Aerobic-anaerobic mixed area
- Anaerobic area.

Compensatory training and basic endurance training 1 are linked with aerobic metabolism. Basic endurance 2, strength endurance and race specific endurance training address the aerobic-anaerobic mixed area. The anaerobic-lactacid area is covered by speed training and the training of race specific endurance, the alactacid area is covered by resilience training.

To describe the individual training fields, mainly the terms used in endurance training didactics have been chosen, such as compensatory training, basic endurance 1/2, strength endurance, race specific endurance. Because of the numerous overlaps with road cycling it was decided not to seek completely new terms for mountain biking.

In cycling literature basic endurance 2 corresponds more or less to the so-called development field, race specific endurance has much in common with the top field. Resilience training is referred to in the nomenclature of the Bund Deutscher Radfahrer (German Cycling Federation) as K 1 training and strength endurance training as K 3 or K 4.

Compensatory Training – CO

As the name indicates, in compensation training a strain or regeneration deficit is compensated for. The aim is active sport-specific recovery. Compensatory training should definitely be carried out when the body is very tired. The CO field has the lowest intensity of all training fields.

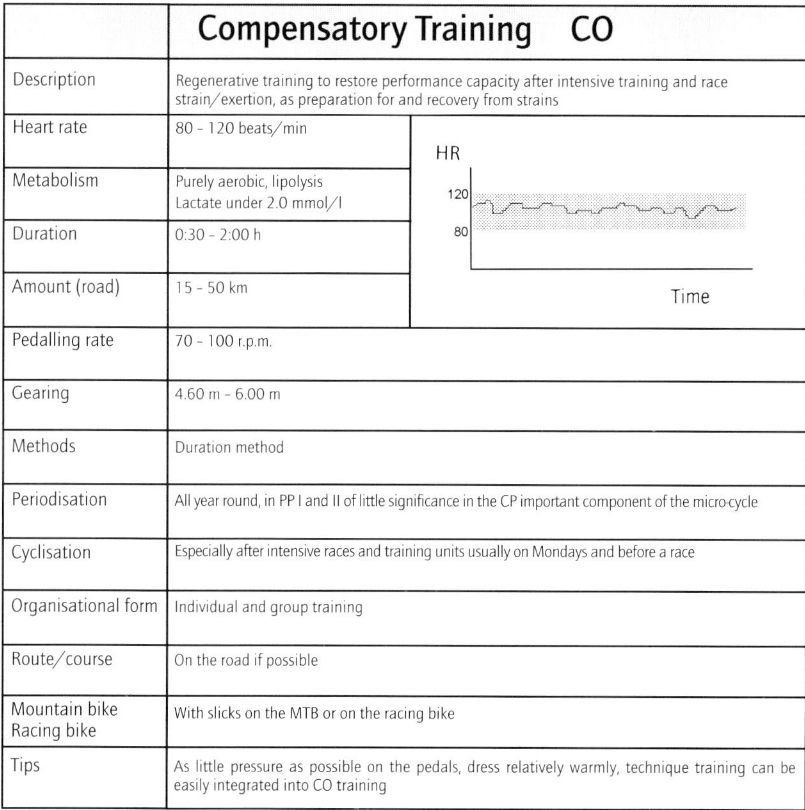

	Compensatory Training CO
Description	Regenerative training to restore performance capacity after intensive training and race strain/exertion, as preparation for and recovery from strains
Heart rate	80 - 120 beats/min
Metabolism	Purely aerobic, lipolysis Lactate under 2.0 mmol/l
Duration	0:30 - 2:00 h
Amount (road)	15 - 50 km
Pedalling rate	70 - 100 r.p.m.
Gearing	4.60 m - 6.00 m
Methods	Duration method
Periodisation	All year round, in PP I and II of little significance in the CP important component of the micro-cycle
Cyclisation	Especially after intensive races and training units usually on Mondays and before a race
Organisational form	Individual and group training
Route/course	On the road if possible
Mountain bike Racing bike	With slicks on the MTB or on the racing bike
Tips	As little pressure as possible on the pedals, dress relatively warmly, technique training can be easily integrated into CO training

Fig. 3.10: Compensatory training

Basic Endurance Training - BE

The most important intensity area, and thus training field in mountain biking is the aerobic metabolism area. This area is also called basic endurance. A high percentage (about 60-75%) of the total annual amount of training is done in this area in order to prevent lactate production, to put it in an exaggerated way. Only when basic endurance is at a very high level can high race strains under aerobic or mixed metabolic conditions be handled. In fitness mountain biking even over 90% of total training is done in the BE field. A major part of cross-training without the bike also takes place in this field. BE training sessions are characterised by very large amounts at low intensity. The basic endurance field is further broken down into two levels of intensity: basic endurance 1 and basic endurance 2.

Basic Endurance 1 - BE 1

When strain lasts for two to seven hours (on the road bike 60 to over 200 km) energy provision is exclusively aerobic with a high proportion of fat combustion. This is the training field in which fat combustion is excellently trained and it is thus the most favourable field from a health point of view as well (overweight). When training on the mountain bike slicks should be mounted.

Basic Endurance 2 - BE 2

In the BE 2 field the lower range of the aerobic-anaerobic transitional area is trained. A difference is made between a strength and a pedalling rate oriented field. Individual

	Basic Endurance 1 BE 1
Description	Most important training field for mountain bikers, to create high aerobic capacity as a basis for high performance capacity, to warm-up before strain
Heart rate	115 - 145 beats/min
Metabolism	Purely aerobic, lipolysis Lactate 0 - 2.5 (3.0) mmol/l
Duration	2:00 - 8:00 h
Amount (road)	50 - 250 km
Pedalling rate	80 - 110 r.p.m., opt. 100 r.p.m.
Gearing	4.70 m - 6.40 m e.g. 42 x 19 - 14 (racing bike)
Methods	Duration method
Periodisation	All year round, important especially in the PPs, in all other compensatory sports in the PPs stay in the aerobic area BE 1, main component of a spring training camp
Cyclisation	Train in blocks if possible: 3:1, 4:1 or 5:1, e.g. 1. 3 h, 2. 4 h, 3. 5 h, 4. 1 h CO; during the CP best from Tue. to Thu., when weekends are race free or in PP from Fri. to Sun.
Organisational form	Individual training is the most favourable form, regulation of intensity with heart rate Group training: frequent leader change to keep intensity constant (1 - 2 min)
Route/course	If possible on the road or on good tracks Flat to rolling
Mountain bike Racing bike	With slicks on the MTB or on the racing bike
Tips	It is a good idea to determine individual heart rate values through performance diagnostics; try not to train at over 150 beats/min, a range of about 20 beats is optimal, speed is not a regulatory parameter

Fig. 3.11: Basic endurance training 1

heart rates in the training fields will be discussed in the next section. It is a good idea to include a few BE 2 intervals in the course of a BE 1 training session. A long training ride (3 h) exclusively in BE 2 tires greatly and empties the glycogen stores, which is desired for example in carbohydrate loading (see chapter 7 "Dietary Considerations"). Altogether the BE 2 field only makes up about 5% of the annual amount of training.

Race Specific Endurance - RSE

As the name says, training in the RSE field is oriented to race speed and race exertion and is thus in the upper aerobic-anaerobic mixed area. Depending on the form, distances are covered at or above race intensity. Training in the race specific field can be

<table>
<tr><th></th><th colspan="2">Basic Endurance 2 BE 2</th></tr>
<tr><td>Description</td><td colspan="2">Training field of medium intensity for the development of race specific endurance and to raise the anaerobic threshold, improvement of lactate elimination and optimisation of the aerobic-anaerobic transitional area, stretch or motor training possible depending on objectives; in strength-oriented BE 2 training use higher gears and lower pedalling rate.</td></tr>
<tr><td>Heart rate</td><td>About 145 - 175 beats/min</td><td rowspan="3">HR 175 145</td></tr>
<tr><td>Metabolism</td><td>Aerobic-anaerobic transition
Lactate 3.0 - 6.0 mmol/ll</td></tr>
<tr><td>Duration</td><td>0:15 - 2:00 h</td></tr>
<tr><td>Amount (road)</td><td>5 - 70 km, flat to rolling</td><td rowspan="2">e.g. 3 x 20 min BE 2 with 15 min CO sections between (HR about 100), important: warm-up and cool down</td></tr>
<tr><td>Pedalling rate</td><td>100 - 120 r.p.m.; 70 - 95 r.p.m.</td></tr>
<tr><td>Gearing</td><td colspan="2">5.60 m - 7.60 m (8.60 m with strength)
e.g. 42 x 16 - 52 x 15</td></tr>
<tr><td>Methods</td><td colspan="2">Interval methods</td></tr>
<tr><td>Periodisation</td><td colspan="2">In the PP II, III and in the CP, here especially in race preparation, the longer the race, the less BE 2 training</td></tr>
<tr><td>Cyclisation</td><td colspan="2">During the CP on Wednesdays or also advisable on Thursdays as well as a short BE 2 course the day before a race</td></tr>
<tr><td>Organisational form</td><td colspan="2">Individual training: self-motivation not easy, intensity regulation using heart rate and pedalling rate
Group training: frequent leader change to keep intensity constant (1 - 2 min)</td></tr>
<tr><td>Route/course</td><td colspan="2">Also possible off-road on tracks. Flat to rolling, or on longer hills</td></tr>
<tr><td>Mountain bike
Racing bike</td><td colspan="2">With slicks or appropriate tyres on the MTB
Racing bike</td></tr>
<tr><td>Tips</td><td colspan="2">Important to determine individual heart rate values with performance diagnostics, range of 10-15 beats is optimal, speed is not a regulatory parameter, use to warm-up for races, the amount relates to the whole BE 2 course.</td></tr>
</table>

Fig. 3.12: Basic endurance training 2

done either at very high pedalling rates and low use of strength, at race pedalling rates and with race gearing, or with high gearing and correspondingly low pedalling rates and greater strain on strength. RSE training with the mountain bike on rough terrain is often subject to great variations in intensity of exertion depending on the course.

Special Training Fields

Special training fields only make up a small percentage of total training and in contrast to the above-mentioned fields heart rates are only a secondary means to regulate intensity. Rather, a concrete movement has to be carried out which, depending on performance level, leads to varying degrees of exertion with varying parameters of strain.

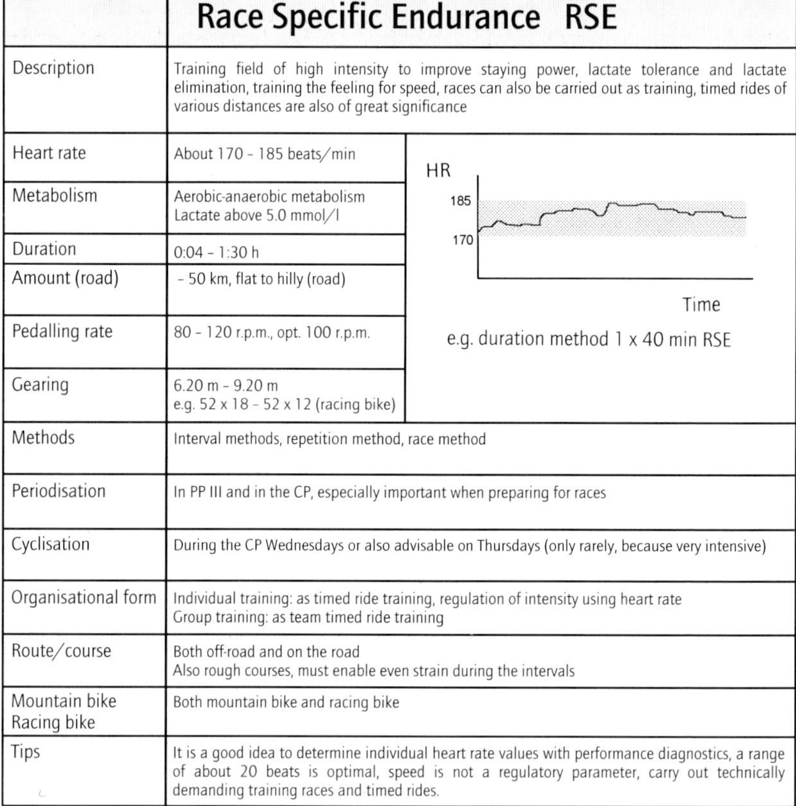

	Race Specific Endurance RSE
Description	Training field of high intensity to improve staying power, lactate tolerance and lactate elimination, training the feeling for speed, races can also be carried out as training, timed rides of various distances are also of great significance
Heart rate	About 170 - 185 beats/min
Metabolism	Aerobic-anaerobic metabolism Lactate above 5.0 mmol/l
Duration	0:04 - 1:30 h
Amount (road)	- 50 km, flat to hilly (road)
Pedalling rate	80 - 120 r.p.m., opt. 100 r.p.m.
Gearing	6.20 m - 9.20 m e.g. 52 x 18 - 52 x 12 (racing bike)
Methods	Interval methods, repetition method, race method
Periodisation	In PP III and in the CP, especially important when preparing for races
Cyclisation	During the CP Wednesdays or also advisable on Thursdays (only rarely, because very intensive)
Organisational form	Individual training: as timed ride training, regulation of intensity using heart rate Group training: as team timed ride training
Route/course	Both off-road and on the road Also rough courses, must enable even strain during the intervals
Mountain bike Racing bike	Both mountain bike and racing bike
Tips	It is a good idea to determine individual heart rate values with performance diagnostics, a range of about 20 beats is optimal, speed is not a regulatory parameter, carry out technically demanding training races and timed rides.

Fig. 3.13: Race specific endurance

Strength Endurance Training - SE

The aim of strength endurance training is to improve resistance to tiring from great, cyclically repeated, exertion. In order to train with increased resistance the training route should lead up a hill or pass with low incline. Using high gearing (large cog) the relatively flat incline is covered sitting on the saddle at pedalling rates of between 40 and 60 per minute. This is also an excellent opportunity to train a rounded thrust when pedalling, in particular the pulling/drawing phase.

In recent years strength training has become increasingly important; especially when using high gearing even greater speeds can be achieved. As a result of the high strain on strength and low rates of movement, intensity remains in the aerobic-anaerobic area.

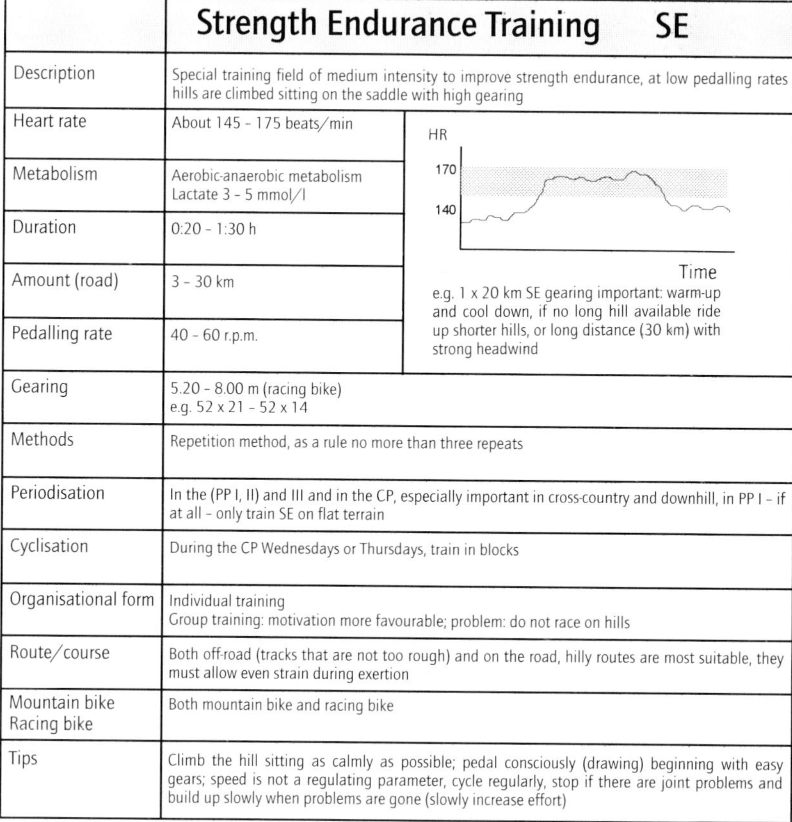

	Strength Endurance Training SE	
Description	Special training field of medium intensity to improve strength endurance, at low pedalling rates hills are climbed sitting on the saddle with high gearing	
Heart rate	About 145 - 175 beats/min	HR 170 140 Time e.g. 1 x 20 km SE gearing important: warm-up and cool down, if no long hill available ride up shorter hills, or long distance (30 km) with strong headwind
Metabolism	Aerobic-anaerobic metabolism Lactate 3 - 5 mmol/l	
Duration	0:20 - 1:30 h	
Amount (road)	3 - 30 km	
Pedalling rate	40 - 60 r.p.m.	
Gearing	5.20 - 8.00 m (racing bike) e.g. 52 x 21 - 52 x 14	
Methods	Repetition method, as a rule no more than three repeats	
Periodisation	In the (PP I, II) and III and in the CP, especially important in cross-country and downhill, in PP I - if at all - only train SE on flat terrain	
Cyclisation	During the CP Wednesdays or Thursdays, train in blocks	
Organisational form	Individual training Group training: motivation more favourable; problem: do not race on hills	
Route/course	Both off-road (tracks that are not too rough) and on the road, hilly routes are most suitable, they must allow even strain during exertion	
Mountain bike Racing bike	Both mountain bike and racing bike	
Tips	Climb the hill sitting as calmly as possible; pedal consciously (drawing) beginning with easy gears; speed is not a regulating parameter, cycle regularly, stop if there are joint problems and build up slowly when problems are gone (slowly increase effort)	

Fig. 3.14: Strength endurance training

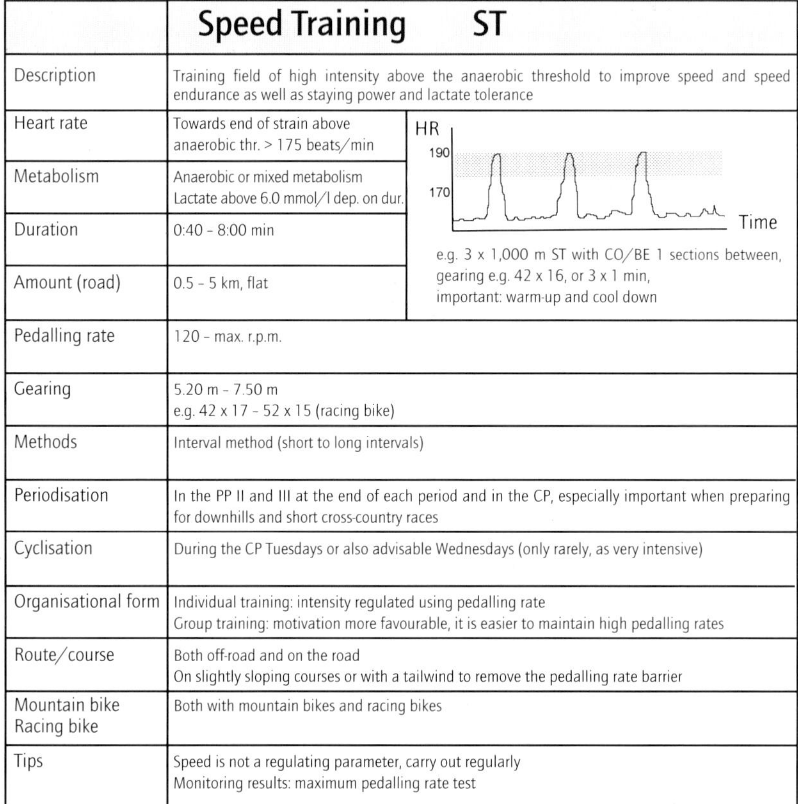

	Speed Training ST	
Description	Training field of high intensity above the anaerobic threshold to improve speed and speed endurance as well as staying power and lactate tolerance	
Heart rate	Towards end of strain above anaerobic thr. > 175 beats/min	HR 190 170 Time e.g. 3 x 1,000 m ST with CO/BE 1 sections between, gearing e.g. 42 x 16, or 3 x 1 min, important: warm-up and cool down
Metabolism	Anaerobic or mixed metabolism Lactate above 6.0 mmol/l dep. on dur.	
Duration	0:40 - 8:00 min	
Amount (road)	0.5 - 5 km, flat	
Pedalling rate	120 - max. r.p.m.	
Gearing	5.20 m - 7.50 m e.g. 42 x 17 - 52 x 15 (racing bike)	
Methods	Interval method (short to long intervals)	
Periodisation	In the PP II and III at the end of each period and in the CP, especially important when preparing for downhills and short cross-country races	
Cyclisation	During the CP Tuesdays or also advisable Wednesdays (only rarely, as very intensive)	
Organisational form	Individual training: intensity regulated using pedalling rate Group training: motivation more favourable, it is easier to maintain high pedalling rates	
Route/course	Both off-road and on the road On slightly sloping courses or with a tailwind to remove the pedalling rate barrier	
Mountain bike Racing bike	Both with mountain bikes and racing bikes	
Tips	Speed is not a regulating parameter, carry out regularly Monitoring results: maximum pedalling rate test	

Fig. 3.15: Speed training

If the heart rate is in the maximum area then the strain on strength is too low and pedalling rate too high; higher gearing must be selected.

To train race specific strength endurance it is a good idea to cycle up a hill that is at least 4 km long with racing gearing and in so doing to simulate several (3-5) break away attempts over 300 m, raising the gearing each time. Finish with a closing sprint over the last 500 m. The latter method should be used very rarely as it is extremely intensive. If there are no hills available for SE training, an alternative is to use a flat route where there is a constant strong headwind; this is, however, only a compromise. When training on the flat like this it is necessary to use high gearing on a racing bike in the top performance field (e.g. 53 x 12).

Because of the high strain on strength there is a relatively great increase in blood pressure, so that strength training to this extent is not suitable in recreational sport.

Speed Training - ST

Speed training is one of the special training fields and is differentiated from resilience training. Speed does not mean cycling speed here, but speed of movement, which in mountain biking is the same as pedalling rate. Speed and speed endurance are trained. Although pedalling rates in mountain biking are relatively low, speed training should be carried out in order to improve economy of movement.

Speed training especially includes intervals of about 1:30 to 2:00 minutes (about 1,000 metres) using low gearing and maximum pedalling rate. Another training form for speed training are so-called wind sprints or "ins and outs". This involves cycling in an easy gear and accelerating 6-12 times in a row for about 20 to 30 metres each time, pedalling only very easily for about 50 metres between accelerations. On a slight downhill slope or with a tailwind it is possible to work with very high-pedalling rates and low use of strength (low gearing).

	Resilience Training RT	
Description	Special training field at high intensity to improve resilience and maximum strength Improvement of anaerobic-alactacid metabolism, with short breaks also of lactacid components, in brackets are the values for short breaks	
Heart rate	Not relevant	HR 170 140 Time
Metabolism	Anaerobic-alactacid Lactate not above 2.5 (4.0) mmol/l	
Duration	6-12 x 6-8 s, 1-3 sets	
Amount (road)	Include within a 60 km BE 1 session	
Pedalling rate	Pedal the maximum from a standing start	e.g. 8 x 6 s RT with CO/BE 1 sections between; gearing e.g. 52 x 15, breaks 1-2 min, important: warm-up and cool down
Gearing	6.20 m - 7.20 m e.g. 52 x 18 - 52 x 15 (racing bike)	
Methods	Interval method (short intervals), length of breaks 3 - 5 min; (with lactate increase 1 - 2 min)	
Periodisation	In the PP II and III and in the CP, especially important when preparing for downhills and cross-country routes full of corners with many accelerations	
Cyclisation	During the CP Tuesdays or also advisable on Wednesdays	
Organisational form	Individual training: regulate intensity using time (6 - 8 s) Group training: motivation more favourable, easier to persevere through the repetitions	
Route/course	Both off-road and on the road Also hilly routes	
Mountain bike Racing bike	Both mountain bike and racing bike	
Tips	Accelerate to the full and only exert for 8 s, but at 100%, starting with easier gearing, speed is not a regulating parameter, carry out regularly, can be done very well off-road.	

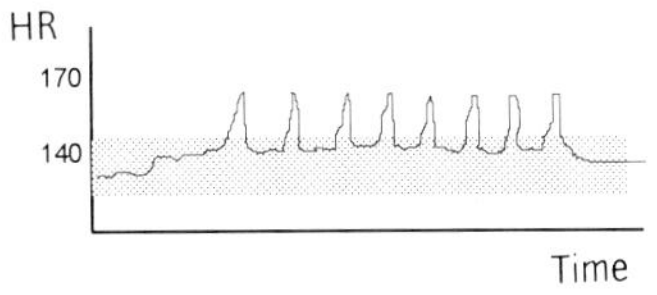

Fig. 3.16: Resilience training

Resilience or Sprint Training – 

Resilience training serves mainly to improve the ability to sprint and accelerate and thus addresses anaerobic-lactacid metabolism. Using medium gearing you go from slowly rolling or standing still to about six to eight seconds pedalling at a maximum and then carrying on easily, after one or two minutes comes the next acceleration. When doing this there is a build-up of tiredness, lactate accumulation and major emptying of the CP and ATP stores because of the short recovery time.

If alactacid energy provision is to be trained in isolation, the breaks must be extended to 3-5 minutes. In downhill especially this training field must be considered when planning training.

Training Programmes

Because it has become apparent that many mountain bikers have difficulty in selecting exertion that corresponds to their level of performance, below are a number of exemplary training sessions for the various training fields.

The training suggestions should be understood as just that and represent something for orientation when trying out unfamiliar training methods.

Your own creativity in changing them is only limited by training methodological restrictions.

Training sessions here are characterised by duration and method, for interval and repetition methods the break lengths are also given. Further details such as pedalling rate, heart rate, gearing etc. can be found in the corresponding charts for the various training fields on the previous pages.

The training sessions are each divided into three or four different classes of strain. As a rule the training fields should be trained in blocks. This is catered for in that the values given in each case correspond to an average strain in a block. In planning a block it is therefore only necessary to formulate a strain below and above that mentioned. In doing so increases in strain should not exceed 15 to 30%.

The classes of strain correspond to the following division. In this way training strains are allocated to certain performance and age categories on the basis of physiological criteria of strain and performance structural deductions. This allocation is, however, only for orientation and can be varied.

a Hobby biker/fitness biker
b Youth (licence)
c Juniors (licence)/women (licence)/marathon bikers
d Men (licence)

CO (no block training)

CO a	30 - 40 min	continuous duration method
CO b	40 - 60 min	continuous duration method
CO cd	60 - 90 min	continuous duration method

BE 1

The shorter BE 1 sessions are also carried out by mountain bikers in the men's class.

BE 1 a	1:00 - 2:00	continuous duration method (fartlek)
BE 1 b	2:00 - 4:00	continuous duration method (fartlek)
BE 1 c	4:00 - 6:00	continuous duration method
BE 1 d	> 6:00	continuous duration method

A training session in the following fields of intensity is always begun with a 20-30 minute BE 1 as a warm-up phase. In the active breaks BE 1/CO strain is applied. After the more intensive strain there must be 20-30 minutes of cooling down.

BE 2

BE 2 a	3-4 x 5 - 10 min	interval method (LI) active break 5 min
BE 2 b	3-4 x 10 - 15 min	interval method (LI) active break 5 min
BE 2 c	3-6 x 15 - 20 min	interval method (LI) active break 5 min
BE 2 d	3-6 x 20 - 30 min	interval method (LI) active break 5 min

RSE

RSE can be trained with the interval, race and repetition methods. Here the race method is described. All classes should train both short and long exertion.

RSE a	10 - 20 min	race method
RSE b	10 - 30 min	race method
RSE c	10 - 40 min	race method
RSE d	10 - 60 min	race method

SE

When long hills are available, the total time per training session can be split into up to four amounts of strain, working with the interval method.

SE a	15 - 20 min (3 x 5 min)	interval method	active break 10 min
SE b	30 - 40 min (4 x 10 min)	interval method	active break 10 min
SE c	40 - 60 min (4 x 15 min)	interval method	active break 15 min
SE d	60 - 90 min (3 x 30 min)	interval method	active break 20 min

ST

ST a	3-4 x 1:00 - 1:30 min	interval method (MI)	active break 5 min
ST b	3-4 x 1:30 - 2:00 min	interval method (MI)	active break 5 min
ST c	4-6 x 1:30 - 2:00 min	interval method (MI)	active break 5 min
ST d	6-8 x 2:30 - 3:30 min	interval method (MI)	active break 5 min

RT

RT a	6-8 x 6 - 8 s	interval method (SI)	active break 1-5 min
RT b	8-10 x 6 - 8 s	interval method (SI)	active break 1-5 min
RT c	10-12 x 6 - 8 s (1-2 series)	interval method (SI)	active break 1-5 min
RT d	10-12 x 6 - 8 s (2-3 series)	interval method (SI)	active break 1-5 min

3.3 Heart Rate Oriented Training

The regulation of intensity using the heart rate has the advantage over "subjective" methods that it is more precise and furthermore makes it possible to recognise developmental tendencies in fitness as well as any complications in building up fitness. Unfortunately the heart rate is also prone to a range of disturbance factors which, however, can be recognised and analysed with a little experience.

With the help of simple formulae individual training fields can be worked out.

The History of Heart Rate Measurement as a Training Regulator

Only 25 years ago training regulation using the heart rate was like a lottery because the heart rate could only be determined by feeling the pulse at certain places (wrist, throat); constant monitoring of the heart rate was thus out of the question. In the years that followed the first pulse watches were only used by a handful of top athletes, who were very successful thanks to this method. The incredible success of GDR cyclists was based among other things on the consistent development and use of heart rate regulated training.

In the mid seventies experiments were already being carried out in the GDR using wireless heart rate measurers. In the mid eighties the first completely functional pulse watches from POLAR came onto the market and today this has become an affordable instrument for training regulation that anyone can use (upwards from about US$ 100/ £ 70). The users range from World Cup professionals to recreational athletes.

In the early years, however, there were great differences of opinion which heart rates should mainly be used for training, but in the meantime many mountain bikers know how to use a heart rate measurer and thus structure their training more effectively.

How a Pulse Watch Works

The heart rate is registered by a transmitter in the chest belt and transmitted to the watch by wireless. The measurement of the heart beat by the chest electrodes in the belt using the ECG method is considered the most exact form of measurement.

More advanced models allow programming the desired training intensity field so that an accoustic or optic signal is given when the athlete is above or below this field.

The top models from POLAR also allow storing the heart rate data and other performance parameters (speed, pedalling rate) during training or a race.

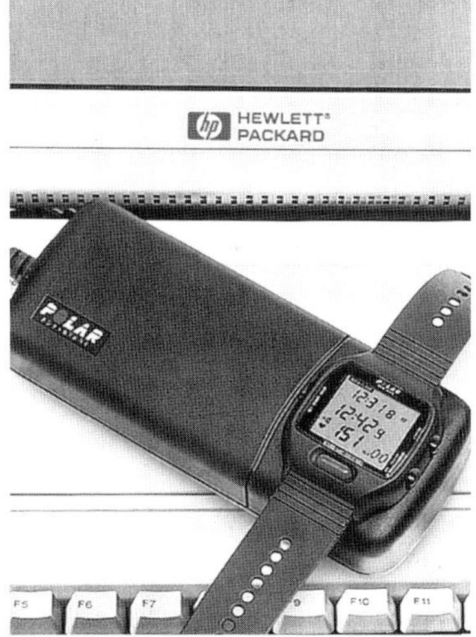

With the POLAR INTERFACE, data transfer is child's play and offers excellent possibilities for heart rate regulated cycling training. Photo: Polar

At home the data can be transferred to a PC using an interface, graphically displayed and analysed.

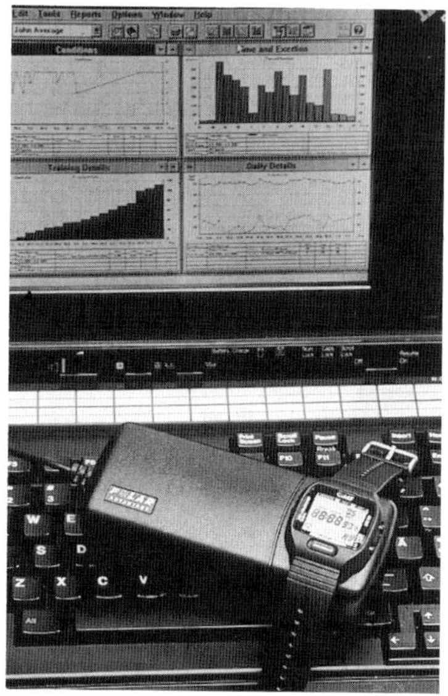

With the POLAR INTERFACE, the heart rates stored in the POLAR VANTAGE NV can be transferred to a PC which, with appropriate software, can evaluate them and display them graphically. Photo: Polar

These readings provide important information for effective regulation of training. When cycling, attaching the watch to the handlebars enables easier monitoring. When using a pulse watch it is important that the belt is fitted correctly and not too tightly; breathing must not be hindered in any way.

The electrodes can only register the heart rate if they are slightly moistened. This is achieved either by wetting them before training, or cycling for several minutes until contact is created through the natural production of sweat.

When very close to strong sources of electricity (high voltage wires, railway lines) very high readings may occur temporarily.

In some cases during training in pairs or groups there can be overlapping and interference with the individual transmitters and receivers. More recent models avoid this by using coded transmitting frequencies.

Heart Rate Behaviour in Mountain Biking

In mountain biking the heart rate is subject to relatively large variations - depending on course profile, weather, track condition - even on flat terrain.

In modern scientific goal-oriented training, intensity is regulated using the heart rate and not speed, which even on flat terrain is not a reliable indicator of intensity.

By matching gearing and pedalling rate the desired field of intensity can be found.

How Does the Pulse Watch Help?

Intensities too high
A necessary consequence of heart rate oriented training is that now, for example, when cycling against the wind or uphill it is necessary to go slower so as not to go beyond the desired field of intensity (e.g. BE 1). The pulse watch is also useful in establishing heart rates that are too high because of infections.

Intensities too low
Certain training fields and methods have to be carried out at high and highest intensities which are very difficult to estimate without a pulse watch. In races too the heart rate shows whether there is still an exertion reserve or whether speed needs to be reduced in order not to produce too much lactate. The prerequisite of course is a close analysis of one's own heart rate behaviour in training and possibly knowledge of the anaerobic threshold.

With a little experience the heart rate also provides information on the cyclist's condition. For this purpose one should closely observe one's heart rate under various degrees of exertion and at rest.

Of course the heart rate fields must not be seen as immovable boundaries that may not be crossed under any circumstances. If the situation calls for it, it certainly is possible to occasionally vary, but the majority of training should take place as planned in the desired field (usually BE 1).

Digression: Resting Heart Rate

The resting heart rate is useful for getting used to using the heart rate measurer. It is not only suitable as an indicator of the state of endurance training, but also as an alarm for developing illnesses, infections and for overtraining.

Changes can only be ascertained if the resting pulse is regularly measured in bed before getting up in the morning. If the resting pulse is usually between 45 and 48 and one morning it is 55, this generally indicates a developing illness even if there are no symptoms yet. If the resting pulse increases slowly over several days this usually means a state of overtraining; in any case it means that regeneration is disturbed.

After hard races, or on stage tours, the resting pulse is often a little higher owing to the very high exertion and only short regeneration times. In general, if there is a variation of six to eight beats per minute, the above-mentioned factors should be checked. In training and competition one should exert oneself carefully, especially if the pulse under strain is also up, and possibly even stop, for endurance training when there is an infection can lead to damage to the heart muscle and other organs.

As figure 3.17 shows, the resting pulse rises slightly during a training camp (1-2 beats). The curve shows, however, the group average of a well-trained group. A mountain biker in bad training condition would have a significantly greater increase under the same degree of effort.

At a basic training camp it is essential that the exertion be adjusted to performance capacity to avoid a major rise and with it a major regeneration deficit.

	Heart rate	Cause	Remedy
Before	Increased resting HR	Infection Tiredness Overtaxing Overtraining	Training break Training to build up again Medical examination
	Low variation in resting HR	Need for regeneration Infection	CO training Break
During	Unusually low maximum HR and general moving downwards of the HR, HR does not oscillate	Beginning of overtraining Regeneration deficit Glycogen poverty	Training break CO training, BE 1 training Possibly training to build up again
	Unusually high HR under strain	Infection Fluid deficiency	Pull out of training or race, fluid intake
After	Unusually pronounced falling of recovery HR	State of overtraining in various forms	Reduced training or break Training to build up again
	Increase of HR after training or race over longer period (several hours)	Great exhaustion Beginning infection Fluid deficiency	Regenerative measures Fluid intake

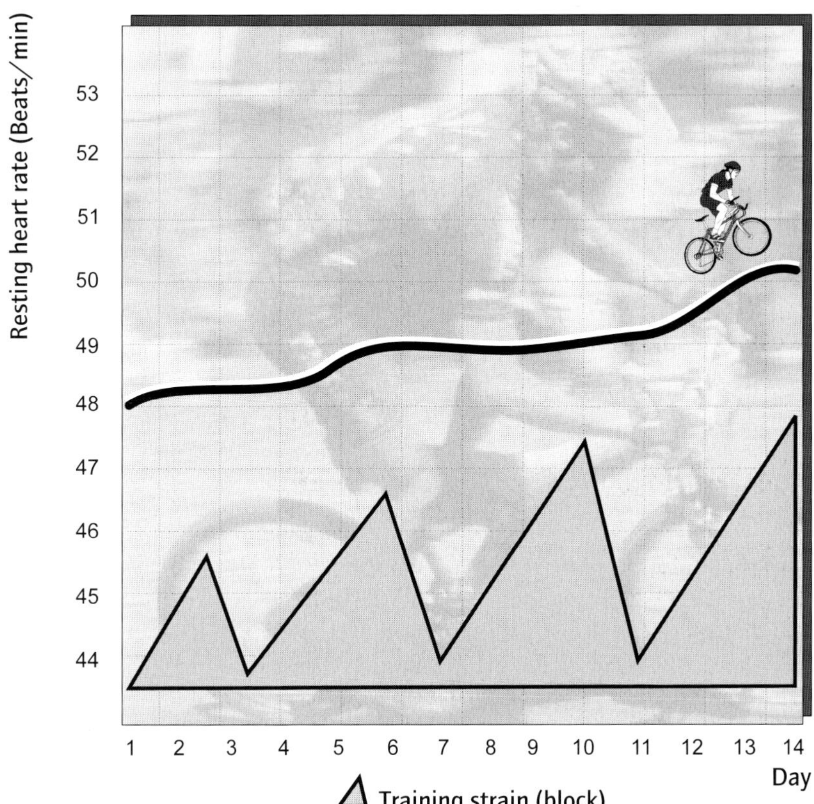

Fig. 3.17: Course of resting heart rates during a 14 day basic training camp (average of twelve participants)

Determining the Training Fields

The training fields explained in the previous chapter mainly use the heart rate as a regulatory means. The values shown relate to an 18- to 35-year old trained mountain biker with a maximum pulse of about 200.

Younger and older mountain bikers, but also athletes with other maximum heart rates, cannot use the values mentioned and would thus end up training in the wrong fields.

Therefore the individual training fields in each case must be determined using performance diagnostics or the maximum heart rate.

Determining the Maximum Heart Rate (MHR)

The most exact and certain method is to determine the MHR during a performance test under medical supervision. Older mountain bikers in particular (40 and above) and beginners should not carry out the maximum test alone because of the risks, but only under medical supervision.

In the health and rehabilitation field, establishing the maximum heart rate would in practice be an unnecessary risk. Here the MHR is calculated using the formula **220 - age = MHR** or an exact medical examination.

This formula, however, only provides a very rough approximation (+/-10) and is of no use at all in performance sport.

Maximum Test

After a 30 minute warm-up phase the test to determine the maximum heart rate can begin.

With the Bike

To reach the MHR exertion must be increased over several minutes (about 4-5 min) and carried out at maximum intensity in the last minute. A hill with a slight incline of three to four kilometres would be suitable; cycle up it at a minimum of race speed and using race gearing. Over the last 600 metres comes an additional finishing sprint at 100% exertion to reach the maximum heart rate.

To reach the MHR a high rate of movement (pedalling rate) is decisive. Shortly after the end of exertion the heart rate is usually highest.

In most cases the MHR is in the area of 220 - age; but here too the exception proves the rule, for trained mountain bikers frequently still have a maximum heart rate of about 200 at age 35 or older.

Measurement is only sufficiently accurate and usable for evaluation if a pulse watch is used, for the extreme exhaustion at the end of the test makes it almost impossible to measure the very high readings manually.

Because in every sport - depending on the muscle mass used - various maximum readings can be achieved, a maximum test should be carried out at least for the most important cross-training types, in any case for cycling. In technically demanding movements such as rollerblading or cross-country skiing, the maximum possible heart rate is often not reached because of lack of technique.

Calculation of the Intensity Fields

Determining the training fields with this simple method is a genuine alternative to expensive and difficult to interpret performance diagnostics which, however, is more exact and is especially used in the top field. Even for good mountain bikers though, the procedure demonstrated here can be used without problems. The formulae used to calculate the intensity fields are based on comprehensive research of many years so that they represent a great degree of accuracy.

To calculate the heart rates under strain the resting heart rate, the maximum heart rate and an intensity factor are used. This factor is a percentage.
Step 1: subtraction of the resting heart rate from the MHR.
Step 2: multiply this value by the intensity factor.
Step 3: add the resting heart rate back to this result.

Example:
1. 200 - 45 = 155
2. 155 x 0.52 = 80.6
3. 80.6 + 45 = 125.6

For the person involved the value calculated would be the upper limit heart rate for the compensatory field (regenerative training).

Training Field		Factor
Compensatory field	CO	up to 0.52
Basic field 1	BE 1	0.52 bis 0.65
Basic field 2	BE 2	0.65 bis 0.82
Race specific endurance	RSE	0.75 bis 0.95
Strength endurance	SE	0.75 bis 0.90
Speed training	ST	0.85 bis 1.00
Resilience training	RT	0.85 bis 0.95

Table 3.1: Intensity factors

The factors give the lower and upper limits of each field. For proper intensity regulation the compensatory field, and in particular the basic endurance field, are especially important.

In the last three mentioned, special highly intensive training fields (SE, ST, RT), training is carried out not so much according to heart rate but rather according to gearing instructions, pedalling rates and movement tasks for predetermined time or distance intervals, for a heart rate of e.g. 180 can be reached using various training methods and strains. Nevertheless, here too the heart rate usually indicates the right degree of strain.

3.4 Performance Diagnostics

Performance diagnostics is a very comprehensive subject and can only be touched on within the framework of this book, therefore the various testing procedures of this complex field will not be dealt with in detail.

In general the "self-training mountain biker" would be out of his depth with regard to the results of performance diagnostics and should therefore turn to an expert right from the start. A number of private training consulting institutions carry out performance diagnostic examinations. At universities too there is often a demand for endurance trained "guinea-pigs". Here you can often get this examination for free as part of a research programme, but as a rule you have to invest considerable time in return.

Mountain bikers especially with a small time budget, low training motivation or beginners hope for miracles from a performance diagnostic examination. But the bottom line is that nothing changes the fact that a large amount of training and a certain training age are necessary in order to achieve high performance, especially in cross-country.

3.4.1 Laboratory Diagnostics

In high performance sport four to six examinations per year are carried out, at the beginning and in the middle of the preparatory periods, and at the beginning and in the middle of the competition period.

Directly before seasonal high points performance diagnostics is used to eradicate any weaknesses that may be found.

A single test cannot provide much information for training, so testing must be done regularly (see above) in order to get the most value. The purpose of laboratory performance diagnostics is to monitor the structure of training so that optimum training stimuli can be applied. The regulatory factors here are heart rate and lactate concentration, not speed.

Stage Test

The athlete is placed under strain on an individually set up cycle ergometer, with strain being increased in stages until it is stopped.

Depending on the school of thought and the purpose of the test, the stages last between two and four minutes with strain increases of 20 to 50 watt per stage. Recently there has been a move towards reducing the strain increases per minute.

A standard examination begins at 100 watt and increases every three minutes by 20 watt. This allows very exact observation of lactate and heart rate behaviour. Tests involving increases of 40 watt or more every three minutes are no longer considered to be appropriate to strain structure, but in the commercial field they are still carried out for time reasons.

In order for tests to be comparable with each other they must be carried out under standardised conditions, for the kind of diet, the training the previous day or the method of measuring lactate immediately have a decisive influence on the test results.

During the tests various measurements can be carried out to determine physiological and biomechanical quantities such as heart rate, electrocardiogramme (ECG), pedalling rate, performance, oxygen intake, breathing volume per minute and lactate, urea and creatin kinase concentration.

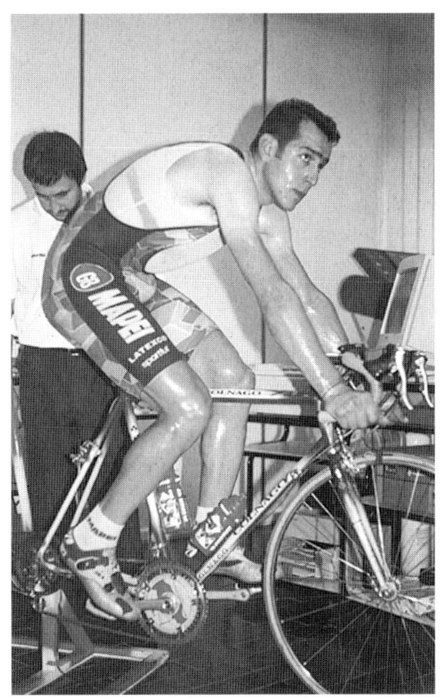

Stage test in the laboratory
Photo: SRM/Schoberer

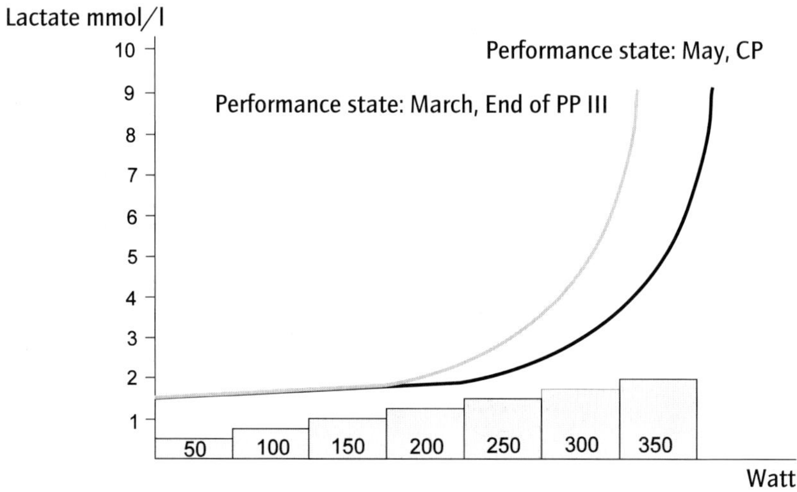

Fig. 3.18: Lactate performance curve determined in the laboratory using the stage test

In the context of this introduction we will not go any further into the exact carrying out of a stage test as such tests cannot be carried out by oneself in any case.

The most important quantities, which in the end are placed in relationship to each other, are performance, heart rate and the corresponding lactate readings as well as, in some cases, spiro-ergometric parameters. If these are displayed graphically the result is a so-called **lactate performance curve** (see fig. 3.18) which can be used to determine the aerobic and anaerobic threshold.

Aerobic and Anaerobic Threshold

On average the aerobic threshold of an endurance trained mountain biker is between about 1.5 and 2.5 mmol lactate/l blood, the anaerobic threshold is between 3.5 and 4.5 mmol/l; here there are, however, considerable differences of opinion among sports scientists. The calculatory determination of the individual thresholds is more exact. As figure 3.19 shows, below the aerobic threshold exertion is purely aerobic, between the thresholds there is mixed metabolism and above the anaerobic threshold mainly anaerobic metabolism. A longer period of strain above the anaerobic threshold automatically leads to an increase in lactate and usually has to be broken off after a certain time (a few seconds to several minutes).

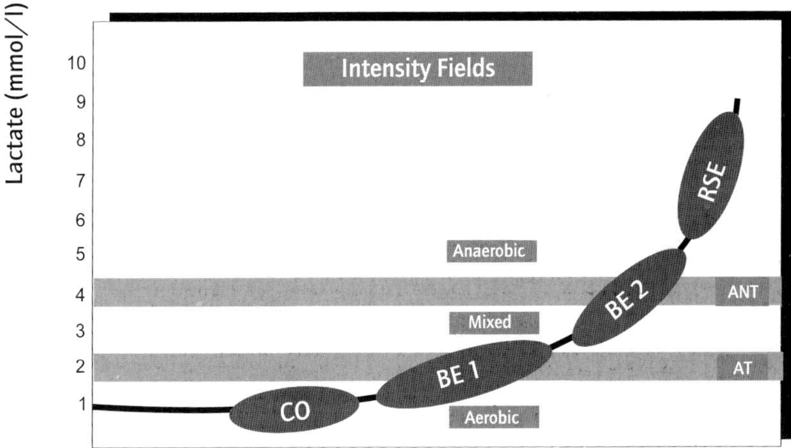

Fig. 3.19: Threshold model and intensity fields. The thresholds are shown here as dark shaded areas which show the possible range of values. The intensity fields are shown schematically. AT: Aerobic Threshold, ANT: Anaerobic Threshold.

Evaluation

In the evaluation the heart rate and the performance are placed in relationship to the lactate readings. The individual thresholds are then calculated. Using several lactate performance curves, performance improvement or general performance development can be traced back exactly.

If one disregards the factors influencing the test results, laboratory diagnostics, when carried out properly, is the most exact method of determining the training fields. Also, only in this way can maximum performance capacity be determined and quantified.

Other Laboratory Tests

Within the complex framework of cycling specific performance diagnostics it is not only possible to measure total performance on the bike, but also to examine individual components of total performance with special tests. The following list demonstrates the diversity of the tests possible: maximum pedalling power, maximum pedalling rate, anaerobic capacity, tractive power in relationship to pedalling rate, pedalling power under varying strains etc.

3.4.2 Field Stage Test

The field stage test is a stage test (increasing stages or levels of strain) which is not carried out in a laboratory under standardised and ideal conditions but "in the field", i.e. with your own bike on the road, in the forest or on the track.

Because of various external factors (wind, distance, temperature, equipment, tyre pressure etc.) it is very difficult to draw comparisons between several tests of one athlete or between simultaneous tests of different athletes. Because of the uniform conditions, if possible such a field test should be carried out on a cycling racing track (always the same lap lengths, wind is predictable, easy to carry out).

In a field test usually only two or three parameter are ascertained, namely heart rate and lactate reading in relationship to speed. Intensity during the test is regulated either using speed or heart rate values. Stage lengths of 4 to 6 km are selected. The long stages are better for determining the training intensities of well-trained cyclists.

The starting speed of for example 30 km/h is increased by 2 km/h every 2.5 km (on a 250 m track: ten laps). The heart rate is recorded by a pulse watch and after each stage the lactate reading is determined. The riders must use their bike computer, or pulse measurer, to maintain the given speed or heart rate as exactly as possible until exertion is stopped.

Heart Rate Method

When the prescribed intensity of strain is determined using the heart rate, you need a little feeling for speed and your body, and above all experience with heart rate oriented intensity regulation. The first stage should be clearly within the aerobic field, the second as well if possible, the third in the mixed region, and the fourth just below the anaerobic threshold.

The last stage can just touch on the anaerobic area. The heart rate sequence 115-130-145-160-175-190 has proved itself. Because of the exponential increase in air resistance at high speeds, preference should be given to the heart rate method over the speed method.

Pedalling Rate

The choice of gearing poses a problem in field stage tests as the idea is to maintain a pedalling rate of 80-100 r.p.m. in all stages if possible, making a pedalling rate measurer necessary.

This means that at lower speeds low gears, and at higher speeds higher gears, are used, the adjustment of which to speeds or heart rates that have to be kept to exactly is not always easy. The "Cross-Trainer" from POLAR is exceptionally well-suited for carrying out field stage tests as it stores not only the heart rate but also speed and pedalling rate.

A field stage test can also be carried out on a mountain bike on flat round, or good off-road, tracks that are well-protected from the wind.

Evaluation

First of all the lactate concentrations are entered on the left axis and the heart rate on the right axis (ordinates). On the lower axis (abscissa or x-coordinate) the speed is entered (calculate for each stage).

Now the individual data pairs are entered. Two rows of data are created; the lactate-speed data and the heart rate-speed data. When the points of a data row are linked two curves are created.

When evaluating the curve you relate a particular lactate reading to the corresponding heart rate on the other curve. You thus get as a result e.g. that the aerobic threshold is at a heart rate of 130. In basic endurance training 1 you should therefore not go above a heart rate of 130.

On the lactate-speed curve the aerobic threshold corresponds to the lowest value measured, as long as there were no mistakes in measuring. To determine the anaerobic threshold you add 1.5 mmol/l lactate to the aerobic threshold value.

The other training fields are determined using the lactate values shown in the relevant illustrations.

3.4.3 A Simple Test to Determine the Anaerobic Threshold

Cross-country races involve aerobic-anaerobic mixed metabolism. Depending on the course and the length of the race, the heart rate is around the anaerobic threshold, usually just below it. This fact can be used to at least determine approximately the anaerobic threshold in a timed ride test.

For this you need a heart rate measurer with data saving ability (e.g. "Cross-Trainer" or "Vantage" from POLAR) and a corresponding computer interface to transfer the saved data to a PC for evaluation.

A timed ride is carried out either on a mountain bike on flat tracks or roads or on a racing bike on flat roads. The course should be planned in such a way that no traffic lights or other hinderances reduce the speed. A five kilometre lap is very suitable.

Varying Route Lengths

The anaerobic threshold should be tested over various distances. Testing is done over 5, 10 and 40 km, corresponding to a duration of strain of under nine, under 18 and under 75 minutes. The test can be carried out as training or as a race. If you enter a race the motivation is usually higher, which leads to faster times and thus higher heart rates.

This Is What You Do

After the timed ride the average heart rate during the timed ride is calculated using the heart rate analysis programme on the PC. This value is divided by the appropriate percentage from the table shown here. The result is an approximate value for the anaerobic threshold. Often it is exactly right. The 40 km reading is most exact because here, if motivation is good, the heart rate under strain corresponds to the anaerobic threshold.

Example:
A biker does a 10 km timed ride (race) in 15 minutes and has an average heart rate of 182 beats.

Calculation: 182 divided by 1.07 is 170 beats/min as threshold value. A 40 km long timed ride or a cross-country race of about an hour should therefore be ridden at 100% of the threshold heart rate, i.e. 170 beats/minute.

Why Do All This?

Because cross-country races often have a definite timed ride character, knowing the level of the anaerobic threshold helps choose the right amount of exertion in a race.

In races of up to one and a half hours you should try to ride at the threshold pulse. In longer races choose a pulse target a few beats below it, in shorter races correspondingly higher.

On climbs before downhills, and in challenges, it is possible to exert oneself a little higher than the threshold pulse because the downhill provides for a little recovery. With the aid of the anaerobic threshold training fields can also be calculated.

Distance	Race	Training
5 km	110% of ANT	104% of ANT
10 km	107% of ANT	102% of ANT
40 km	100% of ANT	97% of ANT

Fig. 3.20: Derivation of the anaerobic threshold heart rate using average pulse under strain when cycling against the clock

Under 73% of the anaerobic threshold is the compensatory training field, between 72 and 84% is basic endurance 1, from 84%-97% is basic endurance 2 and up to 104% is race specific endurance.

Timed Riding Off-road as a Simple Form of Performance Diagnostics

In training the competition method as the simplest form of performance diagnostics should be done as often as possible. Only athletes who have a feeling for their bodies, and also know their heart rate at the limit of ongoing performance, and have gained experience in frequent race specific situations, can make the most of their performance potential in races. With the help of demanding off-road timed rides of race length you can learn to judge your performance capacity better and find out the optimal race heart rate. The use of heart rate measurers with saving ability and the corresponding PC software are a great help here. These also help analyse races. After about 20 races and timed rides it is thus possible to determine your optimal race heart rate for various race lengths and types.

3.5 Periodisation – the Training Year

In endurance performance sport the year is divided into several training periods with varying content and objectives. In contrast to the calendar year a training year usually begins with the 1st preparatory period in autumn. The division of the individual periods is determined by the competition period, which for mountain biking usually runs from April to October. Although races can also take place during other months, the number of races is small and their significance in winter low. In cross-country skiing for example, or cross-country cycling, there is a

	PP I	PP II	PP III	CP	TP
Duration	6 - 9 weeks	6 - 9 weeks	4 - 6 weeks	19 - 23 weeks	3 - 6 weeks
Training fields	BE 1 (BE 2)	BE 1 BE 2 (RSE) SE ST	CO BE 1 BE 2 RSE SE ST RT	CO BE 1 BE 2 RSE SE ST RT	CO BE 1
Training types	• MTB • (Racing bike) • Cross-training • Indoor training • Fitness studio/strength training room • Technique training • Sport games • Squash, badminton Stretching Balancing circle	• MTB • Racing bike • Cross-training • Indoor training • Fitness studio/strength training room • Technique training • Sport games • Squash, badminton Stretching Balancing circle	• MTB • Racing bike • Cross-training • (Indoor training) • Fitness studio/strength training room • Technique training • Sport games • Squash, badminton Stretching Balancing circle	• MTB • Racing bike • Cross-training (a compensatory sport) • (Indoor training) • Fitness studio/strength training room • Technique training Stretching Balancing circle	• Anything that is fun • Cross-training • Sport games Stretching
Methods	Duration methods	Duration methods Interval methods Repetition method (Race method)	Duration methods Interval methods Repetition method Race method	Duration methods Interval methods Repetition method Race method	Duration methods
Aims	↑ General performance foundations	↑ General performance foundations ↑ Special performance foundations	↑ General performance foundations ↑ Special performance foundations ↑ Refining of race form	↑ Refining and stabilisation of race form ↑ Special performance foundations	Regeneration Psychological distance
Mistakes	• Amounts too large • Intensity too high • Monotonous training	• Intensity too high • Regeneration too short • Lack of strength training • Monotonous training	• Lack of strength training • Regeneration too short • No periodisation • Monotonous training	• Amounts too small • Regeneration too short • Wrong choice of race • Monotonous training	• Total training break • Continuing cycling training • Intensity too high

Fig. 3.21: An overview of periodisation

preparatory period in spring with the competition period in winter. The following considerations, however, assume that the competition period is in summer.

The aim of periodisation is to develop the best possible race form within the framework of available time and other considerations. In the top international field, periodisation is often tailored towards a single event, for example the world championships or the Olympics. But also in the top national field certain championships or important races are prepared for in this way.

A real expert at this kind of planned build-up of form is Bart Brentjens who has managed many times to reach his best form exactly at the planned times. In these cases it could be seen that Brentjens had subordinated all training, and in particular all race activities, to the achievement of his seasonal objective. Thus his achievements in the early World Cup events were more than modest. He only reached his form a few weeks before the main race, and at the time of the world championships or the Olympics he was top fit.

In road racing Miguel Indurain was an expert at so-called **tapering** (race preparation); he oriented his annual periodisation to the goal of winning the Tour de France.

This extreme orientation of periodisation to one highlight can be increasingly observed in international endurance sport because the competition calendars are getting longer and longer, and the athletes have to specialise in particular, commercially significant main races. The increasingly high standard of international mountain bike participants has made it almost impossible to ride at the front during the entire World Cup season.

"Normal" mountain or marathon bikers can also carry out this preparation for a single race, or a brief high performance phase of two to four weeks.

The classical sequence of individual periods is:
Preparatory period I-III, competition period, transitional period.

If the periodisation has two highlights, the duration of the individual periods is shortened and as a rule each period is carried out twice, but then with specific contents matched to the current competition phase.

A sequence for double highlight periodisation is:
Preparatory period I and II, competition period I, transitional period I, preparatory period III and IV, competition period II, transitional period II.

Such a double highlight periodisation can be found in road cycle racing with a track or cross-country season afterwards, in mountain biking (rarely) with a summer and a winter season, or in other sports such as athletics, soccer or ski jumping with a summer and winter season in each case. Many top mountain bikers come from cross-country and add a cross-country season from the end of the mountain biking season until late January/early February.

In general, achieving world class performance with double highlight periodisation is very difficult in mountain biking because the lack of regenerational phases has a negative effect on the refining of individual top performance.

The following sections briefly describe the individual periods with their contents and training objectives.

3.5.1 Preparatory Periods PP

The preparatory periods serve to create foundational but also special performance prerequisites for achieving competition form. At the beginning of the training year, usually in November after a regenerative transitional period, the emphasis is on regaining or maintaining basic endurance capacity. During the whole of winter training as many different training means as possible are used for this purpose. Intensities are low, intensive training sessions should be well spread, but need not be left out.

At the beginning of the preparatory period and especially of preparatory period I, training should be structured but nevertheless not too closely tied to an inflexible schedule. A flexible weekly schedule with a basic amount of training that can be extended according to one's wishes and one's time is advisable.

Cross-training

An excellent means for improving basic endurance in mountain biking is cross-training. By cross-training we mean carrying out many different endurance sports which all have the aim of improving basic endurance but also partially strength endurance.

The advantages of cross-training are on the one hand, from a mental point of view, variety and thus the nipping in the bud of boredom, and on the other hand the diverse exertion stimuli applied to muscles and metabolism. The following are excellently suited as cross-training sports:

Rollerblading, cross-country skiing, roller skiing, aquajogging, swimming, aerobics, running, hiking, mountaineering.

Advantages of cross-training

- Improvement in experience of movement and feeling for one's body
- Development of new performance reserves
- Psychological change
- Active recovery
- Prevention of one-sided strain.

Running

Running or jogging, which is a year-round training means for mountain bikers with race ambitions anyway, is especially appropriate in winter. A major advantage of running is that it is not dependent on the weather and daylight, for even on very short winter days it is not a problem to run in the dark on good tracks after a short period of acclimatisation.

This independence is a decisive factor for the continuity of winter training in the preparatory period.

Anyone who does not run at all or only very little during the race season should initially approach the movement of running slowly. In this case slowly means short (30 minutes) and increasingly frequent sessions at low intensity. If you keep to this rule there will usually be no orthopaedic problems in the lower extremities.

The prerequisite for healthy and effective running training is suitable footwear which supports the feet according to their form (supination, pronation). Here it is best to get advice in a specialised store and spend a bit more for good running shoes, which by the way should be renewed regularly.

One should run in an easy, flowing style with strides that are not too long, upright upper body and slightly bent arms. Small strides reduce impact strains in comparison to big strides.

Forest or field paths are ideal for runs. Runs on rough terrain also have a good training effect and above all are fun.

Optimal run duration is between 45 and 90 minutes (men's class). Young people run up to an hour. The training pulse in basic endurance training running is slightly higher than on a bike (see heart rate). After running the leg muscles should be stretched intensively.

A variation of running are **stick runs**. Here you run uphill (meadow or track) and simulate skiing by pushing hard on ski sticks. Stick runs are very intensive and also train the torso and arm muscles.

Cross-country orienteering runs also provide for variety. **Orienteering** is a sport of its own in which you run from point to point using a map and compass and get a stamp at each checkpoint. As in mountain biking, the experience of nature plays a major part in orienteering, whereby nature must be respected and not damaged.

Hikes of several hours in the mountains and rock climbing tours are also excellent for improving basic endurance. Because of the low intensity, fat metabolism is especially addressed.

Aquajogging

Another form of running is aquajogging where the athlete floats in the water with the aid of a buoyancy belt, with only the head and shoulders out of the water. Using a running technique that can be quickly learned under supervision one slowly moves forward. In doing so various forms of training are possible, from regenerative training through basic training to highly intensive training with anaerobic mobilisation.

In many endurance sports and especially in running, aquajogging is used to apply training stimuli that put less strain on the moving apparatus of the body. In other sports too aquajogging is used in rehabilitation at an early stage already when normal running strain is not yet possible because of injuries.

Technique:
Leaning slightly forwards a running movement is simulated in which the water is tread with the feet to create forward movement. As in running the arms are swung backwards and forwards next to the body with the hands in varying positions (various forms of resistance).

An aquajogging training session lasts about an hour; after a ten minute warm-up either various intervals can be inserted, or training can be according to the duration method. A few co-ordination exercises and functional strengthening of stomach and arm muscles complete the session before the cool down (ten min.).

Swimming

Normal swimming training is also a good compensatory sport for mountain bikers. Because of the lack of impact strain, swimming is especially suitable in a rehabilitation phase after injuries. "Clean" technique is important here, however, breaststroke should be avoided because of the same unphysiological spinal column position (overstretching of the cervical vertebrae) as in biking and the scissor movement of the legs, which can be a strain under some circumstances. The crawl (freestyle) or backstroke is better here. These two techniques are also suitable for reducing muscular weaknesses of less used muscle areas such as the arm and torso muscles.

In swimming training is usually done using the duration method, covering distances of 1,000 to 3,000 metres. As a matter of principle it is absolutely necessary to adjust to the exertion form of a new sport gradually.

Note that in swimming and aquajogging, as a result of the hydrostatic pressure of the water, the heart rate is about ten beats lower than under the same metabolic strain (same level of intensity) on dry ground.

Swimming with Flippers

A variation of swimming that is especially interesting for mountain bikers and other cyclists, but is rarely practised is swimming with flippers, which especially involves the leg and rump muscles. The lower rate of movement, and the greater resistance to movement, create a desired strength endurance strain when swimming with flippers. The training method to be chosen is the duration method, with the exercise lasting from 30 to 90 minutes.

Rollerblading

Rollerblading is becoming increasingly popular not just as a hobby sport but also as a performance sport. Speed skating is the racing variation in which proper races are held on closed-off round courses. Rollerblading is so well suited for mountain bikers for training basic endurance, and especially for strength endurance, because the demands on the muscles are so similar to the pedalling movements of biking. As in biking the main form of muscle contraction in rollerblading is concentric and the stretching of the legs is done at similar angles. Because of the long supporting phase and the low rate of movement, the strength endurance strain should not be underestimated either. The static holding muscles, especially in the back area, are also very much involved.

The structure of movement of rollerblading is practically identical to that of ice speed skating. Many ice speed skaters train in summer with a mountain bike, racing bike and rollerblades. In the Netherlands and the USA they even organise rollerblade races for cyclists and cycling races for ice speed skaters and rollerbladers. Ingrid Haringa is one of many well-known cyclists who are world class both on the ice and the bike.

Anyone seriously wanting to use rollerblading as a training form should get rollerblades with a long blade and five wheels for speed skating, although they are not cheap.

A skating training session lasts 45 minutes to two hours and should be carried out on smooth paths with little traffic. Frequently going on a round of several kilometres is also good, especially for group training.

The heart rate for basic training is in about the same area as in bike training. Intervals and sprints can also be done on rollerblades.

Cross-country Skiing

Similarly to stick running, cross-country skiing involves a large proportion of the body's muscles. In addition to the arms, shoulders and legs, the back and stomach muscles are also greatly affected by training. In cross-country skiing a "clean" technique is essential for successful and effective training that is also fun.

Two techniques are differentiated in cross-country skiing. One is the classic or diagonal technique which is very similar to stick running, the other is the newer skiing technique whose leg movements are very similar to rollerblading and ice speed skating and whose arm movements borrow from the double stick thrust of the classic technique. While classic cross-country ski runs can be found in most winter sports resorts, you have to look for a while to find skating runs. Most bikers will therefore initially come to cross-country skiing via the classic style, and later, if interested, learn the much faster skating technique, which, however, requires special equipment.

For those who do not live in the mountains or near winter sports resorts, cross-country skiing is the ideal sport for their winter vacation. Two weeks in January or February with two to four hours of cross-country skiing daily creates a good foundation for the increasing amount of training afterwards back home.

Back to cross-country skiing. In training sessions of one to six hours depending on intensity the heart rates of the corresponding intensity levels are about the same as in running; they are thus higher than in biking.

In cross-country skiing there is a great temptation to ski at very high intensity; the size of the muscle mass used (almost the whole body) plays a part here. In order to reduce intensity you can ski longer distances which are automatically approached at low intensity.

Roller skiing is a proved means of training for basic training. Using special roller skis, sessions of one to three hours can be carried out on flat terrain on roads and tracks with few cars. Both the classic and the skating technique can be used with modern roller skis. Anyone who already has rollerblades, however, can save the large investment for a pair of roller skis and merely purchase a pair of suitable skating sticks of sufficient length with special tips for asphalt. With skates and sticks the skating technique can easily be simulated. If you risk entering traffic on roller skis or rollerblades you must be able to move confidently, brake and move out of the way speedily, otherwise this training would be very dangerous.

Exemplary Weekly Schedules

The weekly training schedules that follow are suggestions for the cross-country classes juniors, men, ladies, seniors and marathon bikers. For youth and hobby bikers the number of training sessions must be reduced. Amounts are not indicated but only amount and intensity sequences. More exact training suggestions with concrete details can be looked up when training the individual classes.

Preparatory Period 1 PP I

PP I goes from November to late December. After two or three weeks of increasing amounts a regenerative week follows with considerably less work. Within a week (micro-cycle) training follows the same principle: two or three days of increasing work - one day of regenerative or no training. For those who are not so keen on such patterns PP I provides the opportunity to train in a less structured way, but it is important to train regularly, for men this means about five or six times a week with a total weekly amount of 8-12 hours. After all, training should still be fun and not obligatory.

This example of the weekly schedule gives an overview of the structuring of training in this phase. The exertion blocks can of course extend beyond the weekly limits depending on individual availability of time.

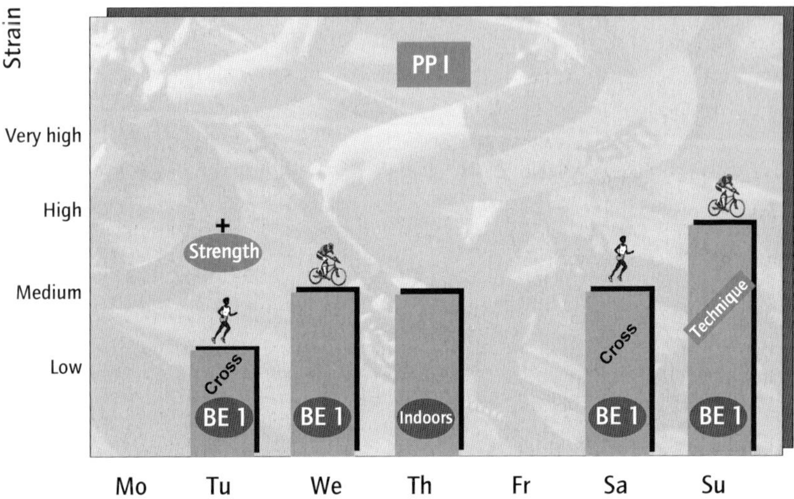

Fig. 3.22: Weekly cycle in PP I, two training sessions as cross-training (BE 1), one indoors

In PP I the basic prerequisites for sporting performance described above are created. Improving basic endurance is the emphasis in this phase. Strength, mobility and co-ordination, however, must also be trained. With the help of well-thought out athletics training indoors and in the fitness room these performance prerequisites can be created.

In winter indoor training, in addition to many games, special strength and endurance programmes are carried out. After a long MTB season the supporting muscles need reasonable compensatory and build-up training to avoid or eradicate posture damage. Furthermore this is an opportunity to show athletes new strengthening and stretching exercises, and to correct already familiar exercises if carried out incorrectly.

Endurance training on the bike is not necessary if one does the other sports described above. Playful technique training in groups with the mountain bike can be useful.

The length of the training session is much less than in summer training and is usually from one to three, at the most four, hours (road training or cross-country skiing), but only at low intensity. Towards the end of PP I the amount of training increases considerably.

The Christmas holidays are especially useful for young people to have a first "training camp" at home or on holiday. There is not as much training as at a spring training camp, but the holidays at least make it possible to train regularly with greater amounts than before.

Preparatory Period II PP II

PP II begins in January and, depending on when the season starts, lasts until about the end of February.

Without restricting the general training means, in this phase specific, i.e. cycling, training (MTB, racing bike) in BE 1 increases. Only in February does cycling training gradually supersede the other sports (cross-training), of which one or two, however, should be continued into the season as compensatory sport. Strength training (February: maximum strength phase) and general athletic training (indoor training) are carried on without change. See chapter 4 for the periodisation of strength training.

As in PP I , two or three weeks of exertion are followed by a week of reduced strain. If the Christmas period was used as a "training camp", it is followed by a regenerative week to begin with. The week should now be divided into a double

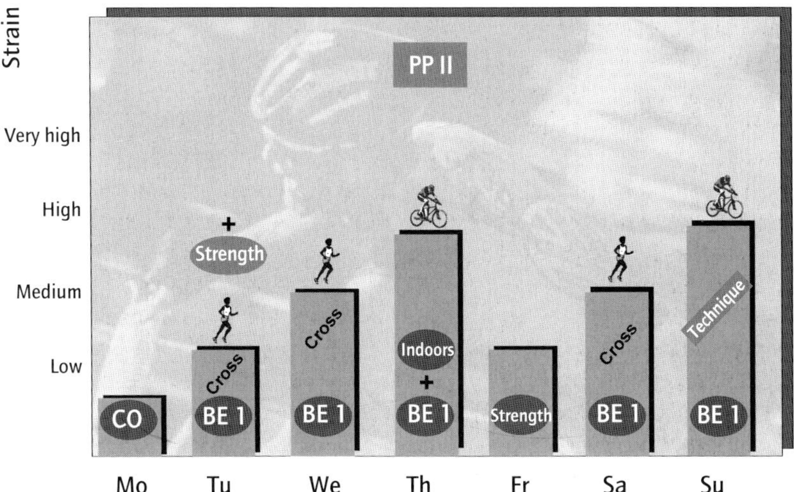

Fig. 3.23: Weekly cycle in PP II *, two to three training sessions as cross-training, the rest on the bike*

and a triple block. The weekends are particularly suitable for a triple block with long BE 1 sessions on the bike.

In the course of PP II the amounts and frequency of training increase while the intensity initially remains mainly in the basic endurance field. During the week, however, there should be some BE 2 training; the weekends are carried out in BE 1 if a triple block is on the agenda. This period finishes with a week or a few days of reduced training for regeneration.

Preparatory Period III PP III

Preparatory period III, which, depending on when the competition period begins, goes from late February to late March/early April and thus covers about four to six weeks, serves specific preparation for the competition period.

First preparatory competitions can be held in PP III immediately. It is also possible to extend PP III until late April if PP I began late or if the season starts later.

As a rule the spring training camp falls in PP III, (chapter 3.8 deals with this separately). If a training camp is carried out in PP III it must be prepared for

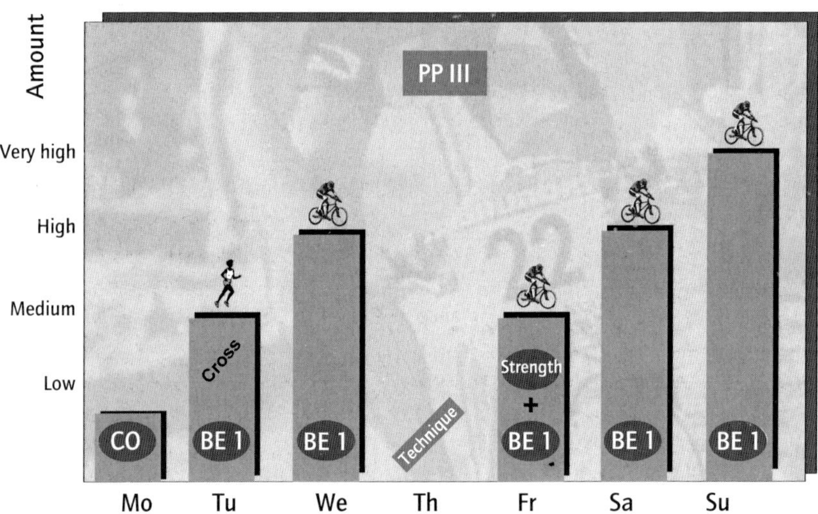

Fig. 3.24: Weekly cycle in PP III, (emphasis on amount) one training session as cross-training (Tuesday or Friday), the rest on the bike

and afterwards integrated. A training camp of two weeks (usually) is prepared for with a comprehensive micro-cycle followed by several days of regeneration, and integrated afterwards with a compensatory micro-cycle.

In most cases such a training camp serves to improve aerobic capacity and thus aims at a great deal of training. In the other weeks of PP III training is done in large amounts and partly at high intensity. The high intensity should be planned for especially after the regeneration week following the training camp and thus create a seamless transition to the competition period. For this RSE intervals and ST and RT training are useful. Strength endurance training on the bike is now increasingly included.

In this phase there is also a gradually decreasing amount of indoor training and cross-training. The training means are now of a specific nature.

As a rule PP III is the period with the greatest training strain. This high training strain can only be placed on the body if a corresponding preparatory foundation has been created in the two previous preparatory periods. If this is not the case, such a PP III will overtax the body and cause a major regeneration deficit, considerably delaying the refinement of top form or even hindering it altogether.

In BE training the amounts are greatest; e.g. up to seven hours per session for men.

Strain is again applied in a double or triple rhythm (i.e. blocks of two or three days), in the high performance field also in quadruple rhythm.

As already mentioned, in PP III first test races can be carried out. In PP III competitions mainly serve the purpose of exact identification of fitness; deficits can be recognised and deliberately worked on in the following micro-cycle.

Special cycling training means such as SE, ST, RSE or RT are best trained in double or triple blocks that build upon each other. For example strength endurance would be trained three days in a row with increasing amounts (e.g. 20 min, 30 min and 40 min SE). Mixed training with the specific cycling training, especially during a training session, should be avoided.

3.5.2 Competition Period (CP)

The competition period that now follows is generally the longest period, lasting from late April until late September or even longer. During these 19-23 weeks a cyclisation must also be planned, for constant form in this period is not possible. Very few other sports have such long competition periods as mountain biking and cycling. In both sports, however, a great number of races are needed to reach top form.

The first weeks of the CP with the first races involve large amounts of training and serve to check on form. Weaknesses and strengths can be recognised and analysed.

In the weeks that follow an attempt should be made to eradicate particularly serious weaknesses such as poor basic endurance, not enough strength abilities or poor anaerobic mobilisation.

Develop Cycles

When dividing up the competition period the same is done as in the other periods. Two to four (five) progressively more exerting weeks are followed by a regeneration week with much less training. This cycle forms a block. Each block should be devoted to one main objective.

A good way of structuring this phase is the alternation of emphasis on amount and intensity. After three weeks of much training there are a few resting days and then two weeks of more intensive training.

This is followed again by a regeneration week. The regeneration weeks in the CP are of very great significance and must be carried out at all costs.

Increase of Strain until Seasonal High Point

The total strain of the block that follows should be higher. This is increased until the high point of the season is reached. This increase ends, however, a week before that high point, for in the last week, apart from two slightly exerting sessions on Wednesday and Thursday, (Sunday: race) training is only in the field of CO / BE 1 .

The competition period weeks with an emphasis on amount differ from those of the preparatory periods in that they are supplemented with intensive exertion in races.

There should additionally be a more intensive training session on days when the amount of training is low, such as on the first day of each triple block.

Competition Free Phase

In particular when there are two seasonal high points, but also in periodisation for a single high point, it has proved to be sensible to include a competition free phase of about two to four weeks which divides the competition period into two halves. In this time basic endurance is trained, at first reduced and then increasing, thus bringing it to a higher level. It is advisable to begin this race free phase with the last week of a block, i.e. the regeneration week. The structuring can be borrowed from the structuring of rebuilding training shown in chapter 6.

Lots of Strength Endurance Training

Strength endurance training in the lower field of intensity should be included in the "amount" blocks during the whole period, for in well-dosed intensity it is not very exerting.

Regular visits to fitness studios or strength training rooms are also part of the training programme of a performance oriented biker. More on this in chapter 4.

Technique Training

During sessions on the mountain bike a technique section should always be included in which a certain technique is practised. These are usually less exerting but should be carried out at the beginning of training in a rested state. In addition, complete technique sessions should be planned for, e.g. as a second session per day. More about technique training in chapter 8.

Weekly Schedule

Also in order to do well in the "preparatory races" or fitness development races, the relevant training weeks, i.e. the micro-cycle, must also be structured. Later in the chapter suggestions for weekly schedules for the various classes can be found. Training must be reduced at the right time before a race so that regeneration can begin. If a race or marathon is on a Sunday, the last major exertion should be on Thursday (Wednesday), if a race is on a Saturday, it should be on Wednesday (Tuesday).

Also, some bikers need more time for regeneration, some less. Here it is a matter of trying out what suits you. On the days following, Friday and Saturday, work is in the fields CO / BE 1.

It is imperative to cycle the day before the race. Brief, intensive exertion as a so-called pre-strain interval gets the body adjusted to the race, activates metabolism and serves to check on form. Furthermore it provides an opportunity to also check on equipment.

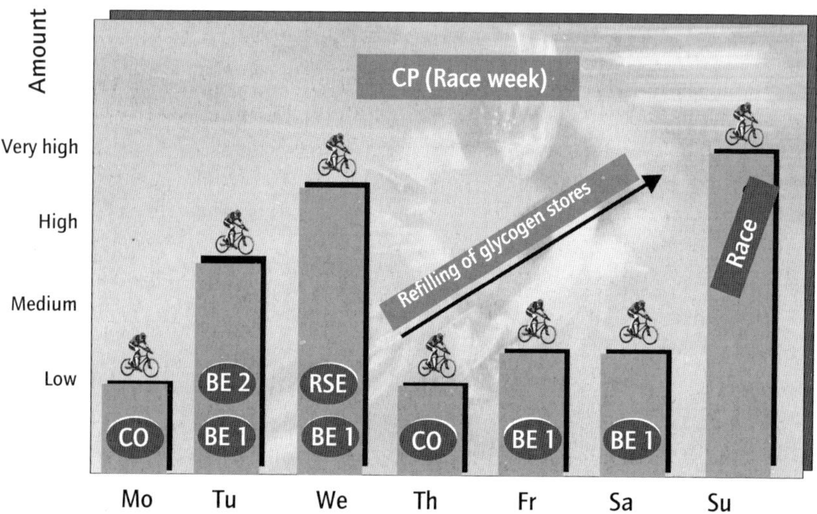

Fig. 3.25: Weekly cycle in the CP, week before the race with high degree of strain on Wednesday followed by a regeneration phase

Exertion Block with a Race

To increase and vary exertion a race can also be included in an exertion block. To do this you start on Friday with a medium length session, ride a long session (low intensity) on Saturday and on Sunday after the race you add another one or two hours, preferably by cycling home. When you do this, make sure you eat enough carbohydrates, especially on Saturday.

A race-free weekend should be used for a longer than usual BE 1 block.

Use Monday as a Regeneration Day

As a rule, on Mondays the emphasis should be on regeneration. To build up form, however, it is possible to follow a race day with a very long BE 1 session in order to increase exertion.

3.5.3 Transitional Period

The transitional period is characterised by regeneration from training and race routine. For performance mountain bikers the annual vacation will usually take place in this phase. Whereas in the other periods training is mainly deliberate and structured, now you do without planning and do what you feel like. Low intensities and amounts aid regeneration. Although some athletes swear by a complete break from all sport for four weeks, it is advisable for medical reasons to keep moving. You should only stop cycling in this period in order to develop motivation for the preparatory periods that follow. As a rule the transitional period lasts about three to five weeks.

Many bikers even stop bike training altogether until early December and devote themselves fully to cross-training in sports that usually get too little attention.

3.5.4 Running Training in the Course of the Year

Do Running Training All Year Round

One training session per week lasting one or two hours continues to serve as cross-training. At least every two weeks this session should include running in order to prepare the muscles for running strains during races.

If running training is completely neglected now and also in the competition period, long or frequent running sections in cross-country can cause serious muscle strain or other damage to the legs. Additionally, regular running training improves economy of movement. Running sessions can be included in the whole preparatory period, but also in summer when the weather is bad. The intensity should be matched to the rest of training, but should not be too high.

3.5.5 MTB or Road Bike

Cycling Training with the MTB or the Road Bike?

A question often discussed is whether a mountain biker has to train on a racing bike or whether he can reach top performance exclusively by training on the mountain bike. To answer this, here are a few details on the background to this question.

After the first mountain bike races and the gradual commercialisation of MTB racing, road racers soon discovered the MTB. Many, but particularly those who were less successful or at the end of their career, changed to the MTB and mainly participated in mountain bike races. Because of their fitness advantages developed through years of race participation, the mountain bikers hardly had a chance against them.

These days many trainers and academics are of the opinion that in order to be successful in mountain biking you have to do road training and even participate in road races. Radical mountain bikers on the other hand say that you certainly can develop the same kind of fitness by training exclusively on the mountain bike as you can in mixed training. The fact is though that practically all successful World Cup mountain bikers came from road cycling or cross-country, but that few of them were absolutely top class in their previous sport (except in cross-country).

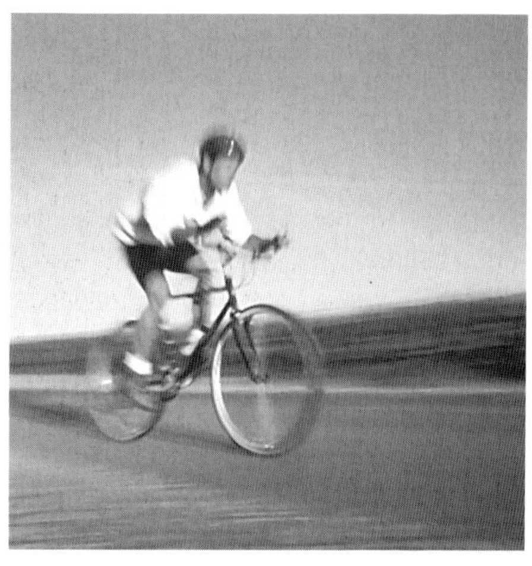

It is also possible to train on the road with a mountain bike.
Photo: Trek Deutschland

This greater performance potential of the "road riders" is not so much because it is not possible to train on the mountain bike to the same degree, but results rather from participation in road races (circuit races and road races). Because they have usually been taking part in such races for years, the road riders are superior to the mountain bikers in all aspects of form (except perhaps co-ordination) and in particular in the areas of endurance and strength.

Thus it appears that it is not the basic training on the racing bike as such that is the deciding advantage, but rather the participation in road races. For the problem of carrying out difficult basic endurance training on the mountain bike can be solved by training on the road with the "mounty" fitted with narrow slicks, which definitely has the same effect. Participation in longer and more frequent road races would, however, not be possible for the mountain biker even with slicks. Mountain bike races are generally too short and too intensive to trigger the same metabolic and muscular adjustment as road racing. Thus much of the evidence suggests that at least in the top performance class you cannot do without road training and racing, unless of course you already have years of experience as a road rider.

Another problem for bikers who only participate in mountain bike races is currently the low frequency of races and the almost total lack of stage races to develop top form.

Circuit races on the road are especially suitable for building up fitness.
Photo: Trek Deutschland

Despite these plausible reasons, young bikers should be given a choice between MTB and racing bike. Only once the junior class has been reached should the coach try to place more emphasis on the racing bike amongst those with serious ambitions and potential.

As mentioned in the introductory chapter of this book, a similar performance explosion to that on the track and in the cross-country field can be expected as soon as good road racing professionals participate in mountain bike races. On courses that are not too demanding technically, road professionals with many thousands of cycling kilometres from classics and stage races would be superior to the MTB professionals of the present.

Mountain bikers should therefore participate, with a road team, in important preparatory races on the road, and if possible also in stage races to get as many racing kilometres as possible "in their legs" before the key mountain bike races (seasonal high points). Stage races often have the effect of an unexpected performance boost and cannot be simulated in training.

Sitting Position on MTB and Racing Bike

In order to avoid or prevent possible orthopaedic problems it is important to match the sitting position on the racing bike to that on the mountain bike. To be precise, the sitting height, the distance between the tip of the saddle and pedal cog centre and the distance from the saddle tip to the centre of the handlebars must be adjusted to match.

If possible the same saddle should be used on both bikes, and only one shoe-pedal system. The pedal crank length of 175 mm typical of mountain bikes should also be mounted on the racing bike if possible.

For mountain bikers it is important to first find the correct position on the MTB and then transfer it to the racing bike. Doing it the other way round, an unfavourable position on the mountain bike could lead to wasting performance potential.

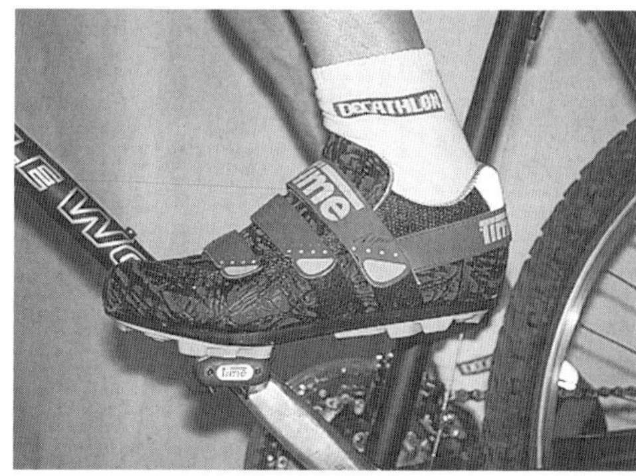

The flexible pedal system from Time allows the freedom of movement necessary for the feet. Photo: Achim Schmidt

When Do You Train on the MTB, when on the Racing Bike?

A simple rule is to carry out greater amounts of training and training camps in spring on the racing bike, and do strength training and other special training sessions, especially technique training, on the mountain bike. Exactly how you train, however, must be decided individually. Essentially, if the sitting position is the same and there are no adjustment problems, all training sessions are also possible on the MTB.

If there are major difficulties in adjusting from one bike to the other you should not change too often, and in particular train basic endurance in blocks on the racing bike. You should investigate what is causing the adjustment difficulties.

Regenerative sessions in the compensatory field should also be done on the racing bike as such a session on the MTB in the forest or rough terrain is usually more intensive, and undesirable bursts of exertion occur again and again.

3.6 Training Mistakes

The main mistakes made in training are listed below:

- Training is too intensive, mainly in basic endurance field 2 BE 2 and in the race specific endurance field RSE. The emphasis should be on developing high aerobic capacity through BE 1 training.
- Because of too intensive training during the week, full performance is not possible at the weekend. A bad state of regeneration (constant exhaustion) and empty glycogen stores characterise this condition.

- Underestimation of occupational strain (or education) which can also lead to a regeneration deficit if training does not take this into consideration.
- Coupled with this is often insufficient training in BE 1.
- Periodisation is not used, mountain bikers have practically the same fitness level the whole year round.
- Ignoring the laws of regeneration.
- Increases and jumps in the level of strain in the course of the year that are too high lead to performance stagnation or even decrease.
- No reduction in training during illness (infections) can lead to drops in performance.
- Strength and strength endurance training are completely neglected.
- Poor cycling technique, no technique training.
- Eating habits not matched to exertion.
- Monotony in the training process often restricts performance.
- Ignorance of new developments in training.

This list could be added to; if you read widely you will come across more.

3.7 Performance Classes

The following description of training of the performance classes is mainly for licenced riders. The training schedules are for orientation and need to be individually changed to suit one's own situation.

The races of the unlicenced hobby classes are correspondingly shorter.

Youth/Female Youth

Depending on the organiser, cross-country races for 15- and 16-year olds last between 30 and 60 minutes. The races for females in this age group are unfortunately usually much shorter.

The short race duration is coupled with high intensity which does not at all mean that youth training has to be very intensive.

The races in the male and female youth classes are often dominated by young people who are physically more developed.

Athletes who are less developed physically, especially those in their first year, have a difficult time here, whereas those mountain bikers already used to success often have motivational problems in the men's and women's classes when they

Male Youth/Female Youth				
Age	15 (m)	16 (m)	15 (f)	16 (f)
Hours per year	250 - 350 h	350 - 450 h	200 - 300 h	300 - 400
Number of races	5 - 10	- 15	5 - 10	- 15
Training duration BE 1 max.	- 4 h	- 5 h	- 3 h	- 4 h
Training fields	BE 1, BE 2 RSE, ST	BE 1, BE 2, RSE, ST, RT (SE)	BE 1, BE 2 RSE, ST	BE 1, BE 2, RSE, ST, RT, (SE)
Tips	• Much technique training	• Careful SE and strength training from 16 on	• Get used to greater amounts	• Important: Much cross-training

Weekly Cycles in PP and CP (15 - 16 years)		
	PP II	CP
Monday	Stretching, gymnastics Strengthening exercises	Stretching, gymnastics, technique training, Strengthening exercises/30 min CO
Tuesday	1 h cross-training 1h indoor training	1 - 2 h BE 1 MTB/racing bike with ST intervals (3 x 2 min)
Wednesday	1 - 1.5 h cross-training	2 - 3 h BE 1 MTB/racing bike with speed intervals (BE 2, RSE)
Thursday	Stretching, gymnastics, Strengthening exercises, technique training	3 h BE 1 MTB/racing bike
Friday	2 h indoor training	1 h cross-training or day off
Saturday	1 - 2 h BE 1 MTB/racing bike with technique training or cross-training	1 h CO/BE 1 (technique training) or BE block when no race
Sunday	2 - 3 h BE 1 MTB/racing bike (technique training)	Race or 2 - 4 h BE 1

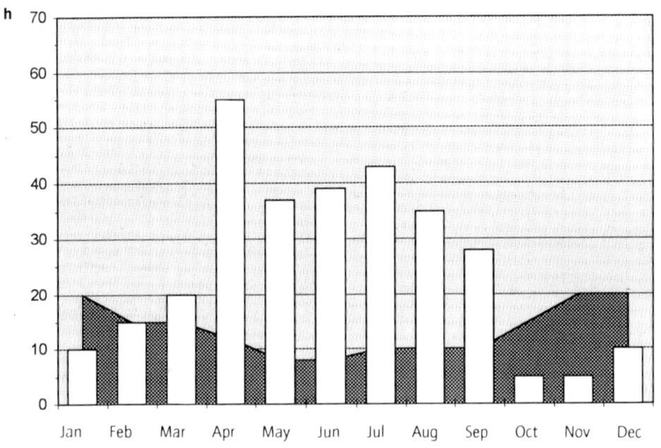

are not so successful; at this time the stragglers usually close the performance gap. Riders who are not so well-developed physically can compensate deficits in endurance and strength with above average technique abilities and therefore can be up the front in races.

Plenty of Technique Training

When training young people one must ensure that there is as much variety as possible which allows them diversity and the possibility to do their own structuring to a certain extent. The broadly based sporting education with its emphasis on the mountain bike should be subordinated to the idea of performance.

This does not mean, however, that an orientation to performance should be avoided, but that young people should be introduced to the performance sport in small doses and with variety. In a sport like mountain biking, which places great demands on technique, technique training plays a very significant role within training as a whole.

To train co-ordination skills on the bike there should be playful training on BMX, track and road bikes (see cycling technique). Linked with this is a not yet realised differentiation in downhill and cross-country which will only be started later at junior age. As a result of this diverse training, basic co-ordination skills can be developed and advanced which will provide the foundation for action and development reserves in the later performance and high performance fields.

Training sessions on the bike are between one and three hours long. Occasionally very long bike tours of four or five hours can be undertaken (assuming an appropriate level of training and stops along the way).

It should be left to the cyclists to decide which bike they prefer to use for endurance training. It would certainly be wrong to persuade young people who only want to train on their mountain bike to do road training on a racing bike. Youth training should be as enjoyable and as free of unnecessary pressures as possible. Furthermore, participation in other endurance events such as cross and road runs, relays, duathlons (with MTB), triathlons is also a good idea.

In addition to daily stretching, functional strengthening gymnastics should be part of training for young mountain bikers. Deliberate strength training on machines should, however, not be included at this stage, especially as strength is already trained enough by the practice on off-road terrain.

When planning races for young people it is important to make sure they do not take part in events too often as this involves major effort. Because of the current small number of races in Europe athletes have to spend a great deal of time in the car.

Ten to 15 mountain bike races a year is plenty; if there is interest these can be supplemented with a few road races.

A one week training camp, or preferably a training course in the holidays, is appropriate in the youth field. It should be diversely structured and should in no way place the emphasis on training with a sports device (road training).

In such a training camp in particular it is possible to carry out a range of endurance activities which allow specific training of basic endurance. Trekking tours with climbing sections or other "adventure activities" taken to a certain extent from adventure education, are excellently suited for this. Young people can thus have a very exciting week of experiences and train their basic endurance with a great deal of diversity.

It is important to develop an understanding of nature at an early age. By providing a variety of experiences in the outdoors, the aim is to teach bikers to live in responsible harmony with nature. The "adventure activities" described above lend themselves particularly well to providing personal and social experiences.

Juniors

Male and female juniors aged 17 and 18 compete in cross-country races with durations of about one to one and a half hours. As in the female youth class the races for female juniors are unfortunately also significantly shorter. Here too many races are still won by those with more advanced physical development, although the disadvantage of the development stragglers gradually begins to disappear.

Junior training is characterised by greater specialisation with regard to the means of training. Whereas in the youth class the emphasis was still on having fun training endurance, now the balance shifts gradually, depending on goals and motivation, to more performance oriented training, although this should not mean that fun oriented elements of training are avoided.

Road training on a racing bike and participation in road races are a good idea but are not absolutely necessary.

Juniors				
Age	17 (m)	18 (m)	17 (f)	18 (f)
Hours per year	400 - 550 h	500 - 650 h	350 - 450 h	400 - 550 h
Number of races	15 - 20	20 - 25	10 - 20	10 - 20
Training duration BE 1 max.	- 6 h	- 7 h	- 5 h	- 6 h
Training fields	BE 1, BE 2 RSE, ST, RT, SE	BE 1, BE 2, RSE, ST, RT, SE	BE 1, BE 2 RSE, ST, RT, SE	BE 1, BE 2, RSE, ST, RT, SE
Tips	• SE and strength training are very important	• Get used to greater amounts	• Participate in road races	• Much cross-training

Weekly Cycles in PP and CP (17 - 18 years)		
	PP II	CP
Monday	Stretching, gymnastics Strengthening exercises	Stretching, gymnastics, Strengthening exercises / 30 min CO
Tuesday	1.5 h cross-training 1h strength/indoor training	2 h BE 1 MTB/racing bike with RT intervals (3 x 10 x 7 s) or ST, SE
Wednesday	1.5 - 2 h cross-training	3 h BE 1 MTB/racing bike with speed intervals (BE 2, RSE)
Thursday	Stretching, gymnastics, Possibly 1 h BE 1/2 MTB/racing bike	4 - 5 h BE 1 MTB/racing bike
Friday	2 h strength/indoor training	Day off
Saturday	2 - 3 h BE 1 MTB/racing bike with technique training or cross-training	1 h CO/BE 1 (technique training) or BE block when no race
Sunday	3 - 4 h BE 1 MTB/racing bike Technique training	Race or 4 - 6 h BE 1

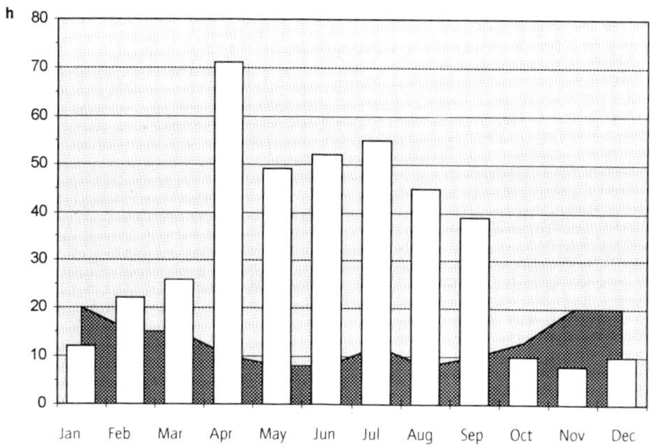

Training sessions last between two and four hours. To develop good endurance capability occasional longer sessions of five or six hours are necessary. Road training is suitable for these extra long sessions. In a one or two week long training camp it is essential to carry out these long sessions at low intensity on even terrain.

Cross-training

In addition to training activities on the mountain bike or racing bike, sound mountain bike training of course also includes cross-training, i.e. participation in other sports such as rollerblading, trekking, cross-country skiing, running, orienteering. Cross-training is particularly valuable in the preparatory periods.

While functional strength training to avoid damage from over-exertion and muscular imbalances continues, at junior age one begins to include specific strength training in the training schedule. This is done initially using the young athletes' own body weight, and then after a while - as described in the chapter "Strength Training" - in a fitness studio and by using dumb-bells.

To perfect technique and co-ordination abilities on the bike, a specific technique session every week with varying content should be introduced. Playful elements should not be left out.

The number of mountain bike races annually for juniors should be about 20. For many this is hard to achieve because of the small number of races held. Here too an alternative is participation in road races and other endurance sports.

Especially recommended are duathlon and triathlon events, cross-runs and orienteering runs which all closely approximate the exertion structure of a mountain bike cross-country race because, in contrast to road races, here athletes determine their own pace and thus the amount of exertion in relationship to their level of fitness and their psychological performance capacity.

When training juniors and young people care must be taken that the intensity of basic endurance training in particular is kept within limits. Juniors like to compete against their training partners which often means they do no basic endurance training at all.

At junior age the decision is often made whether to pursue a course leading to the high performance field or to continue on a regional level, without, however, excluding the possibility of later development. For this reason, junior training is

Large fields of starters in the men's class call for assertiveness right from the start.
Photo: Klaus Eweleit

Men				
Age	19 (m)	20 (m)	21 (m)	22 (m)
Hours per year	600 - 700 h	700 - 800 h	800 - 900 h	900 - 1,000 h
Number of races	30 - 40	40 - 50	45 - 55	> 55
Training duration BE 1 max.	- 8 h	- 8 h	- 8 h	- 8 h
Training fields	BE 1, BE 2 RSE, ST, RT, SE	BE 1, BE 2 RSE, ST, RT, SE	BE 1, BE 2 RSE, ST, RT, SE	BE 1, BE 2, RSE, ST, RT, SE
Tips	• BE 1, SE and strength training are very important	• Maximum amounts of cycling a must	• Participation in road races and possibly circuits	• Cross-training continues

Weekly Cycles in PP and CP (19 - 22 years)		
	PP II	CP
Monday	Stretching, gymnastics Strengthening exercises	Stretching, gymnastics, Strengthening exercises / 1 h CO
Tuesday	2.5 h cross-training 1 h strength/indoor training	3 h BE 1 MTB/racing bike with ST intervals (3 x 12 x 7 s) or ST, SE
Wednesday	2 - 3 h cross-training	4 h BE 1 MTB/racing bike with speed intervals (BE 2, RSE)
Thursday	Stretching, gymnastics possibly 2 h BE 1 MTB/racing bike	5 - 6 h BE 1 MTB/racing bike
Friday	2 h BE 1 MTB/racing bike (technique training) 1 h strength indoor training	Day off
Saturday	4 h BE 1 MTB/racing bike or cross-training	2 h CO/BE 1 (technique training) or BE block when no race
Sunday	5 - 6 h BE 1 MTB/racing bike	Race or 6 - 8 h BE 1

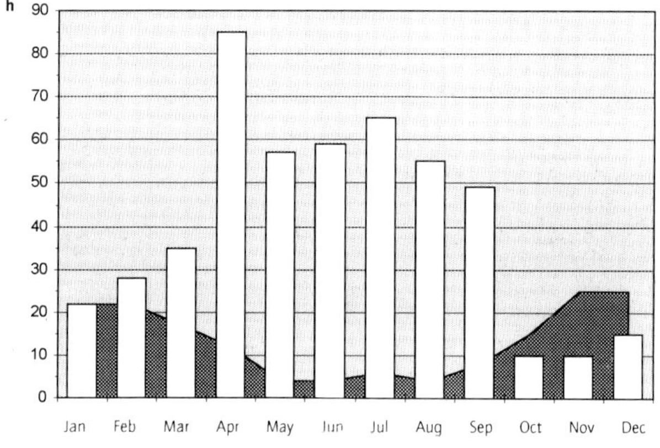

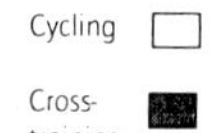

often called "entry training". Anyone wanting to enter the top league nationally will now need to take on the highest degree of training exertion.

Many mountain bikers stop at this age because the increased training requirements no longer suit them, and the race speeds are well above their capabilities. Fortunately, mountain biking also has hobby races which, for most participants, are ridden at a lower level.

Men

At 19 the phase of build-up and entry training is followed by high performance training in the men's field. According to individual objectives, maximum amounts and maximum total exertion is now demanded of athletes. For other athletes entry into the men's class marks the beginning of a phase when they only have limited time for educational or career reasons but still want to take part in licence races.

In many cases mountain bike beginners only discover the sport at this age, which requires a completely different structuring of training.

Those aiming for top individual performance must now ensure that training planning, execution and performance diagnostics, are co-ordinated with each other in order to increase the effect of training. Chapter 6 includes an example of specific training planning.

Race durations in the men's field (licence) are between 1:00 and 3:00 hours (with the exception of marathons) and in some cases more. Cross-country races usually last about two hours.

All training fields increase with constant development. The race proportion of the total number of hours increases overproportionally, for which reason participation in road races is very important. Coupled with this is the necessity of regenerative training after frequent races. Thus the CO field should be increased slightly in relation to the other fields.
The significance of strength also increases in the men's field and must therefore also be trained more.

At the men's level athletes should already have a foundation in technique so that such training can be concentrated on polishing it up and working on difficult techniques.

Women				
Age	19 (f)	20 (f)	21 (f)	22 (f)
Hours per year	500 - 600 h	600 - 700 h	700 - 800 h	800 - 900 h
Number of races	25 - 35	30 - 40	35 - 45	> 45
Training duration BE 1 max.	- 7 h	- 7 h	- 8 h	- 8 h
Training fields	BE 1, BE 2 RSE, ST, RT, SE	BE 1, BE 2 RSE, ST, RT ,SE	BE 1, BE 2 RSE, ST, RT, SE	BE 1, BE 2, RSE, ST, RT, SE
Tips	• BE 1, SE and strength training are very important	• Maximum amounts of cycling a must	• Participation in road races and circuits	• Cross-training continues

Weekly Cycles in PP and CP (19 - 22 years)		
	PP II	CP
Monday	Stretching, gymnastics Strengthening exercises	Stretching, gymnastics, Strengthening exercises / 1 h CO
Tuesday	1 h cross-training 1h strength/indoor training	2 h BE 1 MTB/racing bike with RT intervals (2 x 10 x 7 s) or ST, SE
Wednesday	1 - 2 h cross-training	3 h BE 1 MTB/racing bike with speed intervals (BE 2, RSE)
Thursday	Stretching, gymnastics (technique training) possibly 2 h BE 1 MTB/racing bike	4 - 5 h BE 1 MTB/racing bike
Friday	1 h BE 1 MTB/racing bike 2 h strength/indoor training	Day off
Saturday	3 h BE 1 MTB/racing bike or cross-training	1 h CO/BE 1 (technique training) or BE block when no race
Sunday	4 - 5 h BE 1 MTB/racing bike	Race or 5 - 7 h BE 1

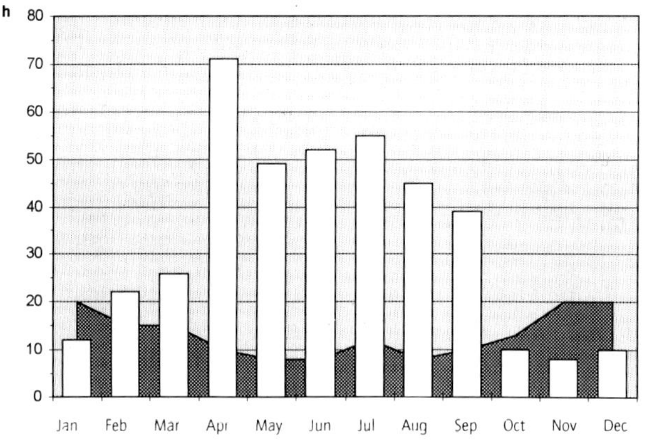

Road or Forest?

At the men's level at the latest, the large amounts of BE 1 make it increasingly difficult to meet the demands of training exclusively on the mountain bike off-road. Road training allows a more precise dosage of exertion and thus becomes in most cases a permanent part of a mountain biker's training.

Added to this is the opportunity of participating in road races (circuit races and proper road races) to achieve the necessary proportion of racing hours, which is either impossible or very difficult to do if you participate solely in mountain bike races.

If you nevertheless try to take part in as many mountain bike races as possible by driving long distances in the car you can easily reach a state of overtraining because medium intensity is much higher than in road races. More about this problem in the section *"Racing Bike or Mountainbike"*.

Because of the sometimes very large numbers of participants in the hobby class in particular, safe cycling technique and a good degree of assertiveness are essential for success here. Good anaerobic mobilisation capability is also necessary in order to have enough reserves for the inevitable overtaking manoeuvres.

Women

Women's cross-country races usually last between one and two hours. With the exception of major international races (World Cup), the fields of participants are very small and the level of performance is not uniform.

In women's racing the main performance deficits, apart from often insufficiently developed basic endurance, are poor to moderate strength abilities and lack of technique. It is thus necessary to improve these two characteristics of fitness in training. With the exception of these peculiarities the same principles apply to women's training as to men's.

It must be ensured that if women train with men they select a training group that matches their own abilities. Often though women ride with very fit men and thus train in intensity fields that are too high so that the desired training effect is not achieved. The same applies to the female youth classes and beginners. Dietary peculiarities are dealt with in the chapter "Dietary Considerations".

Specific and Increased Technique Training

Furthermore, in the female field more technique training must be done because unfortunately in many cases still, as a result of their upbringing, girls and women have poorer technique and co-ordination skills on the mountain bike than boys or men of the same age.

It can often be seen that in all classes many riders with excellent performance diagnostics values lose a great deal of time owing to a lack of skills in cycling technique on downhills and difficult sections which can no longer be made up on climbs and flat sections. This in turn underlines the need for as diverse a training as possible in this technically very demanding sport.

Road races are also an alternative for women. Photo: Trek Deutschland

Seniors

In the senior licence field races are dominated by former top amateurs, often with cross-country experience, who are almost unbeatable because of their technical abilities but also because of their outstanding strength endurance. This applies especially in contrast to newcomers who have gained first experiences in the hobby class.

Thus the group of senior riders can also be divided into two subcategories. This division could be applied in any racing class but needs to be covered more extensively in the senior class because the differences are greatest here.

Next to the above-mentioned group with up to three decades of racing experience there is a group of riders, some who come from other endurance sports and some with no previous sporting experience, who take part in licence events. There could hardly be a greater difference between opponents.

Training of experienced riders is a continuation of men's training but often with a greatly reduced time budget. Specific strength training would still be useful for them, but usually takes a back seat because riders have a high level of strength and strength endurance due to their many years of racing. Long basic endurance sessions are absolutely necessary and should be included at least twice weekly so that the level of basic endurance does not sink too low.

Functional Gymnastics
At senior age in particular, the significance of specific functional strengthening gymnastics increases greatly in order to compensate for posture damage and over-exertion through years of cycling.

A daily stretching programme is also a compulsory element for senior mountain bikers.

Beginners/Fitness Bikers

Beginners first need to specifically train basic endurance in order to apply specific training stimuli to this foundation. They will thus spend a major part of their training time improving basic endurance. Cross-training can help to do this. The emphasis, however, should be on bike training in order to remove deficits in technique.

If endurance capacity is poor, athletes ride races in a higher intensity field which also greatly reduces performance with regard to cycling technique because of the increased demands on the total system "athlete".

A special technique training session needs to be done twice a week, if possible with experienced cyclists.

Another major aspect for beginners is strength training both on the bike and in the fitness studio. Functional strengthening gymnastics and stretching should be part of the beginner's standard programme.

Those who have not previously done any kind of endurance sport will certainly find it hardest. It takes at least two years of concentrated training to achieve well-developed endurance ability with organic adjustments, which calls for a considerable amount of willpower and persistence.

Before taking up mountain bike training it is advised to have a thorough examination by a sports doctor to avoid possible health risks right from the start. Apart from this it is important for a beginner to start training in small doses and pay attention to his body to make sure he does not demand much too much of it, or even cause damage.

Fitness Bikers/Beginners			
Hours per year	150 - 200 h	200 - 250 h	250 - 300 h
Training duration BE 1 max.	- 3 h	- 4 h	- 5 h
Training fields	BE 1, BE 2, RSE	BE 1, BE 2, RSE	BE 1, BE 2, RSE
Tips	• Health check-up • Also long sessions	• Important: compensatory sports, cross-training	• Compensatory gymnastics are important

Weekly Cycles in PP and CP (200 - 250 h)		
	PP II	CP
Monday	–	–
Tuesday	30 min cross-training or 45 min BE 1 MTB	1 h BE 1 MTB or cross-training
Wednesday	1 h BE 1/2 MTB or 1 h cross-training	1 - 2 h BE 1 with BE 1/RSE intervals MTB
Thursday	Stretching, gymnastics Strengthening exercises	Stretching, gymnastics Strengthening exercises
Friday	–	–
Saturday	1.5 h BE 1 MTB with technique training	1 - 2 h BE 1 MTB with technique training
Sunday	2 h BE 1 MTB	2 - 3 h BE 1 MTB or cycling tour/CTF

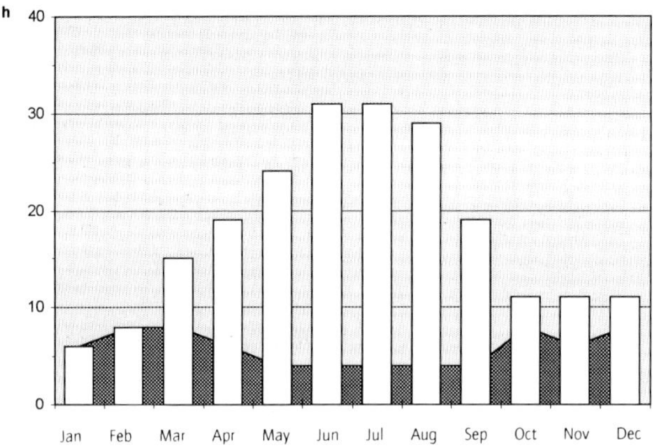

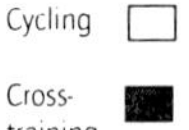

For this reason only the training fields BE 1 and 2 and RSE come into consideration. Specific, highly intensive and goal-oriented training is out of the question for fitness bikers or beginners.

To increase general ability to bear strain both beginners and fitness bikers should do regular cross-training. Strength training is not necessary, compensatory gymnastics and stretching are, however.

Marathon Bikers

The group of bikers participating in marathons gets bigger all the time. In this group too there are great differences in performance capacity and objectives. Marathons are where races and touring events overlap.

Whatever the objectives, all marathon bikers need long training sessions. Long and extra long BE 1 sessions need to be trained in blocks before a marathon. The supply of energy can only be guaranteed for the full marathon distance (often up to six hours) if there is a well-developed aerobic foundation with efficient fat metabolism.

Speed and resilience training take a back seat because of the duration of exertion, but strength endurance is important.

Specific technique training gives marathon bikers a reserve of cycling technique knowledge which can save them from making grave cycling mistakes when they are very tired in the last third of the marathon.

The chart shows the three different groups of marathon bikers classified by the amount of hours. The first group only trains a basic amount and mainly prepares itself for covering the distance by training greater amounts in the last eight weeks before the big day.

In the second, and above all the third group, with a large amount of training a good result becomes more important, requiring greater amounts and intensities which must be spread over the whole year. This total strain, spread over the year, builds the foundation for a higher average speed, and the ability to deal with increases in pace at least for short periods.

Food intake during marathons is absolutely essential and must therefore be practised during training rides to avoid complications during the marathon e.g. with new products.

Marathon Bikers			
Hours per year	200 - 400 h	400 - 600 h	600 - 800 h
Training duration BE 1 max.	- 6 h	- 7 h	- 8 h
Training fields	BE 1, BE 2, RSE, SE	BE 1, BE 2 RSE, SE	BE 1, BE 2, RSE, SE
Tips	• Much technique training • Long sessions also	• Important: compensatory sports, cross-training	• Compensatory gymnastics important

Weekly cycles in PP and CP (400 - 600 h)		
	PP II	CP
Monday	Stretching, gymnastics Strengthening exercises	Stretching, gymnastics, Strengthening exercises
Tuesday	1 h cross-training or 1 h BE 1 MTB/racing bike	1.5 - 2.5 h BE 1 MTB/racing bike 15 min SE or cross-training
Wednesday	1.5 - 2 h BE 1 MTB/racing bike or 1.5 - 2 h cross-training	1 - 2 h BE 1 with BE 2/RSE intervals MTB/racing bike
Thursday	Stretching, gymnastics Strengthening exercises	2 - 3 h BE 1 MTB/racing bike
Friday	1 h cross-training	1 h CO/BE 1 MTB/racing bike (technique training) or day off
Saturday	1 - 2 h BE 1 MTB/racing bike (technique training)	3 - 5 h BE 1 MTB/racing bike
Sunday	3 - 4 h BE 1 MTB/racing bike	4 - 6 h BE 1 MTB/racing bike or marathon

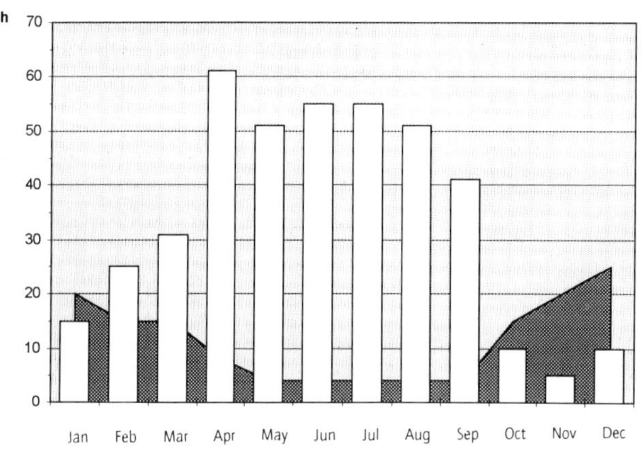

3.8 Training Camps

Fitting the Training Camp into the Annual Plan

If you are planning a training camp, at the beginning of the training year, preferably in the transitional phase, you should start to consider when there will be time for it and above all when it will best fit into the annual training structure.

If the training year is divided up as recommended in the chapter "Periodisation", it is best to place the training camp at the end of preparatory period II or the beginning of preparatory period III.

A training camp at this time should pursue the objective of improving basic endurance; there is time to do even long and extra long sessions in the BE field. In addition, the training camp provides the opportunity to compensate these amounts with appropriate regenerative measures such as stretching, physiotherapy, and in particular with sufficient sleep.

For young people training camps have to be placed in the school or Easter vacations, which correspond to the end of PP III. In PP III, specific elements are usually trained as basic endurance should already have reached a high level. If favourable weather conditions have made it possible to train enough basic endurance in PP I and PP II, or if the desired level has already been reached, it is certainly acceptable to use more intensive training forms at a training camp in PP III during the Easter vacation, but the amount should be somewhat less. Nevertheless, for reasons already mentioned, the emphasis should be on developing or stabilising basic endurance.

More intensive forms of training are better placed in the second week of training after the first week has been used e.g. for two BE 1 blocks and for acclimatisation. In the second week the amounts would then be slightly reduced and broken up by more intensive intervals (BE 2, RSE).

In addition to the spring, or foundational, training camp there can also be training camps in the competition period. For young people the summer vacation is ideal; adults must take the usual restrictions into account.

Preparation

In any case training camps should be prepared and followed up according to training methodology. This preparation and following up has already been covered in the periodisation chapter under PP III.

A number of micro-cycles (weeks) that build up and prepare for exertion should be placed in advance of the training camp so that directly before it just under a week of regeneration can be included. After the training camp there is also regeneration of a few days to a week.

Before a training camp a performance oriented mountain biker (men's class) should have trained at least 1,500 km or 60 hours on the bike. The minimum for hobby and junior bikers is about 800-1,000 km or 30 to 40 hours. These figures relate to PP II beginning in January.

Duration of a Training Camp

Ideally a basic training camp lasts two weeks whereas for a summer training camp one week is enough. In the youth field too, one week camps are suitable, but if the programme is diverse enough they can be extended to two weeks.

Selection of the Location

Southern countries with stable weather conditions are very good for spring training camps. Mallorca, the Canary Islands, the south of France, Italy and Spain generally have good roads, pleasant landscapes and the appropriate climate. If it is not possible to hold a training camp in the south, it can be done in more northern latitudes if certain things are considered. Because of the possibility of bad weather there can be days when training is cancelled. If training is done regardless of the weather, many athletes will get infections of the upper respiratory system because of the high degree of exertion.

Thus for a spring training camp in central or northern Europe you must ensure that there are alternative training areas at the location which allow training when it rains or is cold, for example bodybuilding room, gym, indoor swimming pool or training on the rolling machine.

The coach should make sure there are three to five rolling machines available at the camp location on which the bikers can take turns at training when the weather is bad. Two sessions on the roller (morning, afternoon) as well as indoor games are a good alternative to cancelled road training and also provide for diversity.

The one week training camps can easily be carried out locally. Low mountain ranges are suitable, providing on the one hand a change of surroundings with pleasant scenery and on the other hand ideal conditions for mountain biking.

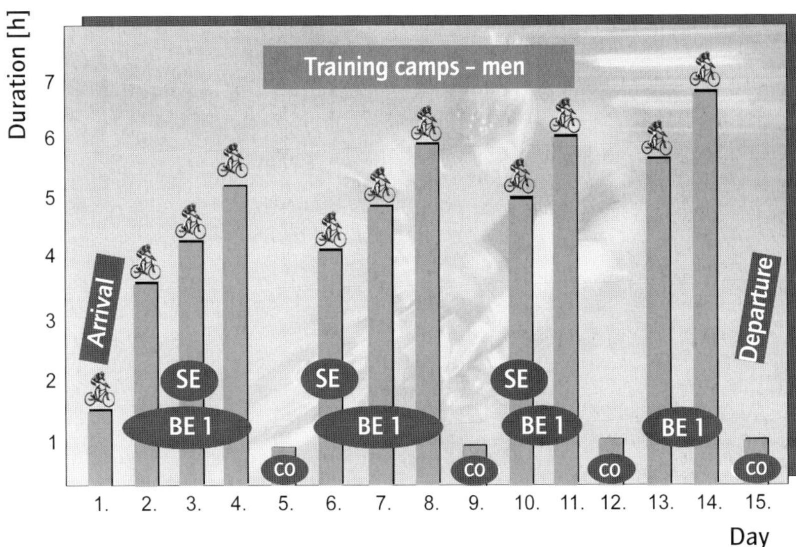

Fig. 3.26: Spring training camp for the men's class (14 days, oriented to amount)

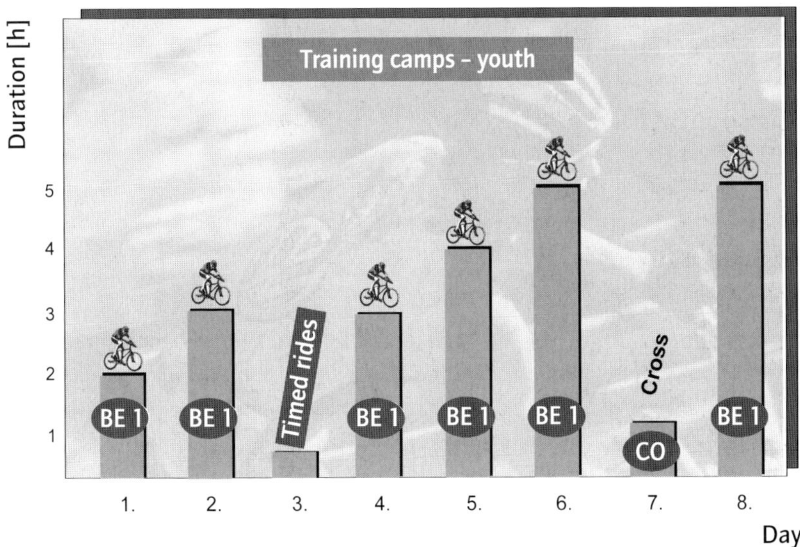

Fig. 3.27: Spring training camp for the youth class (eight days, oriented to amount)

With the increase in professionalism in mountain biking, more and more athletes plan for high altitude training camps in order to develop physical advantages over other bikers.

Which Bike Do You Take to the Training Camp?

At a basic training camp it does not really matter whether training is done on a mountain bike with slicks or a racing bike. Road training, however, is important for maintaining even intensity of strain. Because of the rough surface of tracks and various other reasons it is difficult to maintain even intensity in BE 1 when training off-road. Experience has shown that mixed groups of men and women with mountain bikes (slicks) and racing bikes can train together as long as they have a similar level of fitness.

At the special training camp training should be off-road on the mountain bike in order to place methodological training emphasis on particular aspects. When greater amounts are trained on the bike, low intensity must be ensured. If on the other hand the emphasis is on basic endurance, for example to boost it, training is best done on the road no matter which bike is used.

Structuring of the Training Camp

A two week basic training camp is divided into separate blocks, as are the micro-cycles too. The 14 days are divided into double, triple and quadruple blocks with a day of regeneration between each pair of blocks on which a short CO trip is undertaken.

For young people double and triple blocks have proved effective. In the high performance field quadruple blocks can also be trained, which are both physically and psychologically very hard.

As a rule an individual block is structured as a progression. During a training camp the amounts of training within the individual blocks also rise. The creation of blocks has proved itself because in this way a gradual increase in strain and sufficient regeneration phases are provided for. Mentally there is a clearly recognisable progression of strain which athletes can adjust to and which is cognitively plausible. The first day of a block is usually handled without problems; on the second day the first motivational problems and physical pains occur, and on the third day with the greatest amount of strain the thought of the following day of regeneration gives the bikers a boost.

With bikers who have poorer motivation and fitness, the progressive block structure described here can lead to motivational problems and physical overtaxing. The consequence of this is often a marked shortening of the last comprehensive days of each block. If the order within a block is reversed, the high motivation and the rested state after the day off can be made use of to do a very large amount of training. The two days afterwards then have reduced amounts.

When the block structure is progressive, tiredness accumulates during the block, when the block division is reversed, the decrease in training stimuli leads to an even level of tiredness after the first day. This second method is easier to deal with mentally. This reversed block should not, however, be the first block in the training camp, which is designed to facilitate settling in and acclimatisation.

Training Intensity

The issue of the intensity of strain at a training camp is a crucial one because it is imperative to make sure that the intensity for basic endurance training is maintained. Intensity that is too high in combination with large amounts leads to major deficits in regeneration. Often mountain bikers do not keep to these prescribed intensities and ride up inclines in particular with too much intensity. By doing so they develop a regeneration deficit which is not reduced in the course of the training camp but in fact increases as training amounts increase.

The result is that the desired improvement in form does not take place; even weeks after the training camp the negative consequences of too high an intensity can be seen in the form of reduced performance capacity. If strain is applied at low intensity an improvement in form is usually noticed from block to block and should be tested in the last block.

On one day a hill or another place for fast cycling should be chosen where there can even be a race over several kilometres. A timed trip can also make the training camp more fun and break through the monotony of basic training. Such intensive work does no harm and above all it channels the drive to ride fast and compete against the others.

Double rows with groups of not more than 12 riders are the appropriate training form. Even on rough terrain basic intensities can be realised without difficulty. The prerequisite for this is the correct selection of gearing. Thus gearings of 39/23 or even 25 must be possible in order to be able to manage steep climbs in the BE 1 field.

3.9 SRM Measurement System – Hightech Training

The following brief section covers the SRM training system which has revolutionised academic research in cycling and thus in mountain biking.

In the early years of performance diagnostics, although the relationship between physiological parameters of strain such as heart rate, lactate concentration and oxygen intake on the one hand, and physical performance on the other, was known, owing to a lack of appropriate measuring equipment this knowledge could only be used in the laboratory but not in the field. Thus a compromise was used.

The heart rate corresponding to performance and a certain metabolic situation (determined by measuring lactate) was used as a regulatory parameter. This was done without knowing if the readings determined in the laboratory corresponded to the levels of performance achieved on a bike out on the road or off the road.

For about ten years now it has been possible to reliably measure performance on a racing bike, and more recently also on a mountain bike, with the aid of the SRM training system, a sensitive electronic measuring device (expansion measurement strip) fitted to the pedal crankshaft.

The measured readings are transmitted telemetrically (wireless) to a central unit attached to the handlebars which displays all parameters and dispenses with the need for a cycle computer. The central unit is capable of constantly storing the data measured (performance, heart rate, speed, pedalling rate, time and kilometres) for many hours (> 100) at predetermined intervals, for example every five seconds.

SRM-Powermeter III
Photo: SRM/Schoberer

After a training session or a race the data can be transferred via interface to a PC and graphically displayed and analysed. The graphic display and the statistical

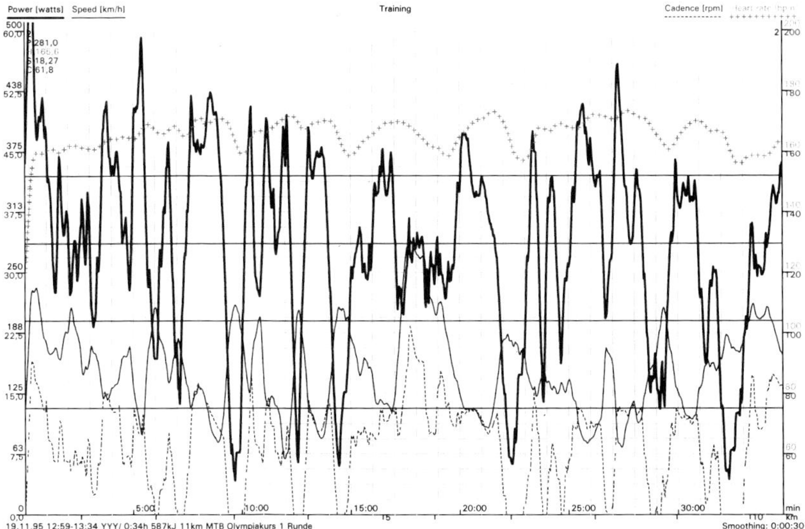

Fig. 3.28: Exertion parameters of the first lap in a mountain bike race on the Olympic course in Atlanta (Nov. 1995, Ned Overend)

evaluation of the data allow detailed conclusions to be drawn about the development in performance of an athlete. The system also allows optimal regulation of intensity during exertion in addition to the heart rate information on the exact level of performance is available.

On the basis of exact performance diagnostics to ascertain the fields of intensity, the SRM training system is currently the only system of its kind to create the prerequisites to efficiently train high performance mountain bikers. Interested amateurs, however, are not able to make much use of the SRM training system because a comprehensive academic education in training is necessary for effective use of the device and analysis of the results.

Meanwhile though there are a number of performance diagnostics institutes offering training guidance with the SRM system, although this is not exactly cheap.

The use of the SRM training system is thus limited to the absolute top class in mountain biking. Furthermore it is used for scientific research.

Analysis of Race Exertion

The detailed analysis of mountain bike races on the basis of evaluation using the SRM system is extremely interesting because it shows a performance structure which even amazes many experts. A detailed explanation here would go too far, however, and has partly been offered in chapter 2.

In figure 3.28 many interesting details regarding race exertion can be recognised at a glance. The data from the Olympic course in Atlanta were recorded during a test race and are those of Ned Overend. They show one lap.

The **heart rate** is between 155 and 175 beats with a core field between 160 and 170. The time gap of about a minute between the heart rate peaks and the performance peaks (e.g. at minutes 14, 18, 22) can be clearly seen. There is thus a delay in the reaction of the cardio-vascular system to exertion because first the performance is achieved anaerobically and then the energy deficit in the aerobic-anaerobic transitional field has to be compensated by increased oxygen intake.

The average **performance** during the monitored period of 281 watt is already relatively high, but more important are the exertion peaks which are not so clear in this smoothed curve. What is clear, however, is that the course of performance

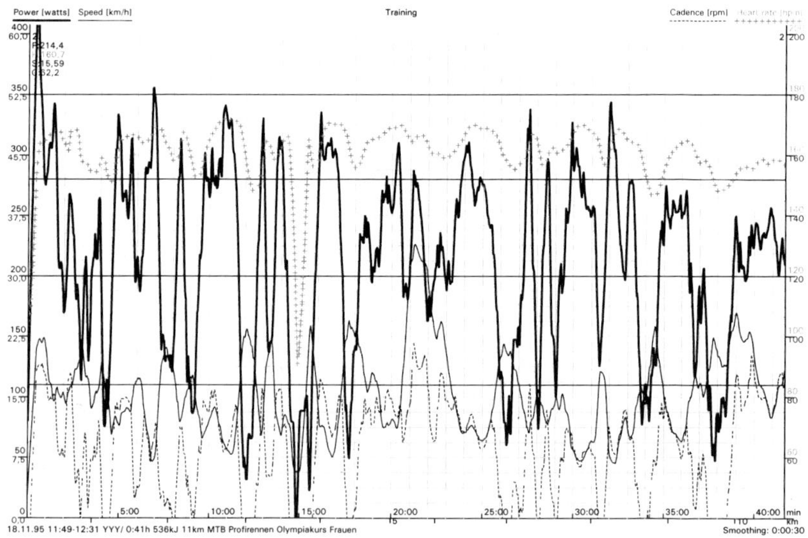

Fig. 3.29: Exertion parameters of the first lap in a mountain bike race on the Olympic course in Atlanta (Nov. 1995, Susan de Mattei)

is characterised by a pronounced variation between very high and very low readings. This oscillating performance is typical of mountain bike races and thus a decisive distinguishing feature from road races (e.g. fig. 3.31). Only on flat and technically easy courses are there longer sections where performance is even. On normal courses performance varies quite considerably because of frequent breaks from pedalling followed by acceleration and climbs. From a training methodology point of view this factor must be reflected in increased strength and resilience training.

In this connection the course of the speed curve is interesting, which is generally a reflection of the performance curve. Where performance shows the lowest values, **speed** is usually highest. These are freewheeling sections going downhill, for the pedalling rate is zero (e.g. minutes 10, 15, 23). At the beginning and end of the section shown, speed, performance and pedalling rate run parallel. This corresponds to the start-finish area where long straight sections allow even performance.

The average **pedalling rate** is only 62 r.p.m. The highest pedalling rate peaks are 100, but the average peaks are only 70. From a training methodological point of

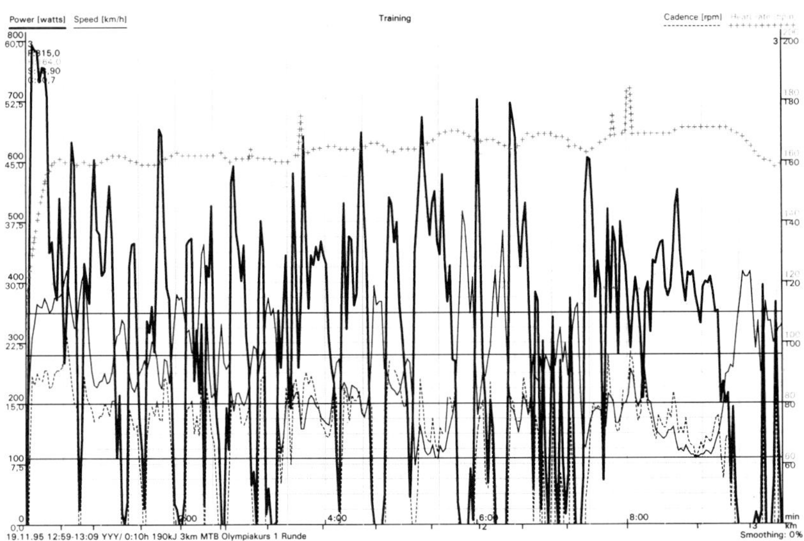

Fig. 3.30: Display of the exertion parameters of the first ten minutes of Ned Overend's race. In contrast to 3.28 the curve is not smoothed and shows the actual performance peaks.

view the significance of strength endurance training at low pedalling rates is emphasised. It is also clear that the speed field ST also needs to be trained to a certain extent to train high pedalling rates so that on flat sections a high frequency can be maintained.

Figure 3.29 shows Susan de Mattei's exertion parameters on the same course in Atlanta. The first lap is shown. Greater variations in the heart rate point to a tactically different race situation. Performance still reaches an average of 214 watt with smoothed peaks of up to 350 watt. If the curve had not been smoothed, the large amount of data and the even more oscillating curves would make an analysis impossible.

Figure 3.30 shows a short unsmoothed ten minute section from Ned Overend's measurement curves. The even greater variations can be seen immediately and the exertion peaks reach 700 watt. Within this short period the rider has to briefly reach 500 watt or more about 18 times. Here the significance of strength becomes even more obvious.

Because of the lower performance level, Susan's average speed (upper left in each case P performance, H heart rate, S speed, C pedalling rate or cadence) is about 3 km/h lower than Ned's. The other parameters, however, are very similar. Pedalling rate is almost identical. Both athletes have conspicuously low heart rates, which has to do with their age and the performance physiological spectrum created by training. This relativises the formula 220 - age as a way of calculating maximum heart rate.

Susan de Mattei on the Olympic course in Atlanta. Photo: SRM/Schoberer

In contrast figure 3.31 shows the progression of the parameters described during a hill section of a road World Cup in the Belgian Ardennes. The much more even curves

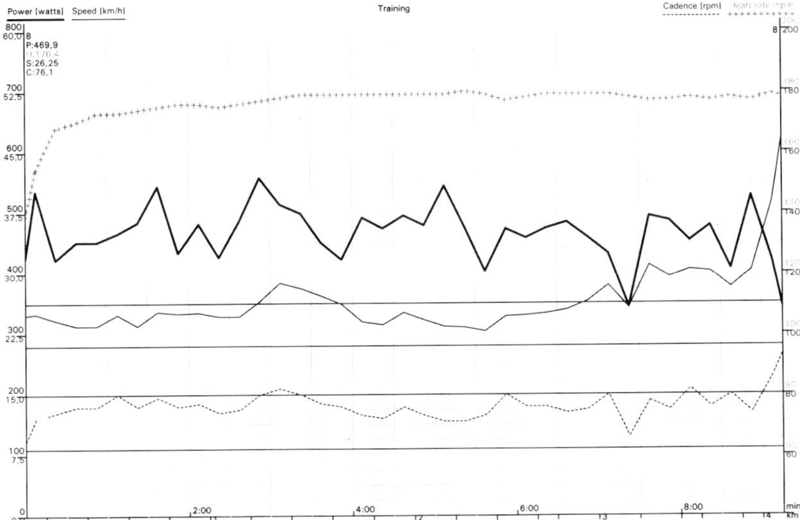

Fig. 3.31: Exertion parameters of a World Cup race (road) on a hill (ten minutes)

show the completely different exertion structure in a road race. This section is characterised by a higher pedalling rate and a more even speed, performance and above all heart rate progression. In the course of this hill, average performance is about 470 watt.

If you consider that the participants in such a race have to deal with about 20 hills like this, as well as constant challenges from other cyclists, it gives you an idea of the incredible performance capacity of good road racing professionals.

The different exertion structure makes it very difficult to say whether such a road racing professional could win mountain bike World Cup races.

Nevertheless, because of his excellent aerobic capacity and strength endurance, after a few weeks of specific training to improve anaerobic mobilisation and to increase the ability to handle extreme exertion peaks, a cycling technically skilled road professional should be able to ride right up front with the top mountain bikers.

4 Strength Training for Mountain Bikers

The requirement profile for the sport of mountain biking described in chapter 2 stressed the great significance of strength for total performance as the most important factor next to endurance capability. A high performance level in mountain biking is increasingly linked with high strength endurance. This gives special significance to strength training.

Although endurance capability has not yet reached the same level in mountain biking as it has in road cycling and there are therefore training and exertion reserves to be found here, strength in its various forms must also be trained in order to be able to make use of individual performance reserves. When endurance capability is the same, a greater level of strength allows one to move to a higher gearing with greater forward thrust. The result is a higher speed or at constant speed lower metabolic strain.

Strength training refers on the one hand to training in the bodybuilding room or fitness studio with body weight, dumb-bells or machines and on the other hand training on the mountain bike. From a functional point of view, strength training on the mountain bike or racing bike is specific strength training while all other strength training is non-specific.

Furthermore, strength training also includes the functional strengthening exercises which on the one hand can have a preventative or rehabilitative character and on the other hand can be specifically used to economise pedalling.

No Exaggerated Muscle Development

The call for strength training in mountain biking does not by any means signify that an increase in muscle mass should be aimed for, but merely getting the available muscles in a better training state.

This improvement in function is achieved by increasing maximum strength

Photo: John Kelly, Trisport

and improving co-ordination within a muscle and between the muscles involved in a movement (inter- and intra-muscular co-ordination). Only after long-term and frequent training with heavy weights or resistance is there an increase in muscle diameter (muscle growth) which is not desirable as it reduces endurance, and also means that additional muscle mass must be provided with oxygen. On top of that, body weight increases.

Muscle Anatomy

The individual muscle fibres are made to contract by so-called "motoneurons" (nerve cells) in the spinal cord. A motoneuron and the muscle fibres it supplies are called a motor unit.

If a motoneuron in the spinal cord is stimulated by the brain, it passes this information on and all muscle fibres it supplies contract. The dosage of strength is determined by the number of motoneurons addressed.

A strength training programme teaches the body to deliberately address as large a number of these motoneurons as possible in order to make maximum use of the theoretically possible strength potential (number of muscle fibres available). A certain area always remains autonomously protected, however, for example for dangerous situations.

Intra-muscular training causes an increase in the number of muscle fibres voluntarily involved in a contraction. In chapter 2 the functioning of the muscles that are very important for strength training is explained.

Importance of Strength Training

Training science is still not quite sure about the question "How should you train?", although very good results can be achieved using the accepted "traditional" methods. In particular there is still division over the definition of individual types of strength and the methods of training them. Some research teams even have completely opposing opinions.

The methods and exercises shown here, however, largely represent the accepted teaching principles. Recent findings indicate that maximum strength has much greater significance for the level of the other strength types (resilience, strength endurance, explosive strength) than has so far been assumed, which applies especially to mountain biking with its high demand on strength.

Strength training is certainly considered more important in mountain biking than in road cycling.

When Should You Train?

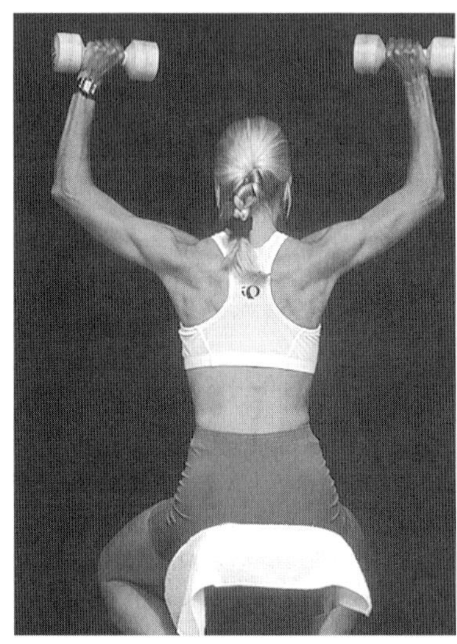
Photo: John Kelly, Trisport

Because of a lack of strength training during the season, often the strength potential trained with great effort in the preparatory phase very quickly goes back to its original level. Even with only one regular weekly strength training session the level of strength could be maintained, and thus bike specific performance capacity improved.

There is therefore every reason to cycle a few kilometres per week less and instead devote oneself to strength training. An hour is more than enough, e.g. on Tuesday, Wednesday or Thursday before or after an easy endurance training session. On days with bad weather too, strength training can be slipped in. The day within the micro-cycle on which strength training is done depends on race planning. If there is a race on Saturday or Sunday there should definitely not be strength training on Thursday.

4.1 Periodisation

Similarly to endurance training, strength training is also periodised. Various cycles with differences in strain and training methods are designed to prepare bikers for their seasonal peak. For bikers without a real seasonal high point, periodisation serves to aid long-term performance improvement and optimal preparation for the competition phase.

The strength foundation is always laid in the preparatory phase in the bodybuilding room or in indoor training. To maintain a basic potential strengthening, gymnastics are done several times a week.

The following periodisation is, however, related to training in the bodybuilding room with machines and dumb-bells. This strength periodisation is based on a single peak competition period in summer. If there are two competition phases, e.g. in summer and in winter, the individual phases are shortened accordingly. During the long competition period training must of course be varied. Individual maximum strength, or strength endurance sessions with medium weights and maximum numbers of repeats, provide both psychologically and training methodologically for diversity. Such intensive sessions must not be carried out in a poor state of regeneration.

With only about 45-60 minutes of training per strength session it is possible to maintain the trained level of strength during the season and thus cycle more effectively, and pedal the high gearing necessary for a high level of performance.

1. Preparatory Period I (Adjustment Phase)

In *November* the muscles are first trained using low weights or resistances, (45-55%) high numbers of repeats (15-20) and two to four sets, and linked to the intensive training that follows. During this time training should be done two or three times in the bodybuilding room. Before and after this phase it is imperative to carry out a maximum strength test to calculate the resistances and weights.

2. Preparatory Period II (Growth Phase)

In *December* and *January* the muscles are exercised more, at 60-70% of maximum strength. Three to four sets with 8-12 repeats are carried out. With only two sessions per week there is no need to worry that the muscles will develop too much.

3. Preparatory Period III (Maximum Strength)

February is used to improve maximum strength, i.e. training is with very high strain (80-100%) and only 1-5 repeats in four to six sets, thus applying considerable stimuli which lead to an increase in maximum strength and resilience. Strength training should be done two to three times per week. In this period, maximum strength ability should be checked several times and strain adjusted accordingly. In *March* training is similar to that in PP II.

During the spring training camp and the regeneration days before and after it in *March*, strength training is left out, but functional strengthening gymnastics continue.

4. Competition Period (Strength Maintenance Phase)

In the competition period from *April* onwards the idea is, as already mentioned, to maintain strength abilities by training once or twice a week at 60-70% with eight repeats in three sets.

	Intensity	Repeats	Sets	Sessions/ week
PP I	45-55%	15-20	2-4	2-3
PP II	60-70%	8-12	3-4	2-3
PP III	80-100%	1-5	4-6	2-3
CP	60-70%	8	3	1-2
TP	–	–	–	–

Fig. 4.1: Annual strength training programme for mountain bikers

During the long competition period, strength training exertion must be cyclised and varied in the same way as endurance exertion is, e.g. by occasionally including a maximum strength session, reducing training after a hard race and also by varying the exercises accordingly.

In the phase of the highest exertion just before the seasonal peak, strength training should also involve more frequent training and increased intensities as in maximum strength training.

5. Transitional Period (Strength Loss Phase)

In the transitional phase - as described in the previous chapter - there is no more specific training. Strength training in the bodybuilding room can and should be omitted completely so that there is a desired sinking of the strength readings which in the following year, among other things, allows a further increase in ability to handle exertion. Strengthening gymnastics should be continued.

In popular and health sport, strength training is restricted to low weights and high repeat phases (phase 1, possibly 2).

4.2 Rules of Strength Training

Because in most cases strength training is highly exerting and if not done properly can cause serious damage, it is important to heed certain training rules and observe that movements are carried out correctly.

- There must be an intensive warm-up programme before every strength training session, no matter what form of training is chosen. The greater the exertion, the longer the warm-up should be.
- Correct and precise carrying out of movements is very important (concentration on the exercise).
- Make sure the back is straight; no strain when the back is hollowed.
- When working with dumb-bells train only with a partner if possible for safety reasons.
- Breathe calmly during the exercises; no forced breathing.
- When training with machines these must be exactly adjusted to the body's dimensions.
- Joints should only be exercised along their physiological axes of movement, evasive movements can cause damage.
- Do not apply strain in joint end positions.
- As in endurance training, the principle of gradually increasing exertion is followed in strength training; only once a muscular foundation has been created can highly exertive maximum strength training begin.
- As in endurance training, here too strain must be varied and cyclised because the same stimuli over and over again no longer trigger any adaptation and thus training effect.
- Strength training must be done regularly (1-3 times a week).
- Strength training must be adapted to performance capability and above all to the athlete's age; up to age 15 athletes should only work with their own body weight; overexercising should be avoided.
- Attention must be paid to regeneration of the body, i.e. there should be no training when the body is very exhausted after a race; during strength training there should be breaks of two to four minutes between sets.
- Do not do strength training after an intensive training session.
- A short training session on the bike with a number of accelerations in the RT field helps develop a positive transfer effect of strength training to the cyclical pedalling movement.
- Strength training causes the muscles to contract; extensive stretching programmes are obligatory after strength training sessions.

4.3 Strength Training Practice

The following exercise suggestions for a strength training programme cannot include concrete individual repeat and set numbers because of the differences between athletes, instead, after a little experience, choose the values in the fields named that feel best for you.

4.3.1 Strength Training Room

The strength training programme that follows covers the entire training year. As an example two strength circuits are shown. The term series or set and repeat are explained in chapter 3.

Ascertain Maximum Strength

The intensity of strain is always indicated as a percentage of maximum strength which first needs to be tested - after an intensive warm-up - on each machine or in each exercise in order to use it as a basis from which to calculate the corresponding levels of effort. In a maximum strength test you carefully approach the maximum weight in three or four attempts.

The values ascertained are noted and on this basis the training programme is calculated and written down. A maximum strength test should be repeated every four to six weeks in order to adjust the exertion to the changing level of strength. An intensive warm-up programme is extremely important before these applications of maximum strain.

Exercises for the Various Muscle Groups

The numbers after the muscle groups refer to the anatomical illustrations of the muscles on pages 20ff. and represent the muscle names shown there. In each case only the most important muscles are mentioned.

Beneath the exercises there are also numbers. These refer to the strength training exercises that follow.

Leg Muscles

- *Knee flexors or extensors* 25, 26 , 31
  Exercises: various leg presses, kneebends with long dumb-bell, not too low, jumps
  ❶❷❸

- *Knee flexors* 36, 38, 39
  Exercises: various pulling machines, bending machine

  Angles of the knee similar to the pedalling cycle should be used. Series with low weights and smaller angles (i.e. greater bending) should also be included in order to make the strength achieved usable on the mountain bike.

- *Lower leg muscles* 32, 33, 34, 39, 44
  Exercises: calf machine, toe stands with long dumb-bell, foot raiser

- *Hip flexors* 24, 27, 30 also 25, 26, 31
  Exercises: the leg press also trains the hip flexors, special machines for hip flexors

- *Hip extensors* 36, 40, 42
  Exercises: leg presses, kneebends with long dumb-bell

Arm and Shoulder Muscles

- *Armflexors* 19, 20, 21, (11)
  Exercises: biceps curls, arm pull lying, pulling machine, pull-ups
  ❼ ❽ ❿

- *Arm extensors* 15, 16
  Exercises: triceps curls, press-ups

- *Chest muscles* 4
  Exercises: bench pressing, straight and diagonal

- *Forearm muscles* 17, 22, 23
  Exercises: wrist curls

  The forearm muscles receive a training stimulus from holding the dumb-bells. A hand press can also be used for training.

Torso Muscles

- *Back muscles* 3, 12
  Exercises: back machine without weights, see section on stretching, press-ups
  ⓬

- *Stomach muscles* 6 , 7 , 8
  Exercises: crunches, stomach machine, stomach exercises in the section on stretching, press-ups.

Working with dumb-bells additionally strengthens the torso muscles. For this reason training with dumb-bells is preferable. The stomach and back muscles can be especially effectively trained with functional strengthening exercises using the body's own weight.

Selection of Exercises

❶ *Leg press*
The leg press must initially be set at a starting knee angle of about 70-80°, angles varying from this should also be used. During stretching the knee must not be stretched out completely (danger of overstraining). With heavy weights be sure of slow and controlled movements; with smaller weights explosive stretching is also possible.

To also place strain on the calf muscles, with light weights the foot is only placed on the ball and the ankle is actively stretched.

❷ *Kneebends with the long dumb-bell*
The long dumb-bell is held by the arms and the upper back. The feet point slightly outwards and the heels can be supported to reduce strain on the Achilles' tendon. It is important to ensure constant muscle tension in the upper body and controlled knee stretching and bending.

The back must be kept straight. To learn the proper technique it is best to start with smaller weights and get the help of an experienced athlete. Both kneebends to about 90° and also low, very exerting kneebends are possible.

❸ *Squat jumps*
The jump in the air is done with both legs, keeping the back straight. After landing on the flat soles, or preferably on the balls of the feet, the knees are bent no further than 70° before another jump follows as quickly as possible. Ten to 30 repeats in three to five series. This exercise is especially good for improving hill and

sprinting performance. In performance sport the strain can be increased by jumping off and onto small boxes. Climbing onto and jumping off boxes with one leg is also good. The strain must only be increased gradually.

❹ *Leg curl and leg pulling machine*

Isolated strengthening of the knee flexors is possible on the *leg curl machine*. The kneecap should be just off the edge and the pivot of the machine should correspond to that of the knee joint. The pelvis and stomach muscles must be tensed.

Training on the *pulling machine* on which several joints are active is better. With the body leaning slightly forward the lower legs, which are held in place by cuffs, are actively stretched back and brought forward again in stages to bend the leg. This also trains the hip flexors. This exercise can also be carried out with a therapeutic sling.

❺ *Toe stands*

Toe stands are carried out for isolated strengthening of the calf muscles. Standing on the balls of the feet facing a wall, the ankle stretches and then relaxes, the other foot is either held in the air or placed on the heel of the active leg.

It is important to stretch the leg being trained at the knee so that only the calf muscles are causing the body to move up and down.

This exercise can be done even better on a step, the top of a box or a ledge. 15 to 50 repeats per leg in two to four sets.

❻ *Foot bending*

The therapeutic sling is fixed to wall bars. Sitting on the floor with the leg stretched out, the foot (without the shoe to avoid damaging the sling) is placed in the loop of the sling.

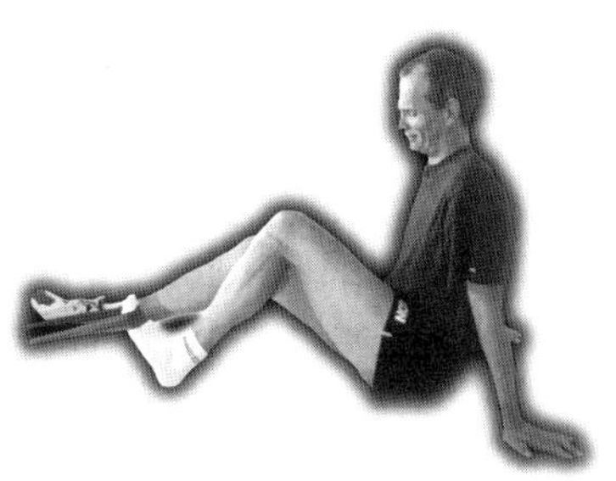

The tip of the foot is now evenly pulled and let go. Therapeutic slings come in various strengths. This exercise can also be done as a partner exercise.

7 *Biceps curls*
Biceps curls are carried out using short dumb-bells in a sitting position with the free arm supported. The back should be as straight as possible.

8 *Latissimus pulling machine*
The multi-joint movement on this machine strains all flexors of the upper extremities concentrically and eccentrically. With the back kept straight the bar is pulled down behind the neck or in front of the chest. The head remains straight and is not bent at the neck. The strain must be released slowly.

9 *Bench pressing*
This exercise can be done either on a machine or using long dumb-bells. The upper body can either lie horizontally or at an angle on an appropriate surface. The legs are bent 90° at the hips and knees. When training with dumb-bells and heavy weights a partner is very important for safety.

10 *Bench pulling*
The other way round, lying on the stomach, the long dumb-bell can be pulled up from the floor. The lower legs are bent vertically to avoid a hollow back.

11 *Wrist curl*
In a sitting position, the elbows are placed on the thighs and the long dumb-bell moved up and down using wrist movement only.

12 *Shoulder raising with long dumb-bell*
Standing, with slightly bent knees and a straight back, the long dumb-bell is held with outstretched arms and moved by moving the shoulders up and down.

13 *Back machine*
Slow stretching of the hanging back and slow, gradual lowering of the back. Make sure of precise movement; the back must not be raised above the horizontal.

14 *Crunches*
a) Crunches: lying on one's back, the legs are raised and the upper body slowly rolled up and unrolled beginning at the head.

b) Crunches crosswise: in the same starting position the hands are placed behind the neck, the body is slowly rolled up, the elbows are moved towards the opposite knee.

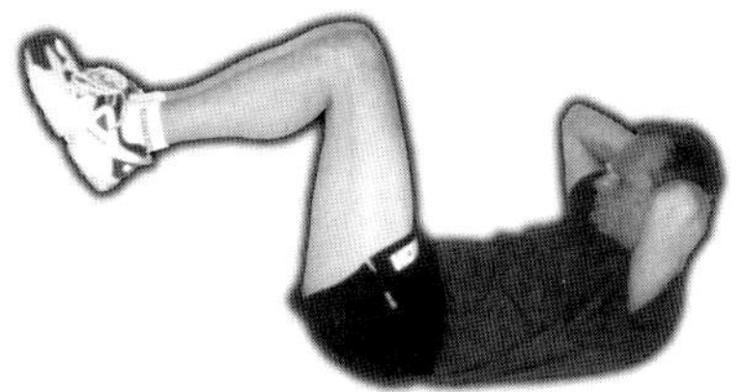

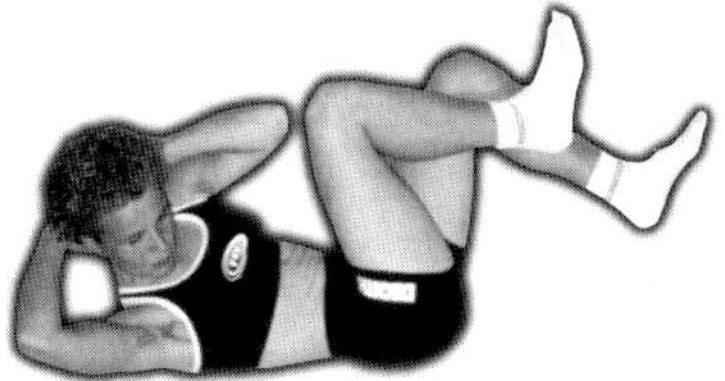

The exercises described above should be explained in a fitness studio or strength training room by an instructor or trainer with strength training experience and combined with exercises from the sections *"In The Gym"* and *"Stretching"*.

A strength training session consists of a **warm-up part**, a **main part (circuit)** and a **cool down part**.

Circuit Training

In the main part a selection of exercises is carried out in the form of a circuit. The exercises in the circuit should place strain on all the muscle groups mentioned if possible, whereby the emphasis is on the muscle groups of the legs and hips. For the arms there are multi-joint pulling and pressing exercises (e.g. pulling machines, bench pressing) which each cover several muscles at once.

When determining the order of the exercises, care must be taken that after a muscle group has been exercised it has a regeneration phase (e.g. by exercising a completely different muscle section).

To avoid one-sided conditioning, certain exercises should occasionally be replaced by other ones. Exercises such as the leg press or kneebends with the long dumbbell should always be included. Exercises for the back and stomach are fitted in between and are part of daily gymnastics anyway.

Circuit programme C_1:
Order of exercises ➊, ➐, ⓭, ➎, ➒, ⓮, ➍, ➓, ➏, ➋

Circuit programme C_2:
Order of exercises ➋, ➑, ⓭, ➐, ➌, ⓮, ➒, ➏, ⓫, ➍

If strength endurance is to be particularly addressed, **station training** is carried out, in which first all sets are carried out at one station. Only then do you move to the next station where a different group of muscles is exercised. In station training there should be about 20 repeats in 3-8 sets. The breaks are about two minutes each. The disadvantage of station training is that it involves a great deal of time.

4.3.2 In the Gym or at Home

Effective strength training - mainly using bodyweight - can also be done in a gym or even at home. If done properly and combined with strength training on the bike it can replace training in the strength training room; even better is a combination with strength training on machines and with dumb-bells.

In strength training in the gym or at home the emphasis is on two different training methods: on the one hand dynamic training (movement training), on the other static strength training (holding training). It is important not only to do exercises for the leg muscles but also for arms, stomach, back and shoulders (in performance sport: whole body training with the emphasis on the leg muscles, in popular sport: emphasis on torso muscles).

The following is a selection of exercises for strength training in the gym or at home, structured by parts of the body.

What Must Be Taken into Consideration?

The number of repeats and sets depends on age, training state and objectives; a recreational athlete will thus prefer the lower repeat and series numbers, while trained performance athletes will opt for the higher figures. If you train so hard each time that you get strained muscles the exertion is much too high; strained muscles or extreme states of exhaustion should be avoided. After the muscle groups the individual muscles named in chapter 2 are again indicated.

Leg Muscles

Calf muscles 39, 44
See strength training exercise No. 5

Shin muscles 32, 33, 34
Sitting on the floor with legs drawn up, bend the ankles by raising the tips of the feet and gradually lowering them; the heels remain on the floor. A partner places pressure on the tips of the feet. Ten to 20 repeats in two to four sets.

Knee extensors, calf, rump 25 , 26 , 31 ,39 ,40 , 44

A whole range of exercises is suitable for the knee extensors.

a) Sit on an imaginary chair at the wall and stay in this position for 15 to 60 seconds. The back is straight and pressed against the wall and the arms hang down next to the body (static exercise).
b) Depending on ability, ten to 30 two-legged crouch jumps backwards and forwards over a bench. 2-4 sets.
c) See strength training exercise No. ❸

Torso Muscles

Stomach muscle training 6 , 7 , 8

See strength training exercise No. ⓮

Back muscle training 3 , 9 , 10 , 12 , 40

Lying on the stomach face the floor and raise the stretched out feet only a little above the floor. With the arms, slow, long pull-ups are done. It is also possible to quickly move alternate arms up and down along the body.

Press-ups 3 , 4 , 5 , 6 , 7 , 8 , 9 , 10 , 14 , 15

When done properly, press-ups are an excellent exercise for the back, stomach and also the arms and shoulders. A high degree of body tension is important, the body must remain straight.

A number of variations is possible, with the arms narrow or wide, fast or slow, or especially high.

The number of repetitions depends completely on individual ability. It is best to do three series with a certain number of repeats.

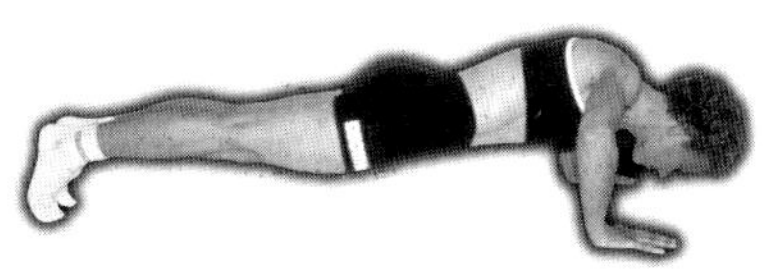

Arms and Shoulders

For the arm and shoulder muscles, in addition to strengthening exercises from back training, medicine ball training is very good. In the context of this book it is not possible to go into back training.

In medicine ball training two athletes throw each other a medicine ball (3-6 kg) using various throwing and thrusting techniques in several sets. A programme to strengthen torso and arm muscles should be carried out daily to avoid posture damage caused by one-sided strain on the bike.

"Jump Garden"

Almost all jumping exercises are suitable for strength training of the leg muscles, whereby one-legged jumps should not be attempted until a high level of strength has been reached.

In the gym a "jump garden" can easily be put together consisting of four to ten exercises carried out in the form of a circle or individually. Jumping exercises also improve resilience. Good ideas for jumping exercises can be found in the book "Sprungkrafttraining" ("Leg Power Training"), also available from Meyer + Meyer Sport.

Skipping is a combination of a strength and an endurance exercise which is especially suitable for improving strength endurance. In a programme for the legs a number of exercises should always be combined.

4.4 Strength Circle

The following circle has proved itself for daily strength training at home with minimal space and time requirements.

The six exercises selected exercise multiple joints and thus train all muscle groups relevant for mountain bikers.

Name of exercise	Repeats	Muscle groups	Aids
1. Press-ups	15	Arms, chest, back	
2. Foot stretcher	30 per side	Calves	Wall
3. Sit-ups	15	Stomach	Bed
4. Press-ups backwards	15	Triceps	Bed
5. Pull-ups on stomach	20	Back	
6. Squat Jumps	20	Leg extensors, rump	

This circle can also be done quickly after training before showering. It is repeated two to five times with very short breaks between sets (a few minutes). The individual exercises are done without a break in the order indicated.

The number of repeats should be adapted to individual ability.

1) Normal press-ups (slow and fast).
2) Facing the wall, stand on one leg and stretch the ankle (calf muscle), i.e push body weight upwards.
3) Legs in the air, 90° angle at hips, knee and ankle.
4) Backwards press-ups at the edge of the bed.
5) Lying on the stomach facing the floor, legs and feet stretched 5 cm above the floor, the arms are used to carry out very slow pull up movements.
6) Squat jumps; a kind of standing jump with absolutely fixed, straight upper body, hands as fists next to the head, knee bends in bending position of about 90°.

Train All Year Round

Year round strength training is called for not only in top class sport but also in "normal" racing and recreational sport, although for differing reasons. Whereas in top class and racing sport specific performance improvement is the main objective, in recreational sport strength training should have more of a preventive character and protect against excessive and unnecessary exertion.

This aspect also should not be neglected in performance sport, for by carrying out specific training of the holding and supporting muscles (torso, shoulders, arms) problems with the moving apparatus can be effectively avoided.

5 Functional Stretching

5.1 Why Stretching?

Many mountain bikers think of nothing but improving their performance capacity and think they can achieve this best with hard training on their bike. Yet training on the bike off or on the road and strength training are only part of a complete and well-thought out training programme.

In addition to these active training forms which are more or less exerting, stretching as a relaxing and regenerative training form is an integral part of a mountain biker's well-planned programme, whether for cross-country or downhill, as a licence rider or in popular sport.

With daily effort of about ten to 15 minutes much can be achieved in stretching and the body will respond to this increased effort by being less prone to injury and thus performing better in races or training. Within the context of mountain biking both stretching and functional strengthening gymnastics thus have preventive significance.

5.2 What Effect Does Stretching Have?

Stretching was popularised in the USA in the sixties by Bob Anderson - to call it a sport, however, would be an exaggeration. Following certain exercise patterns, all muscle sections are stretched. It is best to start with the head and finish with the feet.

Because of the cyclical contractions of pedalling and the continual static strain on large parts of the muscles, mountain bikers' muscles are prone to contraction and tenseness which are increased by the unnatural position sitting on a mountain bike or racing bike.

As a result of muscle contractions, wrong kinds of strain or non-functional compensatory movements are caused which lead to overstraining of other ligaments, tendons, muscles, bones etc. In this case stretching has the purpose of restoring the natural muscle tone, i.e. normal muscle tension.

The most important functions of stretching are:

- Prevention of injury
- Acceleration of regeneration
- Improving performance
- Improving feeling for the body.

The increase in elasticity and the improvement in blood circulation prepare muscles and tendons for exertion and thus make them less prone to injury. In addition, damage to tendons and their links to bones from overexertion, which constant pulling on contracted muscles helps to cause, can be avoided and treated.

After exertion stretching causes an acceleration of regeneration by triggering metabolism.

An improvement in performance is achieved through improved muscle co-ordination and more economical functioning of the stretched muscles. When muscles work the corresponding opposite muscles must also be actively stretched. For the working muscle this means that, in addition to the strength needed for the actual movement, additional strength is required to stretch the corresponding opposite muscle (antagonist) because this is responsible for the return movement.

If this opposite muscle is contracted the stretching work required of the agonist is correspondingly higher. A practical example is the ischiocrural muscle group (back of thigh/flexor) which has to be stretched by the flexors every time the leg stretches. A regular stretching programme loosens up matted muscles, tendons and connective tissue which in turn improves economy of movement.

Finally, stretching improves one's body consciousness and perception. Tiny changes within the muscles are noticed more quickly and intensively so that active injury prevention (by ending or reducing exertion), but also training regulation and body feeling, are supported.

Stretching Techniques

The most important principle of stretching is to concentrate on the part of the body being stretched in order to be aware of the feeling of tensing and relaxing. Breathing should be even and relaxed and in no way forced.

Because of the calm breathing and the listening of the senses to the inner body, stretching is also excellent for relaxation and has thus become an important part of many athlete's preparation and follow up to races in a mental or psychological sense. The stretching exercises should never cause pain; a slight, pleasant twinge, however, is quite normal. There are a number of stretching techniques, of which two are shown here.

Static Stretching

Static stretching is easiest to learn and is the most important and well-known form of stretching. Static stretching is deliberately slow and even. Outwardly, movement is not recognisable and there is no swinging or springing. During the stretching procedure of 10-30 seconds per exercise and side of the body there is a pleasant tensing feeling in the muscles which goes away slightly towards the end. Then the tension can be increased again and the muscles stretched for another 10-30 seconds. At the beginning of training the stretching time can be quietly counted out loud, after a while, when timing has improved, this is no longer necessary. If required each exercise can be done several times to increase the stretching stimulus.

The exercises in the following section relate to the static method, but most can also be done using the CHRS method.

CHRS (Contract-Hold-Relax-Stretch)

The CHRS method is a slightly more complicated method in which the individual exercises are divided into four sections. After contraction of the muscle to be stretched the position is first held, then relaxed, and only after that is the muscle stretched.

This procedure is carried out in a cycle of two to four times per muscle or muscle group. As a rule the muscle can be stretched a little further after each tensing. This method is supposed to be more effective, but it is more strenuous and requires more time. You should try both methods under supervision and then choose one of them.

Stretching has nothing to do with withstanding pain and clenching your teeth. If the tension in the muscles is too great it is reduced by changing the angle of the joints. Springing and swinging cause further tensing of the muscles because of the so-called stretch reflex.

If a muscle is suddenly greatly stretched, e.g. through springing or swinging, the muscle spindles in the muscles are activated, causing an immediate contraction of the muscle via the spinal cord. The stretch reflex protects the muscle from overstretching or even tearing.

Before the stretching programme it is important to warm-up a little, e.g. by running on the spot, hopping or cycling on an unbraked roller (5 min). Stretching is done in comfortable clothing (track suit) on as soft a surface as possible in a room at a pleasant temperature. In principle though, stretching exercises can be done anywhere at any time (e.g. during breaks at work or when waiting). There is, however one restriction, for after an operation to the moving parts of the body stretching should not be done, or only with permission from a doctor.

Performance athletes stretch daily, especially after training, and depending on the kind of training (gym, strength) sometimes before and during the session. Ideally, recreational athletes also stretch daily, but at least on training days.

5.3 Exercise Programme

The figures after the body parts refer to the muscles in the illustrations 2.4 - 2.7.

❶ *Neck muscles*
(m. trapezius, m. sternocleidomastoideus, deep neck muscles) 1, 3, 13

The head is tilted forwards, left and right. In doing so the shoulder axis does not change its position parallel to the floor. After that the head is turned as far as possible to the left, held there, then the same to the right.

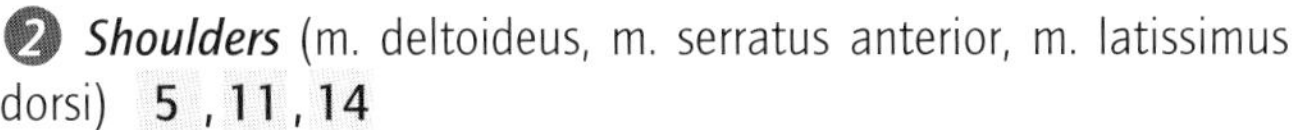

❷ ***Shoulders*** (m. deltoideus, m. serratus anterior, m. latissimus dorsi) 5, 11, 14

To loosen up the shoulders, the arms or the shoulders can be circled. The shoulder belt is stretched by putting the elbow over the head and placing the palm of the hand between the shoulder blades.

This position is maintained for about 10-30 s per side. It considerably increases mobility in the shoulder joint.

❸ *Upper arm and shoulder*
(m. deltoideus, m. triceps brachii) **14 , 15**
A hand is brought past the chin and placed on the opposite shoulder. With the other hand the elbow is pushed towards the shoulder.

❹ *Forearms and wrists*
(forearm and finger muscles) **22 , 23**
Grasping the handle bars tenses the forearm muscles. The wrist is overstretched with the arm straight and raised.

The palm of the hand faces away from the body and the fingers point downwards. In this way the fingers can also be individually stretched.

❺ *Torso* (m. serrati, m. latissimus dorsi) **5 , 11**
The feet are placed apart at about shoulder breadth, the upper body is tilted to the side, one arm is bent over the head and the other pushes an imaginary object into the ground.

❻ *Back and rear thighs*
(m. errector spinae, knee flexors) **12 , 13 ,36 , 37 ,38 , 39**
First stand totally straight and stretch upwards with the arms raised over the head until you are very tall, then bring the arms down and slowly start to bend the head to the chest.

In so doing the back becomes rounded first at the dorsal vertebrae and then also at the lumbar vertebrae, until you are hanging down completely relaxed with legs stretched.

The hands now almost touch the feet. Just as slowly you stand up straight again until you are very tall again. For this exercise, as in the others, you have to turn off and completely go into yourself.

This is easier if you close your eyes. Hanging down is an excellent exercise for the back. You hang from a branch or pole with one or both arms for as long as you can maintain the position.

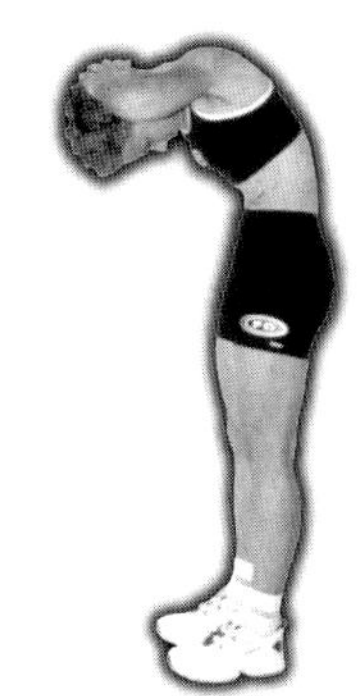

❼ *Calf muscles* (m. gastrocnemius, m. soleus)
39 , 44

With one leg in front of the other, use the hands to press against a wall or similar.

The feet point forwards parallel to each other and the rear leg is stretched. The front leg is bent until a stretching can be felt in the calf. The rear heel must not leave the ground. By bending the rear leg a greater stretching of the Achilles' tendon and the m. soleus can be achieved. Here too the heel stays on the ground. The upper body is somewhat straighter.

❽ ***Rear thigh*** **(flexor) and calves** (ischiocrural muscles, m. gastrocnemius, m. soleus) **36 , 37 , 38 , 39**

a) With one leg in front of the other (feet pointing forwards) bend forwards with a straight back and tip of the foot drawn upwards. In doing this the stretching in the calf and the rear thigh can be felt.
b) With crossed feet bend forwards with the legs stretched. Then change the foot position.

9 *Front thigh* (m. quadriceps) **25 , 26 , 31**
When stretching the quadriceps you can hold onto a wall to keep your balance better. With the left hand grasp the instep of the foot raised to the buttocks and slowly pull it towards the gluteal muscle (rump) until a good feeling of tension is felt in the buttocks. The hips should be brought forward slightly, making sure that the thighs remain parallel to each other and the upper body is vertical; duration 20-30 s per side.

10 *Adductors*
(m. adductor magnus, m. adductor longus) **29 , 35**
In a wide straddle position with parallel feet pointing forwards, one knee is bent until the stretching can be felt in the inside thigh and past the knee. This stretching position can also be done with one leg in front of the other, whereby in this case it is more the rear thigh (ischiocrural muscles) which is addressed.

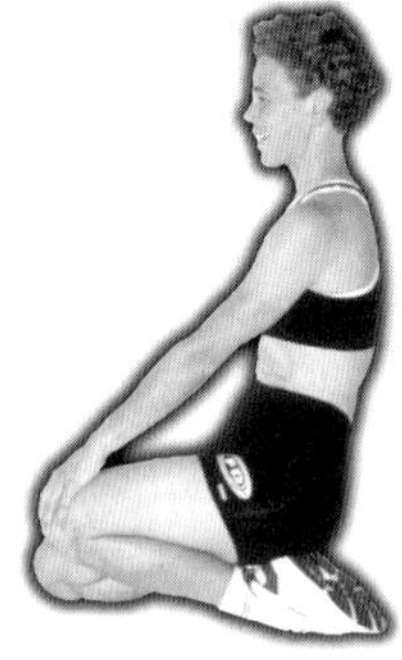

11 *Front thigh and shin muscles*
(m. quadriceps, m. tibialis anterior, m. extensor digitorum longus, m. peronaeus longus) **25 , 26 , 31 , 32 , 33**
Sitting on the thighs and feet, after about 15 s one knee is raised by a hand so that the front shin muscles are stretched.

12 *Gluteal muscles*
(gluteal muscles) **40**

a) Lying down one first stretches out. Then one leg is raised and the ankle of the other placed over the knee of the raised leg. Now the raised knee is grasped with the hand and pulled towards the body a little, the pelvis remains on the ground. If the stretching is not strong enough the knee can be pushed slightly outwards.
b) While sitting, the sole of the left foot is placed on the right knee. Both legs are bent and the upper body is now lain forward on the left leg. You can also support yourself on your elbow. The stretching is especially felt in the left half of the rump and in the upper part of the left flexors. After about 40 s change sides.

The exercises shown in this exercise programme represent a basic programme which can be added to. The exercises explained here can be used both before and after a race as well as in the evenings at home as regenerative stretching.

5.4 Stretching while Mountain biking

During a bike tour the muscles being used can also be stretched. Below a few exercises are explained. They should only be done on flat tracks and not at too high a speed, for example after a strenuous climb or a downhill that tenses the body.

Most of the exercises on the bike are a variation of those shown above. Exercises 7, 8 and 9 can also be used during a race where they mainly serve the purpose of avoiding cramps.

As soon as the first signs of a cramp are felt in the muscles the appropriate exercises should be carried out during the ride, if possible several times.

Exercise Programme on the Mountain Bike or Racing Bike

 *Neck*
(m. trapezius, m. sternocleidomastoideus, deep neck muscles) **1**, **3**, **13**
Overstretching of the cervical vertebrae during cycling often causes tense muscles which can sometimes be very painful. The head is tilted for 5 s each way to the

left and the right. This can be increased by pulling with an arm. Similarly, with the back rounded, the chin is placed on the chest and supported with the arm a little (careful!). See illustration of exercise 1.

❷ ***Spinal column/torso*** (m. trapezius, m. latissimus dorsi, m. erector spinae, small neck muscles) 3 , 11 , 12 , 13
Riding no hands, stretch yourself and reach upwards with your arms to make yourself as tall as possible.

❸ ***Shoulder belt*** (m. trapezius, m. deltoideus, m. subscapularis, m. infraspinatus, m. teres major/minor) 3 , 9 , 10 , 14 , 18
Holding the handlebars in the middle with arms stretched out, both shoulders are raised to the ears (5 s) and then pushed downwards. Then one hand is taken from the handlebars, the arm dangles loosely and the shoulder or the whole arm is circled backwards and forwards a few times.

❹ ***Forearm muscles*** (forearm and finger muscles) 22 , 23
Starting position: no hands.
Forearm muscles that have been tired and tensed by holding, braking and changing gear are to be stretched. To do this stretch an arm with the palm of the hand facing upwards and forwards and pull the fingers towards the ground with the other hand. The exercise is held for about 20 s. See illustration of exercise 4.

❺ ***Hands and arms*** (forearm and finger muscles) 22 , 23
While one hand steers the other is pressed against the waist for about 10 s with the back of the hand and the fingers showing upwards, so that stretching can be felt. The stretching should be felt in the hand, forearm and shoulder. The arm, which is tired from holding the handlebars is relaxed by this. Circling the wrists supports this.

6 *Back*
(m. trapezius, m. latissimus dorsi, m. erector spinae, small neck muscles) **3**, **11**, **12**, **13**

The back is often tense and painful, and thus needs to be moved around.

a) Holding the handlebars in the normal way, first arch your back and then stretch it. Both parts of the exercise are repeated alternately several times.
b) While the left hand holds the handlebars the other arm is passed under the left arm so that the upper body is twisted, thus stretching the torso muscles involved (5-10 s per side).

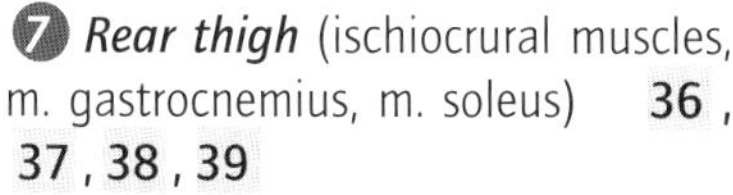

7 ***Rear thigh*** (ischiocrural muscles, m. gastrocnemius, m. soleus) **36**, **37**, **38**, **39**

When cycling the flexors can be stretched wonderfully. Raise yourself off the saddle and bring the left pedal forwards to the 9 o'clock position. With the balls of the feet resting on the pedals lower the heels, stretch your legs and lower your equally stretched upper body forwards (5-10 s). Then change the forward leg being stretched.

8 ***Front thigh*** (m. quadriceps, m. tibialis anterior, m. extensor digitorum longus, m. peronaeus longus) **25**, **26**, **31**, **32**, **33**

The extensors can also be stretched while cycling. This, however, requires a certain amount of cycling skill and a good sense of balance. You take one foot from the pedal and grasp its ankle with the hand on the same side. Then the knee is drawn back a little until the stretching can be felt.

⑨ *Calves and Achilles' tendon*
(m. gastrocnemius, m. soleus)
38, 39, 45

You raise yourself above the saddle keeping the pedal shafts vertical and pressing the lower leg down. In doing so the heel of this lower stretched leg is pushed down until stretching begins. To transfer the stretching to the Achilles' tendon you slightly bend the knee of the stretched leg. The last three exercises (7, 8, 9) are also suitable for getting rid of annoying cramps, especially calf cramps.

Stretching and Running

In comparison to cycling on or off the road, running is a highly exerting form of training because the body weight is not carried by the bike. There are thus major contractions as a result of the high level of mechanical, eccentric strain on the muscles. These need to be balanced out through stretching directly after running training. The leg muscles in particular need to be kept supple with the exercises described. Running training should always include stretching afterwards.

Stretching and Strength Training

Strength training too is highly exerting, even though eccentric components only occur in certain forms of training. To avoid injuries there should always be an intensive stretching programme preceded by a good warm-up. Between exercises the exerted muscles can also be stretched. After the training session, stretching is used as a cool down. A number of recent studies suggest that stretching during strength training reduces the effectiveness of training. This is negligible because the main idea is a sensible way of preventing injury.

6 Training Management

6.1 Being Your Own Trainer

"Be your own coach" is a basic principle typical of the American view of sport, especially regarding endurance sports in the States. You know best about your own body, you feel the exhaustion and the strength and can thus decide better than any trainer what is good and proper for you. But for that you need knowledge, which is what this and other books are trying to give you.

Of course every mountain biker who has a good trainer should be glad. You should definitely not get rid of him for two of you will probably get further together, with the athlete actively involved in training planning and structuring, and your cooperation will be more successful. Absolute beginners will have difficulty on their own and should seek the cooperation of an experienced mountain biker or trainer and then gradually form their own idea of a structured training plan.

Tinker Juarez
Photo: Klaus Eweleit

Sensible, self-structured training on the basis of a few important training rules is a guarantee for good performance development. You have to find your own reasonable balance between liberalness and concentrated training in order to have more fun and be more successful. Mindless, totally serious training following 100% rigid rules cannot guarantee this.

You should "listen to your inner self" and decide what is good for you and what is not. If you do not feel good after training or race exertion, take a day off.

6.2 Your Own Training Schedule

After the important principles of time management which have already been described, the procedure for creating training schedules will now be discussed. First we will take a closer look at the division of the periods.

If you are devising a training schedule for the first time you should take your time and above all get the advice of experienced mountain bikers in order to avoid possible mistakes. Often beginners, and particularly ambitious athletes, tend to overestimate their time budget, but also their motivation and their regeneration capacity. They create schedules which cannot be kept to. A completely false structure, poor performance capacity and potentially overtraining are the consequences.

Fortunately the opinion that only one training schedule or one way leads to the goal of top performance is false. A number of training methods lead to the goal, because everyone reacts to training contents differently, and therefore needs to try out different possibilities. What is good for Bart Brentjens for example and has proved itself will not necessarily help John Tomac find success.

Not only planning and execution are important for the optimisation of performance capacity, but also correction of training. The way to best performance can thus be via a number of variants and needs to be corrected if necessary. With regard to the seasonal goals, performance is stabilised and optimised using systematic periodisation and cyclisation of intensity and amount.

If a training error is recognised quickly then nothing is lost; if, however, training errors or poor performance capacity are ignored, usually it is no longer possible to achieve the seasonal goals that have been set.

Fig. 6.1: Training planning in high performance sport is like walking a tightrope.

Analysis of the Previous Year

Training planning also means analysing the previous year. By using the notes in the training journal many training errors can be discovered and put down in writing. These errors must be taken into consideration when structuring the new training schedule, and if there is a fitness crisis in the following season they should be brought to mind again. Chapter 6.4 contains tips for the annual analysis.

Planning from Year to Year

When putting a training schedule together not only the coming and the previous year should be considered but also long-term development. Constant improvement of performance capacity characterised by moderate increases in strain is much more sensible and causes less injuries and drops in form than excessive rises in total annual strain.

Unstable performance can often be observed amongst young amateurs who cannot yet build on a stable, well-developed foundation of basic endurance. Strain or annual strain is used here to indicate the number of hours annually (in every sporting activity). A high proportion of about 60% BE 1 is assumed.

The principle of constant increase in strain thus calls for a maximum exertion increase of about 15% in the top performance field. Higher increases of over 20% to about 40% are possible in mountain biking at regional level. Only beginners are likely to be able to double their annual exertion in the following year. In other words, the higher the performance level, the more gradually the exertion increases must be planned.

Care must be taken in the fields of health and beginners for here physical training must be done in small doses to avoid potential health risks.

If you decide to stop doing performance sport you must not reduce the amount of strain by more than half per year (de-training) in order to avoid health risks. In the former GDR, when endurance athletes finished their career they were given training schedules for de-training. A basic strain volume of about 200-250 hours per year should be maintained, however.

This Is What You Do

1st Step: Performance/Current Situation

Assuming that the training and competition demands of mountain biking are known, first the current training state must be ascertained. Without a performance diagnosis it is very difficult to formulate training instructions for a mountain biker. Only when the performance level is clear is it possible to estimate whether the planned amounts and intensities will overtax or undertax the athlete.

By diagnosis of the state of training we do not necessarily mean a performance diagnostic examination in a laboratory. The result of a timed ride, the last race result or quite simply an experienced mountain biker's feeling for his body is sufficient to categorise oneself or have someone else do this. If the estimation turns out to be incorrect and the planned training resulting from it overtaxes or undertaxes the athlete, then the schedule must be corrected.

In addition to the performance diagnosis, an analysis of external factors (environment, job) must be made.

Furthermore the strain and the development in form of the previous years must be included in the picture of the state of training. Too great a jump in strain from year to year with regard to the total amounts often has a negative effect on the development of form. A race and training analysis of the previous year round off the considerations regarding the current situation.

2nd Step: Setting Realistic Goals

A very important part of planning is laying down the objectives for the new training year. These should be put in writing. In addition to determining event-specific goals as so-called race goals (e.g. placing in the national championships), fine objectives such as improving downhill technique or strength endurance must be written down.

Even more detailed goal setting can target certain cycling techniques for instance. In the recreational field a goal could be e.g. managing a climb or reaching a hill pass in a certain time. A very important common denominator of all training goals is that they must be realistic. Unrealistic distant goals are soon forgotten, while goals that are too modest do not motivate enough ambition.

The best idea is to discuss goals with training partners, a coach or other experienced bikers. If you are really keen you can formulate goals in all performance components of mountain biking and tick them off as they are accomplished in the course of the training year. It is sensible, however, to change goals slightly in the course of the season.

3rd Step: Competition Planning

The third step involves obtaining and viewing the race calendar (if appropriate also for road racing).

Recreational or touring cyclists note the dates of planned bike tours or marathons. Racing bikers use the race calendar to plan their competition season (beginning/end) and determine their main races, the seasonal high points. Two or three seasonal peaks can be targeted, but one should have priority. It is a good idea to choose a seasonal high point in the late summer. Early peaks, such as certain qualifying races, require that top form is developed very early. This is not easy and requires great effort in the preparatory periods.

4th Step: Division into Periods

The first step in planning is to divide up the individual training periods (preparatory periods, competition period, transitional period) and subdivide them into training sections, so-called cycles or stages (4-6 weeks). As a rule, the division of the periods as described in chapter 3 should not be a problem. Variations from this standard scheme, which aims at achieving top form in summer, can, however, be carried out quite easily. Periodisation is done similarly to the illustrations in chapter 3. Additionally the contents and objectives of the individual periods are worked out. Any possible training camps should also be taken into consideration.

Once the periods have been divided up with beginning and end dates, the number of micro-cycles within the individual periods are calculated. One micro-cycle corresponds to one week.

The micro-cycles are now marked in within the periods. After three (two) to five micro-cycles with increasing strain comes one regeneration micro-cycle.

Now the whole training year has been planned with all the weeks, and concrete training contents have been assigned to every period and every 4-6 week cycle. The races should also be entered as exactly as possible. Detailed planning of the individual training sessions is done immediately before the period begins.

A large DIN A3 sheet of paper is particularly suitable for the annual plan. It is important to record all important considerations in writing or graphically.

5th Step: Detailed Planning of the 4-6 Weekly Cycles

In the last step, the individual training sessions for the next 4-6 week cycles are planned. For planning, use the simple method of forming blocks. After two to four days of increasing exertion comes a day of rest. After two to four weeks of increasing strain there is also a regenerative week.

The individual training sessions are characterised by the following factors:

- Training goal (e.g. improve anaerobic mobilisation)
- Training method (e.g. duration method with details of gearing and pedalling rate)
- Amount (duration or distance)
- Intensity (e.g. BE 1)

Monitoring the Training Schedule with Performance Tests

As described in the following section, performance capacity, and thus the training schedule, must be monitored again and again at regular intervals. To do this, dates to test form are set when the annual plan is drawn up. This can be performance diagnostic examinations or timed rides. These tests are placed at the beginnings or ends of the periods and should be done in a rested state. For example, a form test should be carried out at the beginning of the preparatory period.

6.3 Changes in the Training Schedule

Training should be part of a cycle. At certain intervals the results of training must be checked in order to regulate the cycle with the aid of these results. Race results should also be used to evaluate performance, whereby the multitude of possible other influencing factors on the race result must be taken into consideration.

Heed the Body's Signals

A major factor in assessing individual form is one's own feeling for one's body, with the aid of which it is possible to assess performance capacity very exactly. Many mountain bikers and other athletes have problems with this, however, and have great difficulty identifying certain feelings in their muscles and the rest of their body under strain.

Only after many years of experience in mountain biking do you get a feeling for the little signals from the body which often tell you more than performance diagnostic values. For example, by going upstairs experienced cyclists can judge whether they have "pressure", which means that their muscles are in a regenerated, fit state. Others have learnt over the years that certain muscle pains (twinging or itching) often occur simultaneously with a phase when they are in top form.

The same applies to other body signals such as tiredness, wakefulness, hunger, sleep, desire to train, willingness to put in effort and many others. Monitoring and recording resting and exertion heart rates, body weight and body feeling under strain, also help experienced athletes judge their performance capacity and adjust their training accordingly.

There are, however, a great number of bikers who cannot interpret their body feeling at all or even ignore the signals the body gives them. Here it is extremely

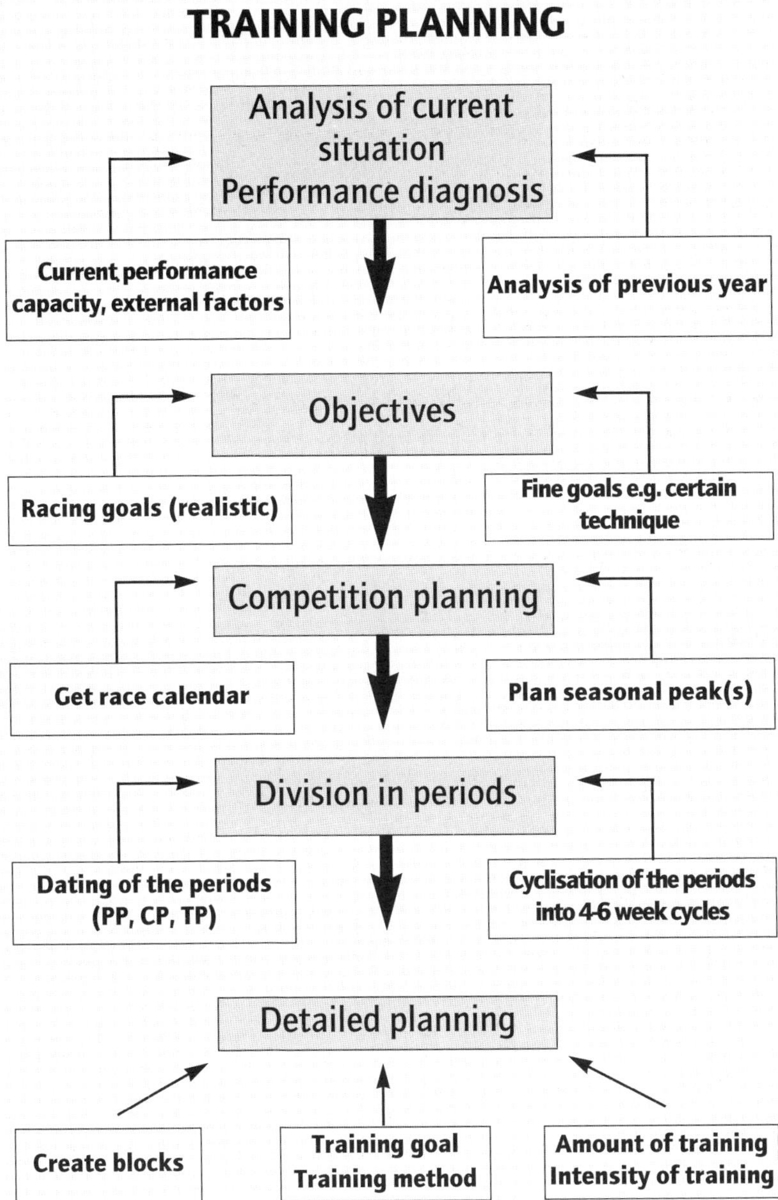

Fig. 6.2: Training planning in five steps

difficult to regulate training because these athletes usually train hard, often and long and psychologically need this high level of training. In most cases such athletes can only be convinced with scientific facts, i.e. diagnostic results, the obtaining of which, however involves much time and money. In view of the performance capacity of these athletes such a course is not justified in many cases.

If stagnation or even a decrease in performance is discovered, you need to think about how this has happened. In most cases a change in training or a break from competition is the consequence of such an analysis. Often the decisive factor is recognised but not changed, especially because of an unwillingness to vary from the training schedule created with such effort, and also because usually a delayed result from training is hoped for. The consequence must therefore be a change.

Emergency Brake – Change in Training Planning

Changing the training schedule is perfectly normal and a part of daily practice in performance sport, for a training year rarely goes the way it was planned. But the more experience you have, the better the planning and the less corrections are necessary. As a matter of principle, in the annual plan only the periods and their contents are worked out.

The detailed planning only takes place a month to six weeks in advance at the most. Changes within the individual micro-cycles are very frequent. If, however, the whole concept needs changes, then something major has gone wrong. Only those who are open to changes and react flexibly to changing conditions can have success with their training.

The following is a practical example with a recommended solution for such a case. A cross-country cyclist could not train sufficiently in the preparatory periods and, as usual, begins in the competition period in late April. Because of fitness deficits in all areas, but especially in aerobic energy supply (basic endurance), the race results leave a lot to be desired. In the races no feeling of fitness arises. In training he mainly does the very intensive programme that corresponds to the period.

In addition the cyclist orients himself towards his team mates with whom he often trains, but they are already in better shape than he is. The result is too high a level of exertion in relation to individual performance capacity, a stagnation of development in form and a motivational crisis on the psychological level. Often athletes then make the mistake of training even more intensively and thus drive themselves completely "into the ground". After participating in three or four races a biker should actually recognise his poor condition and link it with training mistakes. After one or two races this is not usually yet recognised as the races often trigger a development boost as well. At this point there is no avoiding a change in training strategy.

Rebuilding Training

First participation in races should be given up for at least two, better still three or four weeks, in order to concentrate on training and to exclude race strains that are too high in the border area. Often the reason for poor performance capacity is that basic endurance, the conditional basis for high race speed, has not been developed sufficiently.

Anaerobic mobilisation also takes place on the basis of basic endurance and in races is absolutely necessary for challenges, climbs and changes in speed. Apart from the poor aerobic energy provision, strength endurance is not yet at the level it should be.

Here, however, the biker finds himself in a dilemma as the strength abilities are especially improved in races in which he is now not supposed to take part. The goal of the training phase that now follows must therefore be the development of basic endurance. If general condition is good though, strength endurance should be developed in parallel. Supporting this, functional strengthening training (especially torso muscles) should be used to improve general ability to stand strain and also economy of movement.

The new training phase, which can be classed as a building up or rebuilding phase, is begun with several days of physical rest. Stretching and other regenerative measures as well as - at the most - some light compensatory training are the order of the day.

During the build-up phase diet should be especially balanced and nutritious, as often previous training that was too hard has led to a deficit of certain nutrients. Also, such a "new beginning" in training offers the opportunity to begin again psychologically in order to approach the matter with renewed motivation and the feeling of now doing everything right.

This new attitude really does have a positive effect on accompanying factors such as diet, stretching and way of life. Another important factor is time. So as not to train too much and above all not too intensively, it is extremely important to allow oneself time. If a training session has to be cancelled for an important reason, this is all right and the session must not be repeated the next day.

Day	1	2	3	4	5	6	7	8	9	10	11
Amount	-	-	-	+	++	-	+	++	+++	-	+
Intensity	CO	CO	CO	BE 1	BE 1	CO	BE 1	BE 1	BE 1	CO	BE 1
SE	-	-	-	-	-	-	-	-	-	-	+

Day	12	13	14	15	16	17	18	19	20	21	
Amount	++	+++	-	++	+++	++++	-	++	+++	+++	
Intensity	BE 1	BE 1		BE 1	BE 1	KO		BE 1	BE 1	BE 1	
SE	++	-		+	++	-			Test	Test	

Fig. 6.3: Example of rebuilding training (+/low, ++/medium, +++/high, ++++/very high)

After the days of regeneration, a double block of BE 1 training is begun on terrain that is as flat as possible. Another regenerational day follows. Then several progressive triple blocks in BE 1 should follow, with the greatest amount on the third day in each case. The number of triple blocks depends on the length of the period. The regenerational days between the blocks are important, which is not a problem if the bike is left unused. After the second or third block strength endurance training on the bike can begin. The first two days of the blocks are good for this. Here too the idea is to increase slowly and carefully. If desired the blocks can be carried out in reverse order, i.e. with decreasing instead of increasing amounts.

Towards the end of the rebuilding period form should be tested, for example on a hill or on a flat for several minutes, by applying maximum strain and listening to one's body. Especially the feeling in the legs and the heart rate give an indication of form. The heart rate should adjust quickly and exertion values be quickly reached at high strain. A fast drop of the heart rate after exertion is equally desirable (see chapter 3.3). Heart rates that are too high, or that rise too little, hint at a developing infection or a regeneration deficit.

Normally this rebuilding training should have the desired effect. The indication of amounts of training was deliberately left out in the training diagram because they would only apply to one performance class. In this phase the amounts build up until they reach the highest recommended amounts for the particular class.

Rebuilding training is also recommended after a period with many races close together with gradually decreasing basic endurance.

In a case of overtraining the same procedure would be followed, but the rest break should be extended to at least a week and exertion applied even more carefully. The amount would need to be reduced considerably.

Comments

To be successful it is often necessary to go new ways, for not only one but many ways lead to top performance - though within the framework of certain basic training methodology rules. You can only form an opinion as to whether new training methods are suitable for you personally by trying them out and feeling their effects on your own body.

It is recommended that such an experimental phase takes place towards the end of the season, at least after the main race. At this point for example, training can be changed to highest intensity or an extremely high proportion of strength training in order to observe how the body and one's form react.

Through an accentuation and a variation of training, but also through races (race selection) where a jump in form is often possible, performance barriers can thus be broken.

Changes in diet can be tried too.

6.4 Training Journal

In order to document training and competition data exactly, it is a good idea to start and keep a training journal.

The Training Planner

The most important part of the training journal is the actual "calendar" part in which all data and values relevant to training and competitions are entered. In addition to the data relevant to the training session, such as duration, distance, location and content of the training session, the physiological data of the person doing the training must be recorded.

These include values that are ascertained daily, such as resting heart rate, weight, the way one feels (scale of 1-10) and notes on health and the length and quality of sleep. The weather and any other relevant comments should also be noted. In a further block, a note can be made whether a stretching or gymnastics programme was carried out.

This volume of data to be recorded may at first scare readers off, but the effort will pay off for performance oriented bikers. In the end everyone must decide for themselves how many of the spaces are filled out daily and which ones only occasionally or never. In documenting training parameters there are no limits to the detail allowed, so that many other factors could also be recorded. The parameters described here, however, represent a sensible selection.

The last part of the training planner is for the evaluation and analysis of the recorded training and competition data. This part mostly requires a little work if it is not kept up constantly and is only done at the end of the season. On special graphs the weekly averages of the various parameters are plotted and the data points linked to form a graph. Certain events or race results are visually highlighted with arrows and notes.

With the aid of this graphic representation of the training parameters, correlations can often be recognised which would otherwise go unnoticed. If you are unsure about a particular section you can always check the calendar part at the beginning and research correlations in detail.

After the analysis, which will usually be much more detailed in a group, with a coach or with experienced bikers than if you do it alone, you should note the main conclusions and without fail take them into consideration when planning training for the following season.

Only with the help of this data gathered over several years is targeted training planning and regulation possible, which in the final analysis allows one to find the way to top performance.

Starting a Training Journal

Filling out a training journal takes less than five minutes a day, a minimum amount of time with great benefit. If you do not want to use the training planner you can create your own training journal by using photocopied sheets in a spring folder.

Regularity Is Called for

The regularity of the entries is always decisive. For yourself, and especially for young bikers, the keeping of a training journal is a sign of training motivation. As a rule exact entries without gaps mean conscientious training.

Evaluation and Analysis

If entries are made and analysed regularly the training journal can help identify mistakes and errors during the current training year so that they can be worked on straight away.

The first step in training analysis is to compare the actually trained amounts and types of exertion with the planned amounts and types. Are there great discrepancies here?

In a further step, on a weekly or monthly basis the resting heart rate and weight values together with the daily notes on body feeling are placed in relationship to the exertion values. When these are shown on a graph, overexertion through training and phases of too little or incorrect strain can be clearly recognised.

If you now mark the phases in colour when you felt good and achieved good performances in races, it is easy to work out which kind of training and which amounts of exertion lead to good performance capacity. Structures of strain which do exactly the opposite can thus also be found out. Days of illness are coloured in the graphs and in the calendar part.

The Effects of Training Vary Individually

Because training is a very individual process, and the same strains on two athletes can have very different effects, such results can be very valuable for training planning. All specific training tips should thus be relativised and at first individually tested; certain basic principles, however, as presented in this book, have general validity.

A detailed description of the possible groupings of all parameters would go too far at this point, but can be read up on in any training planner. A training journal is especially helpful to mountain bikers who do not have access to an experienced trainer. In the course of several years mistakes can be eliminated and training optimised.

Training Journal on the PC

For some time now various training journal programmes for PCs have been available. Although they take over much of the work (calculations and graphs), they tend to be very inflexible. A major disadvantage is the necessity to own a notebook which must be fed daily with the latest data. For those who find this too bothersome, and also want to have their "database" with them at training camps and races in order to work with it there, a normal training journal made of "paper" such as the training planner in pocketbook format is ideal.

7 Dietary Considerations

7.1 Basic Principles of Nutrition Specific to Mountain Biking

Over the last few years, training amounts and intensity in high performance endurance sports have assumed previously unheard of proportions. With these high demands and performance levels, very large amounts of food are needed and used in contrast to non-athletes. Performance athletes should therefore make particularly sure that the foods they give their bodies are of high quality and as unpolluted as possible. In the following section some principles of diet and physiology must first be examined, on the basis of which we will then discuss the problems of meeting the dietary requirements of mountain biking.

The main functions of food intake:

- Provide energy (for physical activity and vital functions)
- Build up and maintain the organism (cells, tissue)
- Regulation of metabolism and health protection (to keep the negative effects of the environment and of high performance sport on the body to a minimum).

There are four groups of nutrients:

1. *Energy suppliers (fuels)*
   Carbohydrates (starch, sugar), fats, proteins

2. *Building substances*
   Water, proteins (muscles, tendons, ligaments, cartilage), minerals and fats

3. *Regulatory and protective substances*
   Vitamins and trace elements

4. *Food contents aiding bodily functions*
   Ballast materials, scents, aromas and colourings

Carbohydrates

Carbohydrates play a decisive role in sports nutrition. They ensure a supply of energy under high exertion, are easily digestible and in most cases are also healthy. Above all they have two advantages: they are an oxygen saving energy carrier (they provide 10% more energy per litre of oxygen taken in than do fats) and they allow fast access to energy.

In our food we should take in 2/3 of the energy from carbohydrates through complex carbohydrates (polysaccharides), through starch and dextrine. The polysaccharides are multiple sugars, i.e. their molecules consist of a number of simple sugars. Within the group of polysaccharides preference should be given to starch (noodles, potatoes, rice).

At the most simple carbohydrates (mono- and disaccharides) should only make up 1/3 of total carbohydrates; these include the disaccharides saccharose (household sugar), lactose, and maltose, and the monosaccharides glucose, fructose and galactose.

For endurance athletes the amount of carbohydrates as a proportion of total calorie intake should be 60% or more.

Ballast substances play an important role for a carbohydrate rich diet, for a balanced blood sugar concentration in the course of the day, and for digestion, as well as for satisfaction of the feeling of hunger.

Fats

Although the proportion of fats in the total amount of energy should be about 25-30%, the average central European takes in over 40%. Excessive fat intake leads to the development of fat deposits and thus increases the risk of arteriosclerosis. 95% of the fats consumed by humans belong to the group of triglycerides and serve the purpose of gaining energy; about 5% of the fats are phospholipid and cholesterine which are used as building substances. The triglycerides are split into glycerine and free fatty acids, absorbed by special cells in the small intestine and distributed through the circulatory system via the lymph system. Anything not burnt immediately to gain energy is turned back into triglycerine and stored. If the glycogen stores become empty during exertion, the stored fats are remobilised and used to provide energy. The fats can only burn, however, in the "fire of carbohydrates"; if the carbohydrates have been totally used up, fat combustion is also "over a low flame" and performance capacity is reduced.

Fatty foods extend the length of time meals remain in the stomach and thus delay the absorption of nutrients. They slow down the refilling of the glycogen stores after exertion which is so important for regeneration.

Proteins

The proportion of proteins of total energy requirements should be between about 10 and 15%. The significance of proteins for sporting performance ability in

Photo: Scapin

endurance sport was overestimated for a long time. Today the daily steak as the basic prerequisite for a diet appropriate to sport and supportive of performance ability is outdated.

In the cells protein is mainly drawn on as a building and carrier substance and only to a small extent to produce energy.

Proteins consist of chains of various amino acids. 20 different amino acids are known, ten of which humans have to consume with their food, the rest they can synthesise themselves. In the stomach and small intestine the proteins are split by enzymes and absorbed into the blood as amino acids. Once a cell's specific need for amino acid has been met, the amino acids are changed into fat and glycogen to be used as energy.

For endurance athletes the recommended protein requirement is 1.2-1.5 g per kg of body weight. Additional protein consumption for example as supplements is not necessary. If more protein is eaten that in no way means that more muscle mass is built up. Instead, the excess is burnt as third class fuel and excreted again as urea, which puts a great strain on the kidneys. In order to avoid dehydration (drying out) of the body, large amounts of fluids must be drunk if protein consumption is high. The rest of the superfluous protein calories is stored as fat.

Water

Almost all metabolic processes need water as an indispensable medium. In endurance sports such as mountain biking the body loses a great deal of water, through breathing and sweating, so that as a result of this loss the metabolic processes cannot function at their usual speed. Metabolism slows down, a drop in performance is the result.

During intensive physical activity the body can lose between one and two litres of water per hour of exertion. In the course of a training ride the water loss is about a half to one litre per hour, on a training ride of several hours, e.g. five hours training, there is a 2.5 to 5 litres water loss.

The lack of water has the quickest and most serious effect on performance ability of all nutrient deficits. The reduction in sweat production when there is a water deficit can cause an increase in body temperature. For this reason the state of hydration should be sufficiently high before exertion.

The loss of water can be compensated with pure water, which was the usual way in cycling until a few years ago; you can mix your own drink or you can use one of the expensive sport drinks publicised by advertising. The advantage of the sport drinks is that in addition to the necessary water they also contain carbohydrates, minerals and vitamins, which are also lost with sweat. The problem for the drink manufacturers is in the concentration of such a drink; on the one hand it should be absorbed quickly and on the other hand it must contain sufficient carbohydrates to prevent a drop in performance. For most mountain bikers a concentration of 5-8% carbohydrates is best.

Thus 5-8 g of carbohydrates can be stirred into 100 ml of water (500 ml drinking bottle 25-40 g). If the drink is more concentrated (more than 10%) there can be indigestion and stomach problems. Because most fruit juices have a sugar concentration higher than 10%, these should be diluted one to one with a good uncarbonated mineral water containing magnesium, calcium and potassium. The old favourite fruit juice and mineral water is an excellent sport drink which tastes good and also does not cost too much.

Which Drinks Should Be Considered for an Athlete's Daily Diet?

- Mineral water (much Mg, Ca, K, relatively little Na)
- Fruit juices (especially freshly squeezed), no fruit drinks
- Fruit juice and mineral water mix
- Milk, milk based drinks (1.5% fat)
- Tea
- Stout
- Vegetable juice (without added sugar if possible).

After exertion, carbohydrate and mineral rich fruit juice and mineral water or cola in reasonable amounts are especially recommended to refill the glycogen stores.

How Do You Drink during Exertion?

- Slowly, in small mouthfuls.
- About every 15 minutes 150 ml, not the whole bottle at once.
- Never go into exertion with a fluid deficit (thirst).

In training and races you should drink regularly before you feel thirsty. When thirst is felt the fluid deficit is usually already too great. In very high temperatures you can take along a bottle of frozen water and drink the thawing cool water. The other way round, when it is cold, hot tea can be put in a thermos.

Vitamins

Vitamins are organically essential nutrients which influence metabolism in very many places, although they are only present in extremely small concentrations.

They do not belong to the fuels of the body and supply no energy. Often the significance of vitamins for increasing sporting performance capacity is overestimated. If, however a vitamin deficiency has been diagnosed, additional vitamins should be taken.

Minerals

Minerals are anorganic elements and their compounds are of great significance for the human body as building and regulatory substances. They also include the trace elements (iron, zinc, chromium, selenium, copper, iodine, molybdenum, cobalt, manganese, etc.)

7.2 Nutrition during the Various Training Periods

Training Staple Diet

Sports nutrition - endurance (mountain biking)

- Diverse
- Low fat
- Carbohydrate rich (complex carbohydrates as much as possible)
- High in protein

How Do You Ensure a Carbohydrate Rich Diet?

Noodles, rice (both especially as wholegrain products), wholemeal products (wholemeal bread, biscuits, muesli in all variations), potatoes, legumes (beans, peas), vegetables and fruit as well as fruit juices are excellent carbohydrate providers which - in contrast to refined products - additionally also contain a great deal of other valuable nutrients.

White sugar or flour, for example, only contain "empty" calories, because apart from the sugar or starch molecules they contain no other nutrients such as vitamins, ballast or minerals. You should try to eat meals that are as natural and as gently prepared as possible and avoid ready-to-serve meals and products which almost always contain additives (flavour boosters, artificial colouring, preservatives, emulsifying agents etc.).

What Is Important in a Low Fat Diet?

On the one hand consumption of visible fat must be consciously reduced, such as oil, butter, margarine, fat on meat, and on the other hand hidden fats must be recognised and avoided. Hidden fats are found especially in sausages, cheese, eggs, sweets, sauces and (deep) fried foods.

The aim of a low fat diet is not a ban on all fat consumption but rather the conscious choice of foods and thus doing without unhealthy and fatty foods. It is very important to differentiate between saturated and unsaturated, highly nutritious fatty acids, like e.g. linoleic acid, which can lower the cholesterol level in contrast to the saturated fatty acids.

Fats that are liquid at room temperature (oils) are more nutritious than solid fats (frying fats).

Which Foods Contain Highly Nutritious Proteins in Combination with Little Fat?

In this regard ideal protein suppliers are lean or low fat dairy products, wholegrain products, rice and noodles as well as almost all types of fish, poultry and lean parts of beef, pork and lamb. But also legumes and grain products are very good low fat protein suppliers. Increased consumption of vegetable proteins reduces the proportion of fat and increases the intake of ballast, vitamins and complex carbohydrates.

Additional protein preparations are not necessary in mountain biking as an endurance sport if you eat a balanced diet. The specific prescribing of certain amino acids is something only a doctor should do, and should only be done as therapy.

Dietary Practice and Preparational Tips

In order to cover the carbohydrate proportion, the meal plan of endurance athletes, and in particular mountain bikers, should include at least one daily serving of noodles, potatoes or rice (if possible wholegrain products). In the course of the day lots of bread (if possible wholemeal or dark bread) with cheese or a sweet spread (thinly spread) should be eaten as small snacks. Muesli in all its variations without sugar and with fresh grain and fruit is a balanced healthy meal, not only in the morning.

A complete sport diet also includes vegetables and salad. Local seasonable products contain more vitamins and minerals than products from overseas or the greenhouse. Fruit can be eaten at any time of the day.

If the total amount of food is spread over the day in three or four major meals and a number of snacks in between, the blood sugar level and with it hunger can be kept at a balanced level. Keeping weight under control then becomes child's play. Meals should be prepared in a gentle way. Long cooking and roasting reduces the proportion of vitamins and other nutrients and also the taste of meals. Highly nutritious oils with unsaturated fatty acids and a coated frying pan reduce consumption of less nutritious oils. Vegetables should only be briefly steamed or eaten raw.

In general, in performance sport the amount of food should be low but the quality high in order to achieve a small weight reduction or to maintain competition weight. If, however, training intensity is high and there are many races, this course should not be followed. Low food consumption is particularly useful in winter as a way to put on less weight when there is not so much training.

Do not bother working out numbers of calories and calorie composition as this is absolutely impractical and takes up a lot of time.

Preparatory Periods

At the beginning of the training year, when total exertion is very low, there is no need for special techniques to increase the glycogen reserves. Diet should be matched to needs according to the criteria described above. On days with training sessions - whether on the bike, at home or in the strength training room - the supply of protein should be adjusted by eating meat, fish, dairy products or vegetable foods containing protein (legumes).

Competition Period

In the competition period when there is very high exertion, special attention must be paid to diet in mountain biking. In the following chapter best dietary behaviour before, during and after a race will be discussed.

In the training phases during the week the principles of basic training nutrition described above apply. Because the competition period is usually in summer, the increased loss of fluids in high outdoor temperatures means particular attention must be paid to a balance of fluids in the body.

Transitional Period

During the transitional period the principles of diet suitable for sport must not be neglected because often after training camps or intensive training blocks there is a feeling of constant hunger. In the first days of reduced exertion the body - used to high levels of exertion and equally large amounts of food - wants the same amount of food.

In this situation you can only avoid putting on weight through discipline, increased fluid intake and eating foods with a high ballast content.

7.3 Nutrition before Exertion

Here are some tips:

- In the days before the race ensure an especially high proportion of carbohydrates (65%).
- If necessary use "carbohydrate loading" (see below).
- On the evening before the race eat an easily digestible carbohydrate rich, low fat meal (pasta party).
- Ensure sufficient fluids (no alcohol).
- The last solid carbohydrate rich meal should be eaten no later than 3-4 hours before the race and must be easily digestible: do not eat too much, but drink enough, no sweets.

Fluid Intake

In a mountain bike race you should start with a good fluid balance, just as you do when you go on a long tour, for a fluid deficit very much restricts performance capacity and can even be dangerous. A simple method of testing the body's fluid level is to check the colour of your urine.

If it is dark yellow, such as e.g. after long training sessions with low fluid intake, care must be taken and you must drink in order not to enter the race in a dehydrated state. A very weak yellow colouring of the urine is ideal, indicating a good fluid balance.

The urine should be checked the day before the race so that on the evening before the water balance can be at its best with one or two bottles of mineral water.

Be careful with beer, which has a diuretic effect and causes exactly the opposite.

High flying performance thanks to a proper diet
Photo: Stephan Bögli, © by SSG Europe

Pasta Party

On the evening before a race or a long tour it has proved to be helpful to hold a so-called "pasta party" with noodles and a low fat sauce if possible, and plenty to drink. You should not eat and drink too late or too much, however, otherwise you may not sleep well.

In many cases this carbohydrate rich meal is enough to fill the glycogen stores. The method of carbohydrate loading described below should only be used by performance athletes.

Race Day

If your race begins in the morning you will have to get up very early on race day in order to eat a carbohydrate rich breakfast and/or possibly to consume more noodles. This should be done three or four hours before the race to give your body time for digestion. Afterwards you drink a little in small amounts before the start and you can also eat a few small snacks (pieces of banana, muesli bars, etc. but not too sweet if possible, no cola). Sweet snacks such as chocolate raise the blood sugar level which then falls again after the race starts, thus preventing full performance capacity (see Fig. 7.1).

If the start is in the afternoon an early carbohydrate rich lunch should be eaten. The meal on the previous evening, however, is decisive for filling the glycogen stores. Rice pudding has proved to be an excellent supplier of carbohydrates which can also be used between a possible pre- and final run to combat hunger.

Carbohydrate Loading

Carbohydrate loading, also called carboloading, is nothing more than a special filling of the glycogen stores before maximum exertion in order to keep up high speeds for as long as possible. Even for mountain bikers, who already have enlarged glycogen stores in comparison to other athletes as a result of a carbohydrate rich diet, it is possible to load some more.

To do this, after hard training without eating, during which the glycogen stores have been emptied, the following two or three days you should eat very carbohydrate rich food and train only small amounts and intensities, thus filling the glycogen stores - especially in the leg muscles - even more than they were before (super compensation). If the race is at the weekend, exhaustive training can take place on Wednesday or Thursday. Carbohydrate loading then begins directly after the hard training session; now you should hold your first "pasta party".

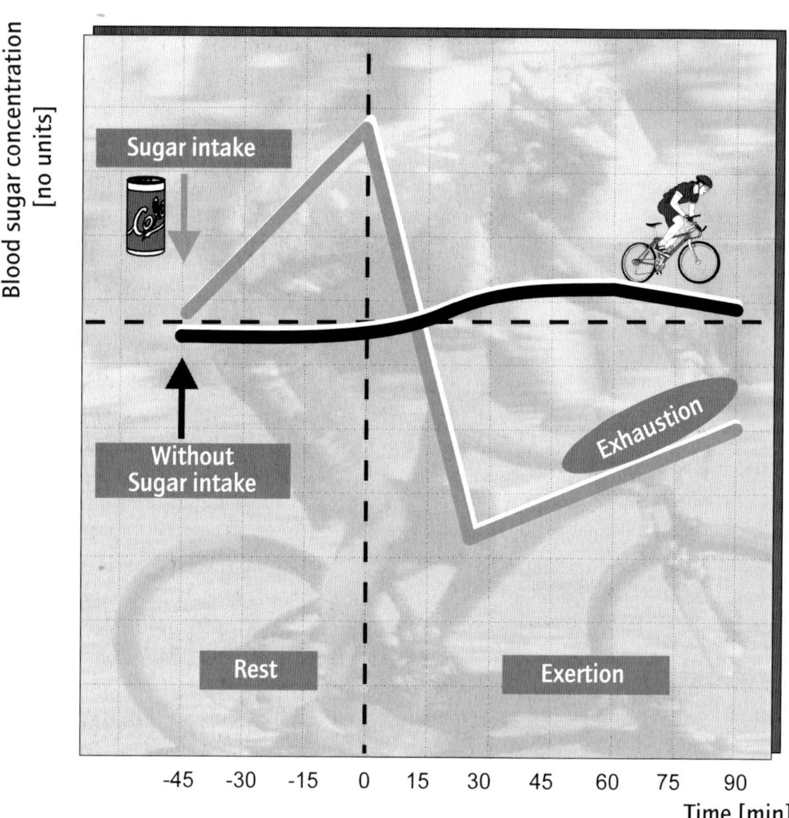

Fig. 7.1: Progression of blood sugar level with and without carbohydrate intake (e.g. cola, sweets) shortly before 90 minutes of exertion

High glycogen concentrations cause increased storage of water in the muscles which often makes the legs feel heavy and fat at the beginning of training, but this disappears after a short time. Carbohydrate loading is only recommended for well-trained athletes as a similar glycogen super compensation effect has not been observed in untrained people, and the large amounts of carbohydrates can even lead to putting on weight.

In the carbohydrate loading described on page 189 the exhausting work is on Thursday. This exertion can also be applied on Wednesday and the "loading phase" extended by a day. This kind of performance diet is sometimes made even more specialised by eating extremely fat and protein rich foods before the phase

Training and dietary plan for carbohydrate loading

Day	Training	Diet
Thursday 3	Exhausting training for 2-6 hours, depending on performance level and age, BE 1/2 with several speed sections (RSE), either on the racing bike or the MTB, do not put too much strain on the muscles	During training: eat as little as possible, drink a lot Afterwards: as many carbohydrates as possible
Friday 2	Depending on performance level and age 1-3 hours BE 1/CO, easy gears, muscular exertion as low as possible	Carbohydrate rich food - little fat Breakfast: muesli, bread Lunch: noodles, rice, potatoes Dinner: noodles, rice, potatoes
Saturday 1	Depending on level of performance and age 1-2 hours BE 1/CO, easy gears, 1 x 1-4 min BE 2/RSE to test	Carbohydrate rich food - little fat As on Friday, but in the evening a "pasta party" = large servings of carbohydrates (not too late!) and drink a lot (water)
Sunday 0	Event	Carbohydrate rich, easily digestible breakfast, possibly a carbohydrate rich lunch, 3-4 hours in advance, do not eat too much, no cola

described here and only then beginning with "carbohydrate fattening". Nutrition and certain diets must not become "scourges"; food must also taste good. It is therefore advisable only to practise carbohydrate loading rigorously before really important events.

7.4 Nutrition during Exertion

Food intake is only potentially necessary in races lasting more than 60 minutes. When exertion lasts over 90 minutes you should definitely consume carbohydrates to avoid a drop in performance. In training, depending on your training state, you will only need a small carbohydrate snack after about two hours.

Ravenous Hunger

In cycling the state of total exhaustion of the glycogen stores is referred to as "ravenous hunger". It is characterised by symptoms such as "fantasies" about food, dizziness, lack of concentration, loss of orientation and greatly reduced performance capacity - a state which can cause problems on a racing bike in traffic and even be dangerous. But it is also dangerous on a mountain bike in the middle of the countryside.

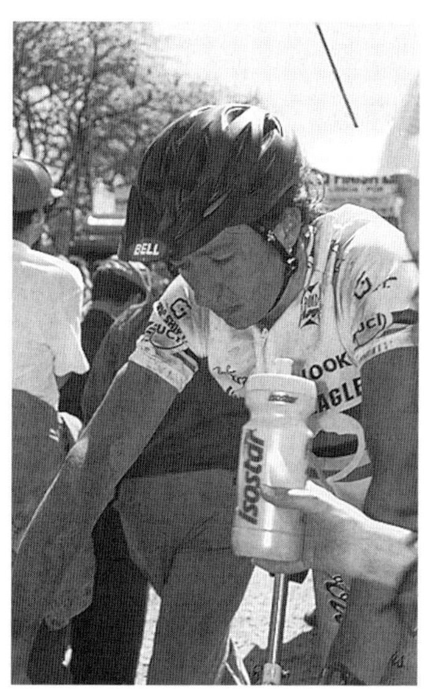

Fluid intake during exertion is extremely important.
Photo: Klaus Eweleit

The then very low blood sugar level can usually be raised by eating a few sugar cubes or some glucose. Although this does not improve performance significantly one does feel better quickly and can head home or in search of food with a clear head. Ravenous hunger usually "attacks" mountain bikers in spring during the first longer training sessions in air that is still cold for the body. By eating carbohydrate rich snacks (especially the various muesli bars, fruit - bananas, apples, pears, dried fruit -, rice cakes, bread - low fat garnishing -, biscuits and also energy bars) it is possible to prevent ravenous hunger and maintain performance.

On longer tours the complex carbohydrates are eaten first and the simple carbohydrates (glucose) only towards the end of the journey. In order to get another energy boost at the often decisive end of a race many racing cyclists drink a coffee with lots of sugar about 30 minutes before the race finishes. As, however, caffeine is on the doping list when it gets above a certain concentration, it is better to do without it.

Half a drinking bottle of cola or a piece of glucose have a similar effect and push performance a little.

Eating during the Race

Eating while cycling needs to be trained as it happens often enough that mountain bike beginners cannot eat anything because of stomach problems during exertion. The ability to eat during exertion is a detail that is often

Food during a race (race duration 2 h)

Time	Solid foods	Fluids
0:00-0:30 beginning	After 15 minutes you can eat an energy bar, a muesli bar	Drink regularly in small sips right from the start
0:30-1:30 middle	In small bites eat an energy bar, muesli bar and drink at the same time	Regularly drink, energy drinks, isotonic drinks, fruit juice/mineral water mixes 30 min before the finish
1:30-2:00 end phase	No more solid foods except glucose (2-3 pieces) 30 min before the finish	perhaps drink some cola (1/2 bottle) spread over several minutes

overlooked, for especially on longer tours, popular marathons and increasingly more frequent MTB stage races, often significant amounts of food need to be eaten while on the mountain bike. Food intake should be practised during training.

If you cannot handle solid foods you must take in liquid carbohydrates, which should be consumed as a balanced mixture of simple and complex carbohydrates. An inexpensive way of making a carbohydrate rich drink is to stir Maltodextrin (available at chemists) into the water in your drinking bottle. High concentrations can, however, lead to indigestion.

The pattern described above represents the ideal course in a slightly simplified form. On demanding courses, though, it is often impossible to eat and drink regularly; here you have to eat and drink whenever the opportunity presents itself. Important: in races up to two and a half hours it is a good idea to drink energy rich drinks as described above because fluid intake is also possible in difficult sections, is much quicker and hinders breathing less.

7.5 Nutrition after Exertion

Nutrition after exertion plays a decisive role in regeneration. The emptying of the glycogen stores leads to increased activity of the enzyme glycogensynthetase. Glycogensynthetase encourages the development of glycogen and its storage in the cells. Because the concentration of this enzyme is at its highest between two and four hours after the end of exertion, and it then goes back to the starting level within 24 hours, the mountain biker must consume sufficient carbohydrates straight after training or a race in order to fill his stores again. If this is forgotten and there is renewed strain the next day, the stores are emptied even further. Glycogen stores are not only emptied by long, intensive exertion, but also through shorter strains several days in a row without refilling the stores in between.

In the first 24 hours after an exhausting event or training there is no difference in the processing of complex and simple carbohydrates, but after 24 hours complex carbohydrates increase glycogen resynthesis much more. Furthermore, complex carbohydrates are more advantageous healthwise because they are consumed together with other nutrients and ballast.

After exertion you should eat foods such as noodles, rice, wholegrain products or fruit. In order to sensibly use the period straight after the race (about two hours) for regeneration, which is usually marked by a lack of appetite, you can drink carbohydrate rich drinks (fruit juice, not too sour, cola).

Normally you do not need special energy drinks unless you are on a trip of several days, or in a stage race where exertion is in the border area and regeneration time is only very limited. The fluid deficit should be made up gradually and not all at once. Ice cold drinks should not be used because of the increased sensitivity of the digestive tract.

Fruit juices (potassium rich, to increase glycogen storage) diluted with a good mineral water provide for replenishment of fluids in the body as well as a good supply of minerals and carbohydrates.

7.6 Reducing Body Weight in Racing Sport

Every endurance athlete knows the relationship between form and weight: the better your form, the lower your weight is too.

The term competition or race weight is used here, which can vary considerably from one individual to another according to constitution and is between two and eight kilograms below "winter weight"; generally your weight should not differ too much from competition weight in winter, the period of reduced training. Often mountain bikers experience a jump in performance after losing weight.

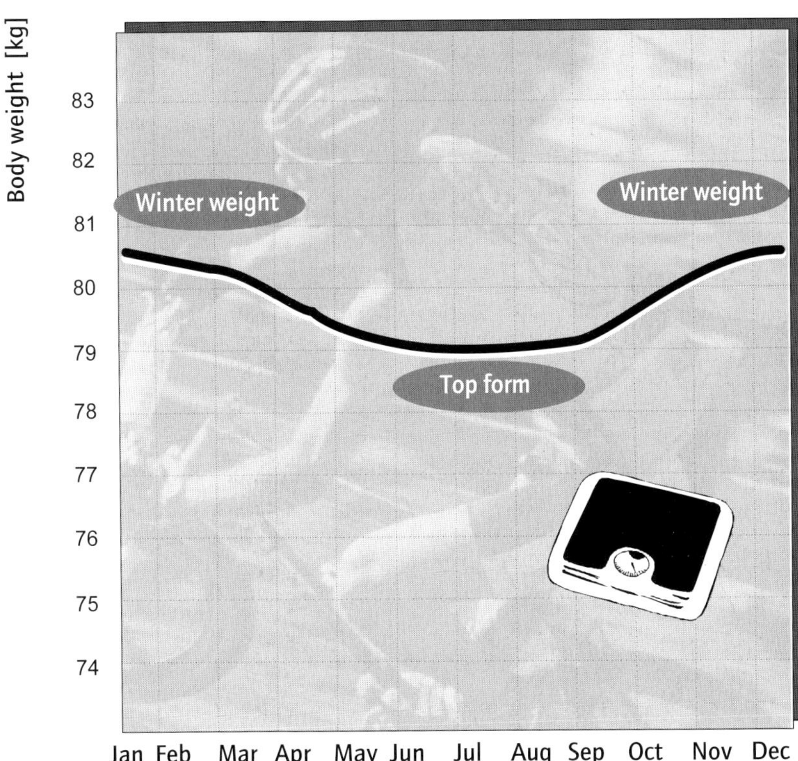

Fig. 7.2: Body weight curve in the course of the year

How Do You Lose Pounds?

Quite a few pounds can be "burnt away" by going on long training rides in the fat combustion field, especially in the preparatory period, and a slightly calorie reduced diet. Food should be especially reduced in fat, yet completely ensure protein provision in order to prevent muscle protein being drawn on for energy metabolism. The supply of carbohydrates must also be sufficient so that glycogen deficiency does not occur.

While carbohydrates are digested very quickly and raise the blood sugar level, fats are digested very slowly and influence the blood sugar level very little, so that a feeling of being satisfied does not occur. The quick feeling of having eaten enough that occurs with carbohydrate rich foods benefits weight reduction in performance sport but also in health sport. Long BE 1 sessions after a very small breakfast also boost fat combustion.

Tips for weight reduction in mountain bike performance sport

- Food that is greatly fat reduced
- High carbohydrate proportion of over 60%
- Carbohydrate rich breakfast (under no circumstances skip breakfast)
- Carbohydrate rich snacks between meals
- Eat the evening meal early, as before sleep calories go into the fat depots
- Try not to eat anything more after the evening meal
  If you do get hungry, only eat fat free snacks (vegetables, fruit)
- Reduce weight slowly

Body weight should be checked every morning after going to the toilet. A balanced supply of energy is reflected in constant body weight. Variations in body weight of 1-1.5 kg (in exceptional cases also up to 2 kg) are normal. What is important is that average weight remains constant.

If an athlete loses too much weight this can indicate a state of overtraining. Weight reduction should be carried out carefully with no more than 1-2 kg reduction per month. Figure 7.2 shows the typical course of the weight curve of a mountain biker (CC-competition) over a year.

7.7 Frequently Asked Questions about Nutrition

How Should Stimulant Drinks Be Viewed?

As is well-known, a number of mountain bike teams are sponsored by manufacturers of stimulant drinks. Unfortunately this implies suitability for endurance athletes. These drinks are certainly capable of mobilising energy reserves to a greater degree - as are cola or coffee - and thus extend performance ability, but they in no way give you wings.

The way they work is individually very different. In the final analysis this is a moral issue just as in doping. If you reject the idea of attacking your performance reserves with doping substances you should also avoid these "legal" substances, for after all, the drop in performance in the course of intensive exertion on the anaerobic threshold has a biological reason. It is a protective mechanism. If you push beyond this natural barrier too often - a barrier which can be moved upwards by training - you must reckon with undesirable side effects.

What Characterises a Good Energy Bar?

Energy bars are available in numerous forms from various manufacturers. Above all, because of its composition of complex and simple carbohydrates, an energy bar should allow a shorter and a longer lasting supply of energy to the working muscles.

Fats and proteins should only be present in very small quantities. Additives such as vitamins and minerals are perhaps sensible, but not necessary if a balanced diet is kept to. Often energy bars are sold whose fat, and in particular whose protein, content is much too high. This kind of bar is usually for bodybuilding where there are other priorities than in endurance sport.

A decisive factor in an energy bar should be its flavour and whether it can also be eaten in cooler weather. The bar must be easy to chew and when fluids are drunk at the same time it should break up quickly in the mouth and be easily swallowed. Energy bars should always be consumed together with fluids in order to dilute the nutrient concentration in the stomach immediately and accelerate nutrient absorption. Ballast rich energy bars such as muesli bars make less sense in races because they are processed too slowly and also have too low a carbohydrate density.

What Must Women Take into Consideration Regarding Nutrition?

Because of their differing physical prerequisites in comparison to men, women mountain bikers who race must also observe a number of basic principles with regard to diet in order to avoid being plagued by deficiency symptoms. In addition to the factors of a diet favourable to sport already mentioned, women must make sure they get enough calcium, iron and vitamin B_2.

The missed periods (amenorrhoe) experienced by some women (10-20%) who undertake endurance sport intensively result from a low oestrogen level which is in turn responsible for a possible development of osteoporosis. There is a "washout" of calcium salts and thus a loss in bone density.

Even in women mountain bikers with normal periods a lowering of the oestrogen level can be observed, so no meal plan should leave out calcium rich foods. The daily requirement of calcium is about 1,200 mg, which can be well met by dairy products, tofu and fresh vegetables. Iron is found especially in meat and lentils. If tea or coffee are consumed at the same time, the tannic acids they contain impair the intake of iron considerably.

The well-known iron deficiency problem of sporting women does not make an exception for mountain bikers, being affected by the loss of blood during menstruation and a diet not adapted to sport. Symptoms include tiredness and decreased performance ability as well as occasional cold spells. In many cases the taking of iron supplements under medical supervision is advisable and necessary.

The deficiency of vitamin B_2 is a problem not only for women but also for male mountain bikers, because endurance training reduces the concentration of B_2. Vitamin B_2 is used to split fats and carbohydrates for energy production and is therefore very important. Dairy products and wholegrain products are rich in B_2. When diet is balanced and nutritious there is no need for B_2 supplementation.

8 Technique Training

8.1 Importance of Technique Training

As already mentioned in chapter 2, co-ordination and cycling technique make up a significant part of total performance in biking. Depending on the discipline the importance of this proportion varies: in the technical disciplines, trialing, slalom and downhill, it is most important, in cross-country less. In comparison to road cycling, however, cross-country races demand much greater technical skills and bike control of the cyclist.

Extreme biking situations must become routine.
Photo: Stephan Bögli, © by SSG Europe

In general cycling technique, i.e. control of the bike, should be trained as well as possible. From a training methodology point of view there should be a weighting, at least in cross-country and partially also in downhill, because other conditional characteristics such as endurance, strength, speed and agility must not be neglected in training practice, and partly (endurance, strength) need a considerably greater amount of time to be developed adequately.

Nevertheless, on demanding cross-country courses, deficiencies in endurance and strength can be made good with well-developed cycling technique, as can often be observed amongst older cyclists in the senior class. Of two physically equally strong cyclists in mountain biking the one with better cycling technique will always do better.

Professionals seem to be part of their bikes and move accordingly out in the field. But in spite of seeming perfection they too must train certain techniques again and again, and thus spend part of their training time on technique training.

Any normal cross-country cyclist who has ever raced down a steep and windy single trail behind a good downhiller will know how great the differences can be particularly in the technical field, and also how great the time differences can be after a long descent. Often it is the technically demanding sections that decide races and many participants lose all important minutes and seconds not in the speed sections and uphill, but here.

Safety Reserves through Cycling Technique Training

With the increasing popularity of mountain biking the number of serious injuries has also gone up, especially those from falls that occur without outside influences. In some hospitals, mainly in alpine regions, there are now more injured mountain bikers than motorcyclists. These falls are usually caused by inappropriate speeds on descents - inappropriate with regard to the course and the cycling technique ability of the cyclists.

Specific and regular training can build up safety reserves which benefit a cyclist in dangerous situations and prevent falls. This assumes, of course, that on dangerous stretches the cyclist does not constantly try to ride at his now increased upper limits.

Co-ordination also decreases greatly with growing exhaustion as race or training duration goes on. Here excellent bike control is also a kind of insurance against a dangerous fall.

Prerequisites for Good Bike Control

Strong and well-trained arm and torso muscles are an important prerequisite for learning and managing difficult techniques. Furthermore the bike should be in excellent condition as technique training can put equipment under great stress. In many cases serious falls have occurred in technique training, or when trying out new movements, as a result of bike defects (broken forks, torn chain, broken handlebars etc.).

Anticipation during Downhills

Good downhillers have the gift of perceiving the course ahead in advance and anticipating the correct action to take (brake, shift weight). Anticipation means unconsciously planning actions in advance in co-ordination with stimuli from the environment. At the slightest change in terrain or other stimuli, processes take place in the brain which steer exactly towards the correct action variant. The action programme can, however, still be corrected at short notice. Anticipation plays a great role in all ball games, for example in tennis in order to be able to prepare oneself for an opponent's shot as quickly as possible.

If downhillers instinctively choose the right line to ride down, they are able to anticipate. At the same time they must also still take in the current situation, process it and act accordingly. These processes automatically taking place illustrate the complexity of actions that are very demanding from a moving technique point of view, and show that co-ordinative talent (quick grasp, short reaction times, good anticipation) is absolutely necessary in order to master difficult sections.

8.2 Selection of the Most Important Cycling Techniques

Co-ordination as the most important main concept of cycling technique abilities comprises more than just the various curve, jump and braking techniques. The movement of pedalling must also be carried out with perfect moving technique in order to cycle as economically as possible. The following list contains a range of activities required for technique training.

The individual fields can be further divided into the various individual techniques. For space reasons, however, a description of the individual cycling techniques cannot be given here. There are many books available though with extensive descriptions.

Type of technique	Specific techniques	Basic skills
Balancing	Attempt to stand on the spot (against a wall and without help) Attempt to stand with one leg Attempt to stand without hands	Balance
Jumping	Bunny hop forwards Bunny hop sideways Bunny hop on the back wheel	Balance Strength (resilience, maximal strength)
Braking	Slide (skid with back wheel) Drifting (back wheel, front wheel) Nose wheelie	Balance Anticipation Feeling for speed
Gear changing	Changing up (adapted to terrain) Changing down (adapted to terrain)	Anticipation
Curve	Cutting Drifting	Balance Braking
Downhill	Speed ride Overcoming steps	Balance Strength, feeling for speed Short reaction time Anticipation
Uphill	Pedalling standing up Sitting Overcoming steps	Balance Strain on back wheel Strain on front wheel Strength
Acceleration	Acceleration standing up Acceleration sitting	Balance Strength
Pedalling	Pedalling standing up Sitting	Pedalling phase Drawing or pulling phase Raising phase Pushing phase

Balance as a Foundation

The foundational skill of good cycling technique is balance on the bike. Only bikers who can keep themselves on their bikes by the slightest shifting of their centre of gravity, and by playing with the brakes and pedals standing up, will also be able to keep control over their bikes when using more complex techniques. Before specific technique training it is therefore first necessary to learn to stand or hop on the spot on the mountain bike. Just like track cyclists you should be able to balance on the spot for several minutes.

In borderline situations you need to still have cycling technique reserves. Photo: Stephan Bögli, © by SSG Europe

8.3 When and How Do You Do Technique Training?

Technique training should always take place in a rested condition, for when the nerve-muscle system has been tired by hard training it does not take in co-ordinative stimuli very well. This leads to the requirement to do technique training either completely isolated from other training or at the beginning of a training session. Especially in group training the time it takes until all participants have arrived can be used for technique training.

Technique training is more fun in groups and also more motivating. In addition it allows discussion and an exchange of experiences, new insights and better understanding of some movements.

Before technique training there should always be a warm-up with several minutes of BE exertion. Stretching exercises are also carried out frequently during training.

With Protective Clothing on a Field or Off-road Terrain

Training of basic techniques and games is done either on off-road terrain in certain difficult places or on a field. A field is advantageous for the inevitable falls. Rollerblading knee and elbow protectors have proved themselves in technique training, are pleasant to wear and prevent most scrapes and bruises. During training a helmet should always be worn.

Execution

The selected techniques are practised again and again and only after progress has been made does one move on to a new technique. A combination of technique and mental training (see chapter 9) is best. If you alternate the two training methods as described you will have most success.

A short circuit of just a few hundred metres in the forest or in an old quarry can be prepared with tree trunks and other measures so that it is very demanding technically. By frequently riding along the circuit in both directions better bike control can playfully be learnt.

A technique training session lasts about 30 to 60 minutes. In longer sessions motor learning abilities deteriorate greatly. Technique training should take place at least once a week.

Start during Childhood

The earlier one begins technique training, the easier it is to learn difficult movements. At adult age one usually needs several times longer to learn a certain technique.

8.4 Practice Course

If you train in a group it is fun to create a practice course. This course can be composed of natural and artificial obstacles. A kind of co-ordination or skills decathlon is also fun and is especially popular with children.

Another way of practising the techniques learnt in the field is to hold training races on a very difficult short circuit. Here timed laps or pursuit rides such as on the track can be carried out.

Ideas for a Practice Course

1. *Seesaw*
   A board is laid over a tree trunk or a beam. When you ride over it the board rocks over to the other side like a seeaw.

2. *Jumping ramps*
   With a board and a beam you can create a small ramp.

3. *A rope as a high obstacle*
   A tightly drawn rope forces you to get off and back on to train the changeover from cycling to running.

4. *Tree trunks*
   Tree trunks of various diameters can be jumped over either with the bike or on foot with the bike raised/shouldered.

5. *Slalom course*
   A slalom section is made using stones, branches or similar.

6. *Ground waves/tree roots*
   Bumpy sections with ground waves or tree roots force you to practise taking the weight off the front wheel in time, compensating jolting movements and keeping your balance.

7. *Valleys/holes*
   Practice for descents and steep climbs.

Skills Competition

1. ***Attempt to stand on the spot***
   (one point for every ten seconds).

2. ***Riding on the back wheel/ wheelie***
   (one point for every five metres).

3. ***Limbo***; ride under a tight cord, the cord is 15 cm higher than the highest part of the bike of each cyclist
   (three points for getting under it).

4. ***Picking up*** small objects from the ground
   (one point per object).

5. ***Balancing*** on a narrow 5 cm beam
   (two points if successful).

Jumps in all variations must be mastered. Photo: Stephan Bögli, © by SSG Europe

6. ***Throw*** a ball at a target from the moving bike (three attempts, one point per hit).

7. ***Drawing;*** a figure, e.g. a large circle, is drawn on the ground with a piece of chalk (two points if successful).

8. ***Timed slalom course*** (establish a minimum time, three points if successful, for every stick knocked over one point is subtracted).

8.5 Little Games with the Mountain Bike

Little games with the mountain bike are lots of fun and allow fear-free, unconscious learning of bike control even when there is body and bike contact.

If desired the protective equipment mentioned above can be worn.

1. Soccer

Soccer on mountain bikes is great fun and works quite well after a while. With only one metre wide goals, goalkeepers are done without. The game should always be played without touching the opponents' bodies.

2. Basketball

Basketball can also be played on mountain bikes. You do not have to dribble the ball but can carry it on the bike.
Variation: When shooting for goal the feet must not touch the ground.

3. Relay games

All forms of relays are excellent as MTB games. Small obstacles can be added to the courses. Small tasks can also be carried out on the way. For example, two slalom courses can be marked which must be covered by both teams at the same time (dual slalom).

4. Pushing away

To learn body contact in biking, two people cycle parallel leaning their upper bodies together and try to push each other away. In doing this they ride at an angle.

5. Touching the back wheel

Two cyclists riding single file alternately try to touch the back wheel of their partner with their front wheel without falling off.

6. (Bike) jumping

A number of different obstacles are built up which must be jumped over one after another in the form of a show jumping course. A minimum time is established and for every obstacle not taken there is a minus point. The winner is the person with the least faults (minus points) and the fastest time. Other obstacles or tasks can also be included.

7. Tag

Many tag games can also be played on the MTB. They are fast, intensive and great fun.

All of the games or exercises named in this event can be put together as you wish to create a different course or a new event. With a little creativity the rules can be altered, new variations or even completely new games devised. The games are most fun in groups of six or more bikers.

9 Psychological Training

In extreme sections fear must be channelled.
Photo: Klaus Eweleit

Anyone who has ever sat on a mountain bike knows only too well situations in which he had a mental block. A steep stage, a descent, a jump or a steep climb trigger fears then. Fear of not being able to manage the section but above all fear of a fall.

With the help of psychological training much more than the mastery of fear can be achieved. In the area of co-ordination in particular, i.e. technique training, psychological training can help achieve astounding successes.

Furthermore, mental preparation for races is vital for optimal performance motivation. But for training too mountain bikers need a great deal of motivation, the foundation of which can be created with mental training. In connection with regeneration the various relaxation techniques do a good job.

9.1 Fear as a Hindrance

Fear as a form of spiritual tension is very often the mental anticipation of a threatening situation which could happen or already has happened (experience of falls). It is the reflection of uncertainty.

In addition to the mentioned concrete fears of falls and their consequences, in mountain biking there are also more complex fears, such as fear of defeat, of victory or of disgrace. The presence of rivals can also trigger feelings of fear.

If you want to do something about your fears it is important to be able to recognise the factors causing fear and describe them in words, for sometimes this is enough to get the fear under control immediately. A talk with a person one trusts or the trainer can help to concretise the factors.

Many bikers are afraid again and again in certain situations which blocks them and prevents them producing their full performance. This fear can have very different forms and causes.

How Is Fear Expressed?

For outsiders the diagnosis of fear in or before certain situations is difficult because the triggers are individual experiences; some external symptoms can, however, give clues to fear:

Physical symptoms: shaking, stomach problems, paleness, rapid pulse
Motor symptoms: poor co-ordination, tenseness, mistakes
Behaviour: abnormal behaviour such as excessive aggressiveness or passiveness.

What Can Be Done About Fear?

Here only the self-regulating methods are mentioned which can be carried out by oneself.

Such training to reduce fear is carried out several times a week and often before a race (especially downhill).

Physical Procedure
On the one hand, fear as a state of mental agitation can be reduced by physical activity such as an intensive warm-up. On the other hand, the relaxation techniques described below usually help get fear under control because **relaxation** is considered the basis of all control of fear.

Mental Procedure
In the mental procedure the negative thoughts triggering fear must be reassessed or given new meaning by trying to think realistically positively. A reassessment and relativisation of the importance of a race reduces the pressure considerably and allows "relaxed" participation in the race.

Great successes in overcoming the very frequent fear of falls are often achieved through visualisation of correct, completely safely and harmoniously carried out techniques such as drifting, jumping or blocking hard blows. The **visualisation,** however, must not lead to increased risk taking.

The relationship of the visualised techniques to reality is important especially in the downhill. Incorrect or unrealistic techniques or falls must be totally kept out of the visualisation programme and out of one's thoughts (think positively).

9.2 Motivation with Realistic Goals

Choose Races of Average Difficulty

To allow a development in mental performance capacity to take place one should choose performance tests that are neither too easy nor too difficult but rather give preference to challenges that correspond to one's physical and psychological form.

A very easy race against weak opponents would lead one to believe physical and psychological performance were higher than they really were, whereas a very difficult race would have the opposite effect.

Set Realistic Goals

Just as care must be taken in the selection of races, it is equally important to be careful about the goals which one really must set oneself as an athlete and towards which one can train. If the goal is many years off (e.g. attaining the title of world champion) and if it is unrealistic into the bargain, it is very soon lost from sight and one becomes goalless. If the goal is too modest, motivation and personal commitment are low (see chapter 6).

Switch off from Cycling

Only those who can switch off from mountain biking when they get off their bike can also mentally relax and maintain their motivation for training and races. Athletes who think of biking day in, day out all year round often have mental blocks and put themselves under too much pressure.

Mental Attitude

Mental attitude has a strong influence both on physical, mental, technical and tactical performance capacity and on willingness to perform. "Winners" are characterised by a very high degree of self-confidence which "losers" often lack.

Thus the first win, the first placing or the first marathon are decisive stages on the way to sporting self-confidence.

Victories Are Won in the Mind

A biker's mind must be prepared to do his best, for victories are first won in the mind and not with the legs.

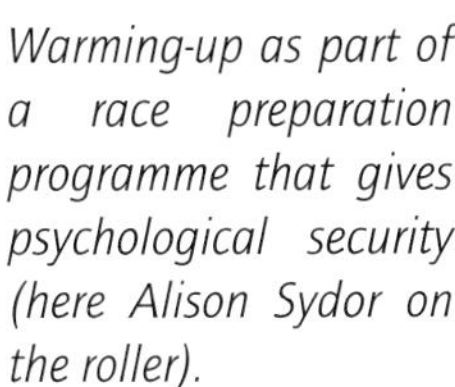

Warming-up as part of a race preparation programme that gives psychological security (here Alison Sydor on the roller).
Photo: Klaus Eweleit

You will not have any success until you are mentally capable of giving everything, unless the exertion situation is below your level. Only optimal mental attitude can explain the successes of athletes who physically do not seem to be "really" capable of them. In such a success situation you are "in the flow", that means that body and mind are in unison and harmonise with each other in an ideal way. When describing this situation of being "in the flow" in retrospect, racing cyclists often say that they did not even consciously notice extreme strains (pain) in a race situation (successful breakaway) or a tour, but rather just cycled relatively calmly and relaxed at a speed that they would otherwise never have been able to cycle at.

Whereas humans are normally only able to make use of a certain percentage of their absolute performance capacity, in certain mental states they can draw on their performance reserves more easily. Through mental training the gap between real and absolute performance capacity can be reduced.

Motivation

Motivation is very much influenced by the evaluation of one's own performance, and in mental training it often makes sense to begin by reassessing this performance because permanent over- or underestimation hinders success. A change in estimation can be arrived at very well by talking to people one relates to (trainer, parents, friends). Through mental training you now try to discover and use available motivation reserves. Simple ways to increase motivation are for example changing the training environment (training camp), planning a break in training (a few days), or practising other sports in winter. You should also give yourself little "rewards" for achieving your goals.

9.3 Mental Technique Training

As already mentioned, **visualisation** (making visible) can be used to improve difficult techniques on the bike. If you imagine such a technique in all its details, the brain sends appropriate impulses to the muscles involved in the movement, very similar to when the movement is concretely realised. These very weak impulses do not cause any externally visible movements, but in some cases they cause discernable movements in the form of twitches.

These impulses can also be ascertained in an electromyogram (conduction of muscular electricity). In this way certain patterns of movement are already stored and prepared for. This form of mental training is especially important for downhillers and trial riders, whom you can often observe before races in a quiet place mentally riding the course only moments before the start. "Mentally withdrawn" athletes before the start can often be observed in sports like ski racing, tobogganing or high diving.

Think in Pictures

When visualising you free yourself from language and think in pictures which can be further supported by imagining sounds, smells and feelings. You let an action pass before your inner eye like a film.

In addition to various cycling techniques it is possible to visualise an ideal race or various desired emotional states (balance, will to perform) and with some practice tactical situations can also be visualised.

It is important to begin with simple movements and only after successfully transferring them to reality move on to more difficult situations. Especially as a beginner in mental training one should practise several minutes at a time as often as possible (daily).

Not every athlete, however, can visualise straight away and some bikers cannot access this kind of training at all.

The technique of visualisation can be practised almost everywhere and above all during forced breaks due to injury.

This Is What You Do

1) Before you begin with visualisation, write down in your own words (extensively) the technique or tactic to be improved.

2) In a second step you read this text through several times in the following days, try to see the situation with your inner eye and if necessary change the text. Before you begin with the preliminary exercises to visualisation each time you should spend a few minutes doing one of the relaxation exercises described in the following chapter to loosen up and calm yourself.

3) When you know the text almost off by heart you begin to imagine the situation with your eyes closed and possibly to support it also in your thoughts with language. In doing this it can be helpful to record the text on a cassette and at first listen to it while visualising. Additionally, the key points of the movement should be marked and described with short words (e.g. push, up, round, hop).

4) The last step is then the visualisation of the movement, during which you can either watch yourself as if an actor in a film (observer's point of view) or - better - see the situation with your own eyes. After a while you try to let the visualisation roll in real time, i.e. you mentally jump from key point to key point.
The action should take place in the present and never in the past, and it must remain realistic. Incorrect carrying out of movements or action processes should be avoided in visualisation because they will be registered as a false picture of movement. In time as you get more experienced at using visualisation you will develop your own individual techniques and methods which come closest to your personal requirements.

5) Only when the short film runs quickly and matches real time (takes about a week) do you attempt the realisation of the movement with the help of visualisation. In technique training the technique of visualisation should be alternated with practical attempts. For example you first twice visualise riding on the back wheel and then make 5-8 practical attempts.

Before Cycling

In the training phase it is useful to train mentally as well as physically by visualising technical, tactical and mental abilities. On the day before a race or immediately before it you visualise the specific tactics and mental willingness to perform for the event.

While Cycling

On the bike too it is possible to call on a visualisation programme, whereby the relaxation phase beforehand is left out. Short tactical instructions (ride up front, follow a certain cyclist), technical movements (drift in the curve or only brake very late) as well as motivational instructions (stay the course, give all you can, ride loosely and easily, pedal fluidly) can be quickly called back to memory and realised with the help of images trained earlier.

Imagine a Motivating Picture

As in other endurance sports, sooner or later in mountain biking too there always comes a point under great strain when there is a struggle between body and mind.

In such a situation where you are almost ready to give up an individual "picture" helps decide the struggle in the mind's favour and makes the job seem easier than it actually is.

Whether you use an imaginary picture of a beach here, a sunny field of flowers, a cord leading to the finish or some other pleasant thought, is something you will have to find out for yourself.

The thought of something nice, a kind of reward after the exertion, can often work wonders and mobilise the last reserves.

After Cycling

After an event or training you should first be aware of any mistakes and then visualise how it should have been, but make sure not to visualise the mistakes. A playful easiness of the movements should always be suggested.

9.4 Mental Race Preparation – Optimal State of Excitement

An optimal situation of excitement is decisive for an excellent mental prerace state. If you are too agitated or almost apathetic, in the race part of your performance capacity is blocked by a psychological barrier.

The aim of psychological training must therefore be an optimal state of excitement.

As a rule, mountain bikers are too agitated before a race, seldom do they show underexcitement, expressed in listlessness and apathy.

Overexcitement is brought under control with relaxation techniques, under-excitement with mobilisation techniques.

9.4.1 Relaxation Techniques

Relaxation techniques should always be used when you find yourself in an emotionally tense state. Tension caused by fear, stress, pressure to succeed or uncertainty is called negative tension, whereas tension resulting from joy, will to perform or self-confidence is positive tension. Before a race the idea is to remove negative tension with the help of relaxation techniques and thus create a situation of optimal excitement. Too much positive excitement can also be brought under control with a relaxation technique. You will have to find out your own individual best state of excitement by experimenting.

Progressive Muscle Relaxation

Progressive muscle relaxation is a relaxation method developed by G. Jacobsen back in 1934 already which is ideally suitable for sport because it is easy to learn and can be successfully applied. In each case individual groups of muscles are isometrically tensed (tensing without moving joints) so that then the progressive relaxing of the muscles can be felt, which has an effect mentally.

It is best to practise ten minutes daily, for example before going to bed or in bed if you have sleeping problems. Before a race there should be at least 30 minutes between the relaxation phase and the start of the race because otherwise you might be too calm when you start. A shortened programme can be used to prepare for visualisation.

Progressive muscle relaxation can be done both sitting and lying; lying is more comfortable and more effective. At the beginning of training it is easier to practise with a partner who gives you relaxation instructions in a calm voice. The technique, which is repeated with each muscle group, is as follows:

1. *Concentration on the muscle group or part of the body.*
2. *Maximum tensing of the muscles involved, held for 8-10 s.*
3. *At a signal relax for about 30 s and concentrate on the area.*

Mountain bikers begin obviously by relaxing the leg muscles, which can also be repeated again at the finish.
A programme looks like this:

1. Left thigh
2. Left lower leg
3. Left foot

4. Right thigh
5. Right lower leg
6. Right foot
7. Stomach
8. Back
9. Left upper arm
10. Left hand and forearm
11. Right upper arm
12. Right hand and forearm
13. Neck
14. Face

To shorten the procedure both halves of the body can also be treated at once. Changes to the programme which treat the individual muscles in the leg area in a different way are possible at any time.

Breathing Exercises

Fast relaxation can also be achieved with conscious breathing. To do this you consciously lengthen breathing out for several minutes. In a practice phase the breathing exercises should initially be done lying down.

Later, relaxation can be achieved in hectic situations by simply lengthening breathing out. Without thinking about it groaning or expelling air has a similar effect.

Autogenic Training

Autogenic training is a form of psychotraining which should only be learnt under the direction of an experienced expert and for which, in comparison to the other techniques described here, a great deal of practice is necessary.

Unfortunately it is only possible to give a brief introduction to the possibilities of psychotraining here; there are however a number of books that go into the subject further (Eberspächer, Baumann). It is important to have an open attitude to psychotraining, the courage to try something new.

9.4.2 Mobilisation

For mobilisation when there is underexcitement above all physical movement is necessary. Especially important for bikers who tend more towards apathy and yawn before a race is a tight preparatory programme beforehand. Periods of slack should be avoided because they provoke an undesired drop in excitement. Extensive warm-up cycling, inspecting the course and a stretching programme help an athlete to mobilise mentally.

A tightly organised preparatory programme always with the same sequence is advantageous to any mountain biker, for this little ritual creates security. And this is what such a programme could look like: get your bike ready, collect your number, inspect the course, mental training (relaxation, etc.), warm-up, stretching, put on your racing clothes, attach your number, final equipment check, final mental preparation, start.

Unforeseen events should not throw an athlete off but should be accepted in good humour.

9.5 The Right Mental Attitude to Training

It is also possible to prepare yourself for training with the various psychological techniques. This is especially important for intensive training sessions when strong willpower is needed for hard intervals. In a short programme on the day before or directly before training, you imagine the optimal progression of the training session with all its planned contents (intervals). This often helps to grind out the last sprints or the last minutes or seconds of an interval. If the mental attitude is poor, training programmes are often discontinued.

Mental training will not help if there is no basic will to train and perform. The original motivation must come from deep inside.

Exhaustion after the race: race result and self-confidence determine motivation for further training.
Photo: Klaus Eweleit

9.6 Regeneration through Relaxation

The various relaxation techniques are also suitable for regeneration, for in addition to physical regeneration, mental regeneration from exertion must be made possible and carried out. In addition, the contraction followed by relaxation in progressive muscle relaxation lowers muscle tone considerably which is very beneficial to physical regeneration. Other relaxation techniques have a similar effect.

9.7 Mental Programme before a Race or Marathon

The following progression can be used to prepare for the effort to come on the evening before and/or on race day itself. There should be at least 30 minutes between the end of the exercises and the start of the race. For this you find a quiet place where you can be undisturbed for about 20 minutes and sit or better still lie down in a relaxed way: the legs lie loosely next to each other, without touching one another; the feet fall slightly outwards.

1. Progressive Muscle Relaxation

With your eyes closed you first relax physically with the help of your own or the muscle relaxation programme described above. In doing so special emphasis should be placed on the legs.

2. Positive Thoughts

You now transport yourself mentally to a beautiful place which suggests calm, security and relaxation. This can be a field, a beach, a forest or similar. The senses should be at this place only and you should concentrate on positive thoughts.

3. Visualisation

In a third step, after successful physical and mental relaxation, you visualise the race or tour ahead. You are on the course or route and you run through your positive promising tactics and techniques. You overcome expected difficulties (uphills, downhills) with playful ease. You try to create a positive approach to the exertion ahead with a desire to perform well, the event should give you joy. A positive race result can also be visualised.

4. Withdrawal

When you have finished visualising your personal success you must withdraw from relaxation by stretching yourself. On competition day you should now begin to concentrate on warming-up. The evening before a race you do not need to shift yourself back to reality so abruptly, especially then when you are going to bed afterwards anyway.

10 Mountain Bike Racing for Beginners

Anyone who has only recently taken up mountain biking will know how difficult it is to get the right information at the right time. As a rule beginners must pay their dues, as in all other sports too, for the racing scene seems impenetrable to outsiders. In the next section a number of tips and tricks have been collated which can help you get comprehensive information and thus save much time and annoyance. The address list allows direct contact to the associations.

Once they have a few hundred kilometres in their legs and their cycling technique has reached a safe level, for most bikers the question of racing poses itself. In stark contrast to road racing, where recreational races are the exception, the MTB scene has a community of beginners. No matter what category you opt for (cross-country, downhill, dual slalom, trial, marathon), at most racing events you will find the appropriate races for many age classes.

The next section portrays exactly the road to the starting signal of your first race with all its preparations, and the clear chart makes it child's play for every ambitious beginner.

A description of the current situation gives an idea of how the racing scene in Germany is organised. As the organisational structures vary from one country to another, it is advisable to check with your own national organisation. In Germany anyone wanting to participate in races of the umbrella organisation BDR (Bund Deutscher Radfahrer, Federation of German Cyclists) must have a licence, the purchase of which is tied to membership in one of the associations affiliated to the BDR.

In mountain biking a beginner's scene tolerated by the BDR has developed which makes uncomplicated race participation possible for the mostly irregularly competing recreational bikers. The performance level of this class can nevertheless be classed as professional because many former licenced riders continue their hobby in these classes.

The upper part of figure 10.1 shows which race forms are offered in the recreational category. The other details are mainly related to the two popular disciplines cross-country and downhill.

If you have decided to take part in a competition the following guidelines will help.

	Children 10-13 years	Young people 15-16 years	Juniors (male) 17-18 years	Juniors (female) 17-18 years	Men 19-35 years	Women 18-35 years	Seniors (male) over 36 years	Seniors (female) over 36 years
Cross-country	X	X	X	X	X	X	X	X
Downhill			X		X	X	X	
Dual slalom			X		X		X	
Trial		X	X		X		X	
Marathon			X	X	X	X	X	X
Road races	X				X		X	
Entry fee		£ 1 - 3.30/ US$ 1.60 - 5.50				£ 3.30 - 10/ US$ 5.50 - 16		
Late registration fee (£ 1.60 - 5/ US$ 2.70 - 8.30)	Rarely	Often	Often	Often	Often	Often	Often	Often
Distances cross-country	1-2 rds. made easier	10-15 km	12-18 km	10-15 km	15-22 km	12-18 km	12-18 km	10-15 km
Course profile		Demanding, mostly with sections made slightly easier (e.g. on climbs and descents)						
Number of participants	10-20	10-20	10-20	1-5	50-100	5-20	10-40	1-5
Frequency	++	+	+	-	++	0	+	-

Fig. 10.1: Recreational races: classes and various information about the types of races (Germany)

First Contact at the Bike Shop

If you want to make a start the bike shop is the place to go because usually the bikers of the region shop here and you can quickly make contacts. Bike shops often organise tours and training trips, or the mountain bikers of the nearest club meet here for training. You should, however, make sure it is a mountain bike or racing bike shop. In large cities this is not always the case.

Magazines Inform about Race Dates and the Racing Scene

You can get detailed information about the racing scene in the various monthly mountain biking magazines. These contain race calendars and race locations, news from the fields of equipment and clothing as well a race reports.

Ask in Shops about Local Clubs

With the aid of the race calendars in the mountain bike magazines, and the address lists attached, you should have no problem finding a race locally in which you can start in the recreational class without a licence.

Race Registration

Participation in races usually calls for registration beforehand which in clubs is handled by the registration official. It is, however, also possible to register yourself or in the recreational class to pay a small fee for late registration (see fig. 10.1).

To start with many are surprised at the sometimes hefty entry fees, but if you take a closer look you will see how much organisational effort goes into running a race. It is best to register for races in writing (fax or postcard). Take note of the closing date, which is usually one or two weeks before the day of the race. Late registration ususally costs more.

If you do not wish to take part in races many European countries now fortunately have mountain bike touring trips which are well-organised and involve none of the stress of races.

Mountain bike marathons are often ridden by racers as "races", but they give everyone the opportunity to participate in a big mountain biking event without having to be "infected" by racing stress. In order to manage the long distances it is necessary to be in good training condition.

Licence Races

If, however, you wish to start in the licence class straight away, which is only recommended for young beginners, you should ask your bike dealer for club addresses.

Another way of getting club addresses is to call the regional, municipal and state sporting associations (can be found in the phone book) which often have full-time staff and are glad to give information. Finally, the cycling associations of the federal states or the cantons and their umbrella organisations at federal or national level are also glad to provide information about mountain bike clubs nearby. Mountain biking is always affiliated to the cycling organisations.

In order to participate in licence races you have to have a valid licence which is only available in clubs. You should choose a club that is as close as possible to your home so you can also take part in training activities. Meanwhile there are quite a number of purely mountain bike clubs.

A certain level of fitness and cycling technique are absolutely necessary prerequisites for the first race. Photo: Klaus Eweleit

Often cycling clubs have mountain biking sections, which has the advantage that there is a selection of training groups and partners available for the somewhat boring basic or road training sessions.

The First Race

Once you have decided to take part in a race you should start preparing for it according to training methodology.

Chapter 3 describes how to do this. The day before the race the equipment is cleaned and checked. Brakes and gears must be in perfect order.

Because the courses are sometimes very demanding you should only enter with a proper mountain bike.

On the morning of the first race eat a carbohydrate rich breakfast, prepare your drinking bottle and race food supplies (also for before and after the race) and pack your bag. It is best to make a list the day before otherwise you are sure to forget something important. Only with increasing competition experience will you be able to pack your things practically blindfolded.

When you arrive at the race location first assemble your bike, get your back number, or if necessary register, and inspect the course. In mountain biking the course inspection is of major importance and must be planned for whatever else happens. You should be at the race location about two or three hours before the start in order to prepare for it calmly and not be put off by anything unexpected. Then you put on your cycling gear and warm-up. The exact procedure before races should become a ritual, which also gives you the necessary psychological security (see chapter 9).

If you try to keep to these guidelines there is nothing to prevent a successful first race. You should not, however, exaggerate your expectations regarding the result, for as a rule you can be satisfied with just completing the course without any falls or defects. For top performance in such a demanding and training-intensive sport like mountain biking you need a great deal of time and experience.

Bibliography

Anderson, Biken.: Stretching. München 1991.
Anderson, K.: Cycling for Women. Emmaus 1989.
Appel, H.-J./Stang-Voss, C.: Funktionelle Anatomie. Berlin 1991.
Baecker, K.: Nutrition for Cyclists. Emmaus 1991.
Baumann, S.: Psychologie im Sport. Aachen 1998.
Bohlmann, J.T.: Injuries in Competitive Cycling. In: The Physician and Sportsmedicine 1981.
Burke, E.R.: Medical and Scientific Aspects of Cycling. Champaign 1988.
Burke, E.R.: High-Tech Cycling. Champaign 1996.
Edwards, S.: Leitfaden zur Trainingskontrolle. Aachen 1993.
Eberspächer, H.: Mentales Training. München 1995.
Ericson, M. et all: Power Output and Work in Different Muscle Groups during Ergometer Cycling. In: Eur. J. appl. Physiol. 55 (1986), S. 229-235.
Faller: Der Körper des Menschen. München 1995.
Gould, T./Burney, S.: Mountainbikesport. Bielefeld 1992.
Geis, K.R./Hamm, M.: Handbuch Sportler Ernährung. Hamburg 1990.
Harre, D.: Trainingslehre. Berlin 1985.
Jacobsen, G.: Progressive Relaxation. Chicago 1938.
Lippert, H.: Anatomie. München 1989.
Marées, de H.: Sportphysiologie. Köln 1989.
Markworth, P.: Sportmedizin. Hamburg 1986.
Matheny, F.: Beginning Bicycle Racing. Brattleboro 1988.
Neumann, G.: Alles unter Kontrolle. Ausdauertraining. Aachen 1993.
Neumann, G./Berbalk, A.: Umstellung und Anpassung des Organismus – grundlegende Voraussetzungen der sportlichen Leistungsfähigkeit.
In: Bernett/Jeschke (Hrsg.): Sport und Medizin. Pro und Contra. W. Zuckschwerdt, München 1991.
Pickel, H./Pecher, S.: Fallstudien. In: BikeSportNews 6/97.
Radcliffe, J.C.: Sprungkrafttraining. Aachen 1991.
Schmidt, A.: Handbuch für Radsport. Aachen 1996.
Schmidt, A.: Stretching für Radfahrer. In: Radfahren extra 2/1993 Bielefeld.
Silbernagel S./Depopoulos, A.: Taschenatlas der Physiologie. Stuttgart 1988.
Sleamaker, R.: Systematisches Leistungstraining. Aachen 1991.
Tobias, M./Sullivan, J.: The complete Stretching Book. London 1992.
Ungerleider, S.: Mental Training for Peak Performance. Emmaus 1996.
Zintl, F.: Ausdauertraining. München 1990.
Zorn, H.: Radsport. Hamburg 1984.